Economics
of the
Mortgage Market

Economics of the Mortgage Market

Perspectives on
household decision making

David Leece

Department of Management
Keele University

Blackwell
Publishing

© 2004 by Blackwell Publishing Ltd
Editorial offices:
Blackwell Publishing Ltd,
9600 Garsington Road, Oxford OX4 2DQ, UK
    Tel: +44 (0)1865 776868
Blackwell Publishing Inc., 350 Main Street, Malden, MA 02148-5020, USA
    Tel: +1 781 388 8250
Blackwell Publishing Asia Pty Ltd, 550 Swanston Street, Carlton, Victoria 3053, Australia
    Tel: +61 (0)3 8359 1011

First published 2004 by Blackwell Publishing Ltd

Library of Congress Cataloging-in-Publication Data
Leece, David.
Economics of the mortgage market : perspectives on household decision-making / David Leece.
    p. cm.
Includes bibliographical references and index.
    ISBN 1-4051-1461-4 (pbk. : alk. paper)
1. Mortgage loans. 2. Mortgages. 3. Housing–Finance. I. Title.

HG2040.15.L44 2004
332.7'22–dc22   2003019585

ISBN 1-4051-1461-4

A catalogue record for this title is available from the British Library

Set in 10/13pt Trump Mediaeval
by Kolam Information Services Pvt. Ltd, Pondicherry, India
Printed and bound in India
by Replika Press Pvt. Ltd, Kundli 131028

The publisher's policy is to use permanent paper from mills that operate a sustainable forestry policy, and which has been manufactured from pulp processed using acid-free and elementary chlorine-free practices. Furthermore, the publisher ensures that the text paper and cover board used have met acceptable environmental accreditation standards.

For further information on Blackwell Publishing, visit our website:
www.blackwellpublishing.com

Real Estate Issues

Series Managing Editors

Stephen Brown RICS Foundation

John Henneberry Department of Town & Regional Planning, University of Sheffield

David Ho School of Design & Environment, National University of Singapore

Real Estate Issues is an international book series presenting the latest thinking into how real estate markets operate. Books have a strong theoretical basis – providing the underpinning for the development of new ideas.

The books are inclusive in nature, drawing both upon established techniques for real estate market analysis and on those from other academic disciplines as appropriate. The series embraces a comparative approach, allowing theory and practice to be put forward and tested for their applicability and relevance to the understanding of new situations. It does not seek to impose solutions, but rather to provide a more effective means by which solutions can be found. It will not make any presumptions as to the importance of real estate markets but will uncover and present, through the clarity of the thinking, the real significance of the operation of real estate markets.

Books in this series

Guy & Henneberry *Development and Developers*
Adams & Watkins *Greenfields, Brownfields and Housing Development*
O'Sullivan & Gibb *Housing Economics and Public Policy*
Couch, Fraser & Percy *Urban Regeneration in Southern Europe*
Allen, Barlow, Padovani, Maloutas & Leal *Housing and Welfare in Southern Europe*
Leece *Economics of the Mortgage Market*
Evans *Economics and Planning*
Evans *Economics, Real Estate and the Supply of Land*
Byrne & Matysiak *Real Estate Investment*
Ball *Markets and Institutions in Real Estate and Construction*
Dixon, McAllister, Marston & Snow *Real Estate in the New Economy*
Adams, Watkins & White *Planning, Public Policy & Property Markets*

RICS **FOUNDATION**

To my much loved wife and inspiration Jan and
my two great boys Steven and Alan

Contents

Preface

My first encounter with mortgage market economics was in the process of researching and writing my PhD on the impact of financial deregulation on housing and mortgage demand in the United Kingdom. Two salient points became apparent during the completion of that work. One was the large extent of research into mortgage market issues in the United States, a volume of literature that has been added to significantly since the completion of my thesis in 1995. The second point was the dearth of comparable research on the microeconomic foundations of mortgage choices for the United Kingdom.

This book represents both my own personal, post PhD, journey deeper and wider into the microeconomics of the mortgage market and the significant progress made in this field, particularly in the United States, over the last few years. The book has several important aims. One of these is to inform and motivate further research into the microeconomics of mortgage markets. The second is to provide an organised research resource encompassing the voluminous literature in this area of study. This includes the highlighting of key research findings and outstanding issues. The work will also present some of my own, mainly empirical, work on household mortgage choices in the United Kingdom.

The emphasis of the book is undoubtedly upon the microeconomics of mortgage choices, including mortgage demand, contract designs, rationing and separating equilibrium in the mortgage market. Other choices include choice of mortgage instrument, amortisation and payment flexibility and default and prepayment behaviour based upon the embedded put and call options in mortgage contracts. It is these microeconomic areas that have been the main focus of study in the United States. There is no attempt to duplicate the excellent work of economists such as Miles (1994) who review the importance of mortgage designs for national economic performance, though these issues will be kept in mind. Neither does the book focus upon the theory of financial firms or market structures. Instead, lender behaviour will be evaluated indirectly, for example through issues in contract design, mortgage pricing and separating equilibrium.

The growing importance of the secondary mortgage market and mortgage securitisation, with cash flows originating from pools of individual mortgages, has heightened the need to understand the microeconomics of consumers' mortgage choices. Indeed the growth in the securitised mortgage market in the United States is no doubt partly responsible for the dramatic growth of interest in mortgage market issues. The United Kingdom and European secondary mortgage markets are also growing and a book on the microeconomics of the mortgage market provides a timely resource to those active and interested in this extremely important financial market.

The book will be of direct interest and assistance to housing and real estate economists, the general economist interested in this important market-place, financial economists, decision-makers in financial institutions and real estate thinkers and practitioners. Though aimed primarily at post-graduate research and teaching, the book would be a useful resource for undergraduate specialist courses in real estate economics and finance. It is hoped that the book will also appeal to professionals active in the mortgage market, including investment analysts and professional market participants in secondary mortgage market activity. Though some of the issues covered invite mathematical treatment and a little knowledge of the language of econometric analysis, the general line of argument should be accessible to the non-mathematical reader with a general background in finance and economics.

Acknowledgements

I would like to thank the administrative staff in the Department of Management at the University of Keele for their support while I was prepossessed with the completion of this book, in particular Vickey Lello, the undergraduate secretary. I would like to thank Jim Shilling, Abdullah Yavas, and Janet Leece for their comments and advice and Dwight Jaffee for his assistance and permission to use online documents. Thanks are also due to Madeleine Metcalfe the *Real Estate Issues* editor who has provided invaluable support throughout.

The author would like to thank the following publishers for permission to reproduce material. Elsevier for permission to reproduce as Figure 7.1, Figure 1 from Posey, L. & A. Yavas (2001) Adjustable and fixed rate mortgages as a screening mechanism for default risk, *Journal of Urban Economics* 49: 54–79. MIT Press for permission to reproduce as Figure 5.1, Figure V from Jaffee, D.M. & T. Russell (1976) Imperfect information, uncertainty, and credit rationing, *The Quarterly Journal of Economics*, 90(4): 661–6. Kluwer Academic Publishers for permission to reproduce as Figure 9.2, Figure 1 from Quigley, J. M. & R. Van Order (1995) Explicit tests of contingent claims models of mortgage default, *Journal of Real Estate Finance and Economics* 11: 99–117; and as Figure 5.2, Figure 2 from Brueckner, J.K. (2000) Mortgage default and asymmetric information, *Journal of Real Estate Finance and Economics*, 20(3): 251–74.

1

An Introduction to Mortgage Market Economics

General background

For those countries with large and extensive mortgage markets, such as the United States (US) and the United Kingdom (UK), mortgage finance can be the single most important source of personal borrowing, dominating the balance sheets of many households. Thus the size, extent and the contractual features of mortgage finance are bound to have important implications for the national economic performance of many countries, along with individual and social welfare. Given the benefits of owner occupation, access to mortgage credit can significantly effect life chances, for example equity can be withdrawn to finance education and owners have access to an asset which materially effects wealth (Stephens 2000). Equity extraction can also be used to finance the purchase of business or other assets (Disney *et al.* 2002; Jones 1993, 1994, 1995) complicating the link between mortgage and housing demand.

Governments in developing economies have begun to recognise the importance of a mortgage market for channelling funds into the housing sector. Mortgage loans can expand housing to meet the needs of lower income households, deepening capital markets in such countries. In some cases developing economies have been assisted by the introduction of a secondary mortgage market which has increased liquidity, facilitating further mortgage market development, for example programmes in South Africa and Argentina.[1] The study of mortgage markets in developing economies is receiving increasing academic attention (Lea 1994). Alvayay & Schwartz (1997) study the case of Chile, while Lea & Bernstein (1996) demonstrate the importance of mortgage contract design for Mexico. Jaffee & Renaud (1998) consider the advantages of a secondary mortgage market and the conditions required for its development in the transition economies in Eastern Europe. Thus the study of mortgage contracts and mortgage markets is a truly international concern.

The growth of secondary mortgage markets, and their refinement through securitisation where pools of mortgages are packaged for sale to investors who receive interest and capital payments, has been a major spur to research into the mortgage choices of households. For example, both the prepayment of mortgage debt and default on payments have implications for the cash flows accruing to mortgage-backed securities (MBS). These phenomenon then effect the valuation of these financial instruments. The MBS market is now substantial, particularly important in the US, and of growing significance in other countries and Europe. Securitisation can lead to the integration of mortgage markets with other capital markets, reduced interest rates for borrowers, with a reduction in mortgage credit rationing. When mortgage markets are inefficient they place restrictions and implicit taxes on the operation of other capital markets. However, efficient mortgage markets facilitate efficiency in other capital markets, the market for housing and labour markets (Jaffee & Renaud 1995, 1998). Thus household behaviour is more integrated with the broader capital market picture. To gain a thorough understanding of MBS valuation we must consider the mortgage choices of households.

The mortgage choices of households covered in this book include the size of mortgage, the rate of debt repayment (amortisation), choice of mortgage instrument, prepayment of mortgage debt and default. We shall have to consider these choices in the context of both perfect capital markets, and imperfect capital markets with asymmetric information and credit rationing. Chapter 2 will show how the demand for mortgage debt can provide a focus for the study of other mortgage market choices. This current chapter provides some of the important background to understanding household decision making in mortgage markets, presenting the structure of the book.

Actual mortgage choices cannot be entirely divorced from the housing finance systems and broader economies of which they are a part, so we briefly consider some important institutional and policy differences between markets. Given the source of most of the research reported in this book, particular attention will be given to comparisons between the US and the UK, with comparisons of research results for the two economies also presented in the majority of chapters.

A key theme of the book is the importance of mortgage contract design; for example, the potential impact of different mortgage instruments on housing demand, the sharing of risk between borrowers and lenders and the role of contract choice in signalling borrower characteristics. Empirical research in the US has enquired into the impact of the adjustable rate mortgage on the stability of the housing market (Brueckner & Follain 1989; Goodman 1992; Gabriel & Rosenthal 1993). In the UK there has been concern over the prevalence of variable rate debt which effects the sensitivity of economic conditions to changes in short-term interest rates (Maclennan *et al.* 1998; Chinloy 1995; Britton & Whitley 1997; Munchau 1997). Prescribed loan-to-value ratios are an important feature of mortgage contract design that can impact upon a households' tenure choice and savings behaviour (Slemrod 1982; Hayashi *et al.* 1988). These are all examples of different mortgage designs having wider economic implications. Why we observe different mortgage contracts and how households choose are important topics for this book. Moreover, the choice set that consumers face can vary significantly between different housing finance systems.

The different mortgage markets

Roche (1999) notes how debt financing has emerged as the 'nearly universal alternative' to paying for a house outright, obtaining the generally valued benefits of home ownership. She evokes the sense of an international phenomenon nicely by citing examples of the many names given to mortgage debt throughout the world, *financiación de la vivienda* in Mexico, *credit au logement* in France.[2] Internationally there are a variety of mortgage instruments. This variety reflects the degree of competition in the respective mortgage markets, together with the institutional and regulatory features of the housing finance systems which delimit the risks faced by lenders and borrowers. This book adopts the view that the fundamental nature of mortgage contracts, their variety and household choices, can also be understood in theoretical terms, and that the extant empirical studies offer insights along with methodologies which can be applicable in many economies. However, we do need to note the significant differences between the main housing finance systems.

This section of the book motivates our study of mortgage market economics by noting the importance of variations in the form and use of mortgage finance in different parts of the world. Because most econometric research is located in North America (the US and Canada) and the UK, there will be an emphasis upon comparisons of the housing finance systems of these countries, with the UK market placed in its European context. Identifying some of the key characteristics of these markets is important for the interpretation of empirical studies. Finally, mortgage markets are not static but ever changing and produce heterogeneous mortgage products. The reasons for the heterogeneity of mortgage contracts, with the implications of this variety, form another key theme of this book. Though mortgage markets are dynamic and complex, the conceptual tools presented should assist in the continuing analysis and study of this important marketplace.

In the UK in 1998, mortgage debt constituted 57% of Gross National Product. This figure was as high as 69% in Denmark, and 65% in the Netherlands. Austria, however, had mortgage debt of just 5% of GNP[3] demonstrating that there can be significant international differences in the importance of this market (see Table 1.1). For the US the volume of residential mortgages is estimated at $3 trillion dollars (2000), representing a doubling of the figure over 10 years. This is compared to a US figure for government borrowing of $5 trillion.[4] Outside of Europe and the US, Canada has mortgage debt on residential properties of 33% of household net worth (1999).[5] In Australia in 1999 there were 2.3 million homeowners with a mortgage (that is 31% of all Australian households).[6] Thus for many economies the mortgage market is very large and important. For some

Table 1.1 Outstanding Residential Mortgage Debt In the European Union

Country	Outstanding residential mortgage debt/GDP 1998[1]	Trend in outstanding residential mortgage debt (1990–1998)[2]
Belgium	25	6.9
Denmark	69	7.0
Germany	53	8.6
Greece	7	16.3
Spain	24	13.8
France	21	1.3
Ireland	27	15.5
Italy	8	11.7
Luxembourg	26	–
Netherlands	65	11.4
Austria	5	–
Portugal	26	24.6
Finland	30	2.4
Sweden	50	4.7
United Kingdom	57	5.7
Norway	42	4.2

Notes:
[1] The figures for Austria include commercial mortgages
[2] The figures for Germany and Sweden relate to the trend growth in residential and commercial mortgages

Source: Hypostat, 1988–1998, Mortgage and Property Markets in the European Union and Norway, European Mortgage Federation (Tables 3 and Table 4).

countries beginning at a low base, such as Greece and Spain, the trend rate of growth in this market is high (see Table 1.1).

Several factors explain international differences in the size and economic significance of mortgage markets. Explanations include differences in the size and quality of the housing stock, variations in the proportion of houses that are owner-occupied properties, together with the range of mortgage instruments available. Variations in the legal and regulatory frameworks can also limit or encourage this market effecting the range and type of mortgage design. Differences in the general economic environment (e.g. monetary and fiscal factors including the subsidisation of mortgage interest payments), and the history of the housing finance systems can also create variety. The location and amount of research on the economics of mortgage choice reflects the sophistication and size of the mortgage markets concerned. Thus the US has provided the most prolific output of research in this area, a factor reflected in most of the literature referred to in this book.

Why differences in housing finance systems are important

Lea (2000) describes an evolutionary path for a housing finance system. It begins with informal lending for house purchase with this role eventually adopted by specialised financial intermediaries. These intermediaries may be mutual societies, owned by shareholders, or 'special circuits' provided through government-backed agencies. The final phase is mortgage market securitisation and the integration of the housing finance system with other capital markets. Different economies will be at different stages in this process so we will observe significant differences in housing finance systems, including prevalent mortgage designs. For Europe, Maclennan *et al.* (1998, p. 62) observes that '[h]ousing finance lenders within Europe have evolved within national boundaries, and reflect the influence of localised origins and national policies'. Even with financial deregulation post–1980, these histories have been modified to different degrees. So different housing finance systems provide the background to mortgage choices.

The implicit subsidisation of fixed rate debt via Federal guarantees in the US, with the role of government sponsored agencies in standardising products for securitisation, might explain the prevalence and popularity of the fixed rate mortgage (FRM). The subsidisation of life insurance premiums on UK endowment mortgages, up to 1984, and tax relief on mortgage interest payments at source (MIRAS), until April 2000, might explain the initial popularity of the endowment mortgage. The UK has seen several shifts in the nature of property taxation; prior to the current council tax there was a shift from a system of rates to a poll tax, which was estimated to have had a significant impact upon housing demand (Rosenthal 1999). Stephens (2000) notes how offering cheap funds to some financial intermediaries prevents the convergence of European mortgage markets, also different legal systems inhibit the emergence of a standard mortgage product.

The theory of mortgage demand to be discussed in Chapter 2 will suggest a common decision-making framework for utility maximising consumers. In a perfectly competitive no arbitrage economy, with perfect capital markets and no information problems, a comprehensive model of mortgage choices might suggest a common choice of mortgage instrument, or at least an indifferent choice. The reasons why we do not observe a single common contract design are explored throughout this book, and in Chapter 7 in particular. However, differences in housing finance systems, and government involvement, clearly offer part of the explanation for the different contracts that we observe together with the borrowers' menu of choices. Housing finance systems will differ in efficiency and these differences will effect borrowers' choices, investors' opportunities and the degree of integration with other capital markets.

There is a body of research that has been concerned with the comparative efficiency of housing finance systems (Diamond & Lea 1992; Lea *et al.* 1997; Stephens 2000). This efficiency can be viewed in the strict economic sense of cost minimisation. Alternatively, it can be viewed as intermediation efficiency (Diamond & Lea 1992; Stephens 2000). The measure of intermediation efficiency used by Diamond & Lea is the difference between the costs to society of mortgage finance, measured by mortgage interest payments plus origination fees, less the theoretical minimum cost, which is the rate of interest on government debt of the same maturity. This margin reflects the extant market distortions evident in the competitive structure of the mortgage market, and any taxes and subsidies.

There are clearly technical difficulties associated with calculating intermediation efficiency and using it to compare housing finance systems. For example, it is difficult to find comparable mortgage contracts with which to compare interest rates. Other factors such as the underlying market conditions (e.g. competitiveness) that facilitate efficiency are also difficult to evaluate. Diamond & Lea incorporate a number of qualitative judgements to ascertain the impact of such factors. From the perspective of this book the measure of intermediation efficiency also leaves out an important dimension. That is the fact that through regulation and market distortion some housing finance systems exclude particular contracts from the consumer's menu of choices, or discourage them, e.g. long-run fixed rate mortgages in the UK. In principle, the measurement of the consumer's willingness to pay for excluded contract designs would provide a measure of any welfare loss (Diamond & Lea 1992).

The overall efficiency of a housing finance system can be judged by how well it matches the preferences of both borrowers and investors. Thus a mortgage finance system should be able to repackage the mortgage debt of borrowers to create securities of interest to investors. Investors may be better placed to bear the risk of holding mortgages than borrowers. The extent to which this risk is repackaged for investors is another perspective on housing finance efficiency (Jaffee & Renaud 1998). In the perfectly efficient system the propositions of Modigliani & Miller hold and borrowers would be indifferent between the choice of gearing and other features of mortgage contracts. In fact, with complete markets even the securitisation of mortgage debt cannot be justified, as investors could package their own securities. With incomplete markets, and markets with liquidity and information problems, we need to make a general judgement on how well borrowers' and investors' needs are met.

To take an example of how an efficient housing finance system, with some constraints, might operate, we consider the following. Residential loans with high loan-to-value ratios and higher risk of default could be sold to investors who wish to have some exposure to real estate markets. Low loan-to-value ratio loans, with lower risk of default, would be sold to investors such as pension funds who wanted a better match with their liabilities. Even if borrowers were constrained by facing a standard loan-to-value ratio, investment bankers could still package the mortgages and issue junior and senior debt to match the preferences of each client group. This would meet the need to repackage risk for investors, but a fully efficient housing finance system should also meet the needs of borrowers. When capital markets are imperfect this implies a variety of mortgage instruments to reflect risk positions and cash flow needs.

Diamond & Lea found both the US and UK housing finance systems to be high in comparative efficiency, though both systems have regulations and distortions. For example, regulations on capital adequacy have limited securitisation in the UK. In the US there are geographic limitations on setting mortgage underwriting criterion for loans to be securitised. However, financial deregulation and increased competition in both economies has led to a better match of contracts with consumer preferences. In the

UK the innovative use of credit derivatives has facilitated the supply of short-term fixed rate debt. In the US the emergence of the adjustable rate mortgage (ARM) has provided borrowers with a choice of risk exposure. Consumers needs appear to be well met in competitive mortgage markets.

Some contracts might be less prevalent due to labour market and housing market imperfections that inhibit residential mobility. For example, more mobile households might be less willing to pay a premium for the risk to the lender of prepayment (or risk incurring penalties) and thus choose an adjustable (variable) rate mortgage rather than a long-term fixed rate contract. Also, information asymmetries prevent the development of innovative contracts that require specialised underwriting skills. The lack of specialised underwriters then further exacerbates the information problem.[7] Primary mortgage markets require underwriting and property valuation skills to underpin any secondary mortgage market development. Thus observed and excluded mortgage contracts can reflect other market imperfections and information problems.

A source of variation in available mortgage contracts that has major implications for household choices is the maximum loan-to-value ratio. Diamond & Lea note that the down payment required of borrowers varies significantly between housing finance systems. In a life cycle decision-making framework a large minimum deposit can defer entry into owner occupation. This requirement can distort life cycle consumption as households save to purchase the house (Artle & Varaya 1978). Tax incentives to borrowing, in the form of a subsidy on the mortgage interest rate, encourage early entry into owner occupation, but this contradicts the desire to postpone consumption to accumulate a deposit (Slemrod 1982; Hayashi *et al.* 1988). Theoretical work has demonstrated the importance of down payment requirements for the timing of entry into own occupation, and its impact upon house price cycles (Stein 1995; Ortalo-Magné & Rady 1998, 1999, 2002). Combinations of loan-to-value ratios and interest rates can also form the basis of separating equilibrium in the mortgage market (Brueckner 2000). This source of variation in mortgage contract design will recur in discussions throughout this book.

In summary, housing finance systems exhibit different degrees of efficiency. In a general sense efficiency can be viewed as the capacity to meet both the needs of investors and borrowers. Incomplete markets, information problems, market distortions and subsidies explain both the prevalent contract choices that face consumers, along with the choices that are not made available to them. Mortgage choices must be viewed in the context of the menu of contract designs that households face, and the characteristics of the housing finance systems in which those choices are made. However, we shall find that competitive pressures in the major systems of housing finance have generated extensive mortgage contract menus. Studies of both the US and UK mortgage choices provide insights into the behaviour of borrowers in highly evolved financial systems, with broad menus of contract choice. We now consider the major and pertinent characteristics of the mortgage finance systems that feature most in this book, that is the US and Canada and the UK and European mortgage markets.

North American mortgage markets

The US market for residential mortgage debt has several important characteristics that will be referred to when evaluating research into mortgage choices. There are a variety of available mortgage designs, with the key instruments being fixed rate debt (the FRM) and the adjustable rate mortgage (the ARM). Fixed rate mortgages fix the rate for 15 or 30 years, while for adjustable rate debt the adjustment period can vary from 1 to 5 years. This compares with fixed rate debt in the UK and Canada which is typically fixed for 1 to 5 years, with some longer periods available, but which reverts back to a variable rate of interest after the period of fixity. These differences will be seen to be significant when we examine household behaviour regarding the choice of mortgage instrument and the impact of mortgage contract choice on housing demand. For example, UK borrowers appear to focus much more on expected movements in short-term interest rates than long-run interest rate expectations.

The mortgage banks that have generally superseded the Savings and Loans institutions dominate mortgage finance in the US. These mortgage banks originate loans, which are then sold to government sponsored agencies (GSEs). That is, the mortgage debt is passed on to the secondary mortgage market. The mortgage banks came to prominence after the Savings and Loan crises in the US. One advantage of this system is that the mortgage banks do not need large amounts of funding to conduct their business, as the debt is sold on. They are also able to pass on the risks of holding mortgage debt to investors, and the risks are largely outside any regulatory framework.

A critical factor in understanding US research is the importance of the securitised mortgage market, where mortgage loans are packaged into securities. Lenders in most economies traditionally originate, fund and service loans. The securitisation of debt separates the functions of originating, funding and servicing. The benefits of securitisation for lenders and borrowers will be briefly discussed below but it is useful to consider the main reason for the growth of this market in the US. During the 1980s there was a crisis for the Savings and Loans institutions that were the main providers of mortgage finance. These thrift institutions borrowed short-term and loaned money for long periods at fixed rates of interest. Subsequent high and volatile interest rates left the thrifts short of capital. It is perhaps not surprising that subsequent developments favoured funding by selling off packages of mortgages as securities (Coles 2001), increasing the lenders' capital base. This is also a prime lesson in the importance of risk sharing, a key feature of mortgage contract designs. For example, a move to adjustable rate mortgages shifted the risk of interest rate variatiations onto the borrower.

A further important feature of the US mortgage market is the role of the GSEs, the Federal National Mortgage Association (FNMA or Fannie Mae), the Government National Mortgage Association (GNMA or Ginny Mae) and the Federal Home Loan Corporation (FHLC or Freddie Mac). The standardisation of pools of mortgages by these agencies also encouraged the rapid growth in the secondary mortgage market. GNMA is on the federal budget and so receives direct government insurance against mortgage default, the other two agencies have implicit government guarantees. It is argued that these guarantees allow the issuing of mortgage-backed securities at lower interest rates.

The development of the GSEs has increased the liquidity and depth of the securitised mortgage market, underwriting a good deal of US mortgage lending, and possibly contributed to lower borrowing costs. A key research issue is the extent to which mortgage interest costs are lower for the borrower in the US, due securitisation *per se*, or to the underwriting by government agencies (Hendershott & Shilling 1989; Kolari *et al.* 1998; Cantor & Demsetz 1993). The continuing growth of the GSEs and the secondary mortgage market reflects a lower cost of cash flow management and mortgage funding (Van Order 2000). Jaffee & Renaud (1995) argue that the development of the securitised mortgage market is a 'revealed preference' for the lower cost of funds involved, and the ability of lenders to hedge against interest rate risk, that is falls in interest rates when lending at a fixed rate. The introduction and development of such agencies may be necessary to expand housing finance systems that wish to achieve efficiency through the development of a secondary mortgage market.

The role of the Federal Housing Administration (FHA) is important in placing US research on mortgage choices in context. The FHA insures the mortgage debt of the secondary mortgage market institutions against default. For conventional lending outside of this system Savings and Loan institutions and banks have recourse to private insurers. The interesting point is that the FHA prohibits variations in underwriting criterion (that is loan-to-value ratios) by geographical region, so that they cannot be changed to reflect local economic conditions, say, increased to choke off excess demand. This is not a constraint applied to conventional lending. Here we have an example of the securitisation of debt leading to the standardisation of mortgage contracts. This disparity has led to some interesting research on the existence of credit rationing in the US, an issue to be explored fully in Chapter 5 (Ambrose *et al.* 2002; Duca & Rosenthal 1991).

One important aspect of the valuation of mortgage-backed securities is the prepayment behaviour of borrowers. MBS investors are insured against default risk but not interest rate risk, that is the risk that borrowers refinance if interest rates fall. There are ways of creating different classes of security for investors that reflects this risk. However, the analysis of prepayment behaviour remains a major concern in mortgage market research. From the lender's perspective, prepayment risk can be partly covered by charging up-front points. This has led to financial institutions offering different combinations of points and interest rates, which can then attract different types of borrowers. This trade off has formed the major focus of research into asymmetric information and the signalling properties of different mortgage designs. In the UK prepayment risk has been covered primarily by redemption penalties, which penalise borrowers for 'prematurely' exiting from a deal, say on a discounted or fixed rate contract. Once again we will find that these different features of housing finance systems have a bearing upon observed household choices, though our understanding can emanate from a common theoretical base.

Canada is another economy where there has been substantive mortgage market research (see Zorn & Lea 1989; Jones 1993, 1994, 1995; Breslaw *et al.* 1996). The Canadian market is interesting in having so called 'roll over mortgages' which are essentially ARMs. Since the early 1980s Canadian fixed rates have typically been adjusted every three years. Canada also mirrors the UK market in having penalties for prepayment of debt, though these typically relate to partial prepayments of over 10%. When reviewing Canadian research we will have to recall a system with these characteristics and few long-term fixed rate mortgages. However, in common with other mortgage markets there has been considerable innovation in Canada. There are now many examples of fixed rate products, discounts, cash backs and flexible or 'open' mortgages. Mortgage finance in Canada is becoming increasingly separated from retail funding, and characterised by increasing use of securitisation.

A further interesting feature of the Canadian mortgage market is the fact that mortgage interest payments are not tax deductible. In the US there is tax relief for mortgage interest payments, though this is complicated to the extent that the US tax reform act of 1986 has meant that for many taxpayers tax gains on mortgage debt have been significantly reduced (Follain & Dunsky 1997). The point is that the tax treatment of mortgage interest payments differs between countries and can have a significant impact upon housing and mortgage demand. The UK is now like Canada in that tax relief on mortgage interest payments was abandoned in April 2000, though its presence will feature in a number of the studies referred to and discussed in later chapters. UK and European mortgage markets vary in a number of other key ways that bear upon the analysis of household choices.

The United Kingdom and European mortgage markets

The UK mortgage market is one of the most sophisticated and liberal markets in the world. The UK economy and its housing market also have their own particular characteristics. There are high levels of owner occupation, high levels of indebtedness and high proportions of mortgages where the interest rate is variable rather than fixed. These features of the UK housing and mortgage market have led to high sensitivity of consumer spending, and savings decisions, to changes in interest rates (Earley 2000). However, high levels of owner occupation and indebtedness are features of other economies–recent reports for both Canada[8] and Australia[9] have featured large amounts of mortgage borrowing as posing a potential afford-ability problem for borrowers. This demonstrates the importance of under-standing the basis of mortgage demand, the key focus of Chapters 2 and 3 of this book.

The funding of mortgage finance in the United Kingdom has been primar-ily through retail deposits though there has been an increase in off balance sheet financing and the securitisation of mortgage debt. Securitisation has been primarily used by so called centralised mortgage lenders who entered the UK market during the late 1980s (Pryke & Whitehead 1991; Pais 2002). Some of these lenders were of US origin, a competitive incursion to be repeated later with the development of the UK sub-prime lending market (e.g. the entry of Money Store in 1997). The centralised lenders were competitors to the traditional building societies and banks. Recently the share of lending by the centralised sector has declined having dropped below 10% during the 1990s,[10] but increasing competitive pressures are leading more traditional providers to consider mortgage securitisation.

European mortgage markets offer more examples of size, role and funding of mortgage debt,[11] and provide an interesting comparison with the UK. Germany and Denmark rely mostly upon mortgage banks which issue mortgage bonds, thus allowing longer-term fixed rate deals to what is a smaller mortgage sector. France has a whole range of legal restrictions and regulations that make its mortgage market less heterogeneous. France also relies upon retail savings to finance mortgage lending, as does the UK, the Irish Republic and Spain. The Netherlands has a system similar to the UK. The existence of such varied housing finance systems has created impediments to convergence towards a single European mortgage market (Munchau 1997; Stephens 2000), so that in empirical work we must note the features of the particular housing finance system concerned.

The UK mortgage market is an example of a mature and deregulated mortgage market where competition has generated a large variety of mortgage contracts. This competition has encouraged discounting of interest rates (teaser rates), cash back arrangements, indexing to the base rate of interest and the emergence of flexible/lifestyle mortgages. Here we have an important dimension of housing finance efficiency discussed above, which is matching consumer preferences. However, the basis of this heterogeneity is something of a puzzle. If lenders are risk-neutral and borrowers risk averse, then the FRM is the optimum mortgage instrument with the lender bearing interest rate risk (Brueckner & Arvan 1986; Brueckner 1993). Explanations lie with housing finance systems and imperfect markets.

We have already noted how differences in funding, regulations and underwriting risk might explain why some contracts, in this case the long-term FRM in the UK, may not be generally available. Housing finance systems vary according to how the risk of interest rate changes is shared. In the UK the borrower has typically borne this risk through the prevalence of variable rate debt. The management of credit risk, where the borrower may default, is also an important driver of differences in mortgage designs (Roche 1999). In France this has led to the imposition of low loan-to-value ratios. In the UK households are liable for any shortfall if they sell a property that is in negative equity, so that deliberate default may not be wealth maximising. The heterogeneity of mortgage contracts might also reflect affordability and information problems which again may vary by housing finance system.

One important aspect of most mortgage markets is that they are constantly subject to change. Considerations of mortgage market futures have even suggested the eventual demise of the specific mortgage instrument, as mortgage borrowing becomes indistinguishable from other forms of debt, with financial planning taking the form of a universal account (Roche 1999). There has been an observable trend towards combining mortgage debt with liquid bank accounts and other lines of credit, certainly in the UK and Australia. There may be other forces leading to a more common future, for example it has been argued that the Canadian mortgage market increasingly resembles that of the United States. Lending has moved away from the traditional banking sector and there is increasing securitisation of mortgage finance. The imperatives of securitisation might eventually impose a degree of uniformity on contracts across a number of countries. The role of secondary mortgage market development and the securitisation of mortgage debt is clearly critical to present and future contract choices.

The secondary mortgage market

The essence of secondary mortgage market development is the separation of the origination, funding, holding and servicing of mortgage loans. In traditional lending, for example by building societies in the UK, each of these functions is carried out by the provider. Secondary mortgage markets do not require securitisation, though this is the ultimate refinement of secondary mortgage market development and capital market integration. The key characteristic of securitisation is that when a pool of mortgages is packaged for sale to investors then the funding of mortgage debt is moved off balance sheet and is separated from the origination and servicing of that debt.

The key feature of securitisation from the investor's point of view is that they now face the risk of early prepayment or default on the debt. Thus prepayment and default behaviour will be relevant to the valuation of mortgage-backed securities. We have already seen how secondary mortgage market investors are explicitly or implicitly insured against default risk in the US. Indeed the lack of such insurance in the UK and Europe has been noted as a major inhibitor to secondary mortgage development (Jaffee & Renaud 1995). However, prepayment remains an important source of risk to cash flows to mortgage securities, even in the US.

Mortgage securitisation has been argued to have many benefits, including the noted lower cost of raising funds and thus increased efficiency in both the cost minimisation sense, and in terms of intermediation efficiency. Potential benefits include the reduction in interest rate costs for the borrower, increased credit availability and reduced credit rationing, improved liquidity for lenders along with greater degrees of geographical diversification. Later chapters will raise these issues again, for example, how far has securitisation facilitated speedier mortgage market adjustment, reducing some forms of credit rationing? Securitisation has raised other significant research questions. What are the costs and benefits for borrowers and lenders? Do mortgage rates now react more quickly to interest rate changes? Has securitisation increased the degree of integration between the market for housing finance and other capital markets, such as the bond and share markets? How do different mortgage contract designs impact upon MBS valuation and how do the dictates of securitisation effect contractual features?

The growth in the secondary mortgage market in the US has provided a spur to research into mortgage market economics. The development of the securitised mortgage market should lead to the integration of the mortgage market with other capital markets; there is a stream of research that considers this question (Goebel & Ma 1993; Allen *et al.* 1999). The enhanced liquidity and credit controls that follow from securitisation should also lead to benefits for borrowers, including lower mortgage interest rates (see Black *et al.* 1981; Hendershott & Shilling 1989; and for a different view see Todd 2001). Jaffee & Renaud (1995) note how the benefits of securitisation will be shared among mortgage borrowers, capital market investors and the lending and securitising agencies. Given a competitive lending market, and the relatively more elastic demand for securities by investors the benefits of securitisation are considered to be higher for borrowers (Jaffee & Renaud 1995). However, securitisation might lead to mortgage rates reflecting current interest rate changes much more quickly.

An example of how the nature of securitisation can effect loan contracts are loans which exceed the limit for conforming loans suitable for securitisation in the US, termed 'jumbo' mortgages. Jumbo loans have a positive rate differential over conforming loans (Hendershott & Shilling 1989; Cotterman & Pearce 1996) which might be attributable to the greater liquidity afforded to conforming mortgages through purchase by the GSEs (Cotterman & Pearce 1996). However, other explanations have been advanced for this interest rate differential, including differences in the price volatility of the houses that provide collateral for the loans (Ambrose 2001). The volatility of underlying assets effects the contract rate on the mortgage, a matter to be further explored in Chapters 9 and 10 of this book where we examine mortgage valuation and pricing.

Here we see the importance of variations in microeconomic factors (in this case, characteristics of the property) for mortgage valuation and a way that securitisation has effected the pricing of loan contracts.

So exactly how quantitatively important is the securitised mortgage market? This market is most fully developed in the US. Figure 1.1 shows the rapid growth in the mortgage-backed securities issued by the US federal home loan agencies. During 2001 the issue of mortgage-backed securities by the major US agencies reached a peak of $1,092.6 billion. This was a feature of a fluctuating market, for example, there was an issue of $482.4 billion in 2000 having fallen from $685.2 in 1999.[12] The new issues of mortgage debt depend upon changes in the prime market for mortgage finance and the varying figures emphasise this link. The total amount of outstanding mortgage-backed securities in the US was $3,041.9 billion as of 30 June 2002, indicating a phenomenally large market.[13]

The Canadian mortgage market is argued to be undergoing a dramatic, if not revolutionary, change in funding and loan provision. Traditionally mortgage lending has been based upon a few large financial institutions. Mortgage rates in Canada, as in the United Kingdom, do not always respond to changes in market interest rates, and adjustments when they arrived were often large. However, increased securitisation and off balance

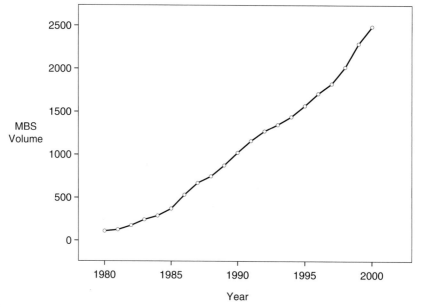

Figure 1.1   Outstanding volume of agency backed mortgage-backed securities (US$ billions).

Source: The Bond Market Association.

sheet financing is creating a more rapid response in mortgage rate adjust-ment.[14] Securitisation has also developed in the Australian mortgage market being led by government house building programmes in the 1980s, which used securitisation as a source of finance. Non-deposit taking institutions entered the Australian mortgage market during the 1990s taking up to 20% of new home loans in 1995,[15] thus adding further impetus to growth via competition from the retail banking sector.[16] Securitisation is a truly international phenomenon.

European mortgage lenders predominantly use mortgage bonds or retail savings deposits to finance mortgage loans. However, the securitised mort-gage market has shown quite rapid recent growth in some European countries. For example, France has a growth of 226.47% (in US dollar terms) of issues of MBS securities between the second quarter of 2001 and the second quarter of 2002. The equivalent figure for the UK was 18.24%, and for the whole of Europe a growth rate of 14.92%.[17] The European market is of particular interest, since attempts at integrating mortgage markets can be evaluated and lessons drawn for the possibility of truly global housing finance systems. For example, extensive securitisa-tion should lead to the equalisation of mortgage rates across countries.

Stephens (2000) notes that there has been little evidence of convergence of mortgage markets in Europe and that cross-border selling has not been very successful. The main difficulty appears to be that lenders in some countries have access to 'privileged sources of funds'. It is an interesting, but at the moment, speculative, point as to whether increased securitisa-tion, and the competitive pressures which underpin it, will erode barriers to convergence on both a European and worldwide scale. Of course, simi-larity is not the same as convergence and while barriers to cross-border selling may remain, some similarities might develop. Generally however, we are looking at a market of international significance. The maturing home finance market is playing an increasingly important, if not yet complete, role within international capital markets.

There is a danger that securitisation, or the possibility of its increased use, is seen as a panacea for removing inefficiencies in housing finance systems, and housing markets. Indeed, there is a theoretical argument that in a perfectly competitive economy with no information problems, packaging mortgages for investors is unnecessary. Securitisation only makes sense if there are information or liquidity problems which it over-comes. There may be problems with securitised mortgage markets if primary mortgage markets are not adequately developed. For example, there needs to be the legal and real estate underpinnings necessary for primary market development. Evolving housing finance systems might be damaged by too early exposure to international capital markets, and foreign competition that hampers domestic lending and banking institutions. Globalised capital markets also increase the susceptibility of national housing finance systems to international disturbances.

The UK securitised mortgage market is not yet as fully developed as that in the US, and there are still some impediments to the expansion of this market in Europe, for example, lack of state guarantees as in the US, and varied legal and regulatory frameworks (Coles 2001). However, many of the research questions and findings that the growth in the MBS market has encouraged are applicable to understanding mortgage market issues in the UK, Europe and many developing economies with emerging and growing mortgage finance markets. For example, the fair pricing of redemption penalties to offset prepayment risk (see Skinner 1999), or the valuation of the various components of mortgage contracts (Pereira *et al.* 2002, 2003). Thus, this book takes the view that mortgage market economics, as currently conceived and researched, is of international importance. However, this is not a 'one size fits all' philosophy, and, in fact, a major argument of this book is the importance of meeting and analysing the variety of needs and preferences, both within and across evolving housing financing systems.

Why study household behaviour? The rationale of this book

Radical changes in housing finance systems give the study of consumer behaviour in mortgage markets extra imperative. Financial deregulation during the 1980s paved the way for major structural changes in mortgage markets. In both the US and the UK the right to sell mortgage debt was extended to a wider range of financial institutions. Recent history has seen the rise of specialist mortgage banks, securitisation, the cross-border sale of mortgages, the growing importance of information technology and the emergence of new mortgage instruments. An impetus to these changes has been the development of fiercely competitive mortgage markets. Neven & Roller (1999) found econometric evidence of an increasingly competitive environment across European mortgage markets.

Though not the only explanation, increasing competition in the provision of housing finance has led to product and cost cutting innovations. The UK and US consumer now faces an extensive, and potentially bewildering, menu of mortgage contracts. A taxonomy of mortgage instruments for the US and the UK must include fixed and adjustable, interest only and annuity, capped and collared, discounted and standard variable, flexible and balloon mortgages, etc. Mortgage characteristics can be combined in a 'pick and mix' fashion, and within each category there may be a choice of interest rate and risk exposure, or other contractual features.[18] How consumers react to this complexity and make their mortgage choices is a key focus of this book. Household behaviour takes on a more central role.

In the US a major innovation in the mortgage market was the introduction of adjustable rate mortgages (ARMs) during the 1980s. In the UK a key change was the creation of short-term fixed rate contracts (FRMs), during the early 1990s. Volatile and unanticipated inflation prompted the issue of ARMs in the US, while a depressed and risky housing market, together with financial deregulation, encouraged fixed rate debt in the UK (Miles 1992). These contract choices have major implications for risk sharing between borrowers and lenders with potential impacts upon the housing market and general macroeconomic management. Interesting is the emergence of the sub-prime lending market, where lenders advance mortgages to the so called 'credit impaired'. There are a number of interesting agency problems, issues concerning asymmetric information, and questions relating to credit rationing that arise out of a consideration of the growth in sub-prime lending. This is a market that is also growing in the UK, primarily led by US providers.

Lenders have not only increased the variety of mortgage instruments available to consumers. The more productive processing and use of information, together with establishing databases to analyse the behaviour of borrowers, have become increasingly important. In the US pressures from secondary mortgage market investors, eager to preserve their cash flows, has led to a focus on the management of payment delinquency–mainly with a view to avoiding mortgage default. Improved information on consumers' credit histories has facilitated this management process (Ambrose & Capone 1996, 2000). Once again, the emergence of the secondary mortgage market has given an imperative to research into consumer behaviour in the mortgage market.

Bennet *et al.* (1998, 2001) have argued that the supply side of the US housing financing system has undergone fundamental structural changes over the last 25 years. Competition has reduced the points[19] and fees attached to mortgage transactions, and shortened the duration of the process from application to the closing of the contract. The increased visibility of competitor prices has also been a key development. These factors have all encouraged the refinancing of mortgage debt, and formed one explanation for refinancing waves in the US (Bennet *et al.* 1998, 2001). Refinancing, or prepayment, is one of the important determinants of cash flows to mortgage-backed securities, and therefore contributes to their valuation. Figure 1.2 highlights both the behaviour and numerical significance of refinancing behaviour in the US, with a peak of 70% of mortgage originations in the fourth quarter of 2001. The reasons for the apparent waves of refinancing activity will be explored in Chapter 10 of this book. Understanding this phenomenon is critical to understanding the relationship between household behaviour and the wider mortgage and housing markets.

The UK mortgage market has also seen a reduction in search costs with internet personal finance sites and a proliferation of mortgage consumer magazines. This may partly explain the increase in refinancing activity as consumers switch between providers. For example, CML figures for January 2001 show 33% of total advances were remortgages. The UK is interesting in having redemption penalties for prepayment of fixed rate and discount mortgages, a form of cover for prepayment risk that is actually illegal in some American states. Valuing such redemption penalties is a good example of how concepts applied in mortgage valuation still have relevance to mortgage pricing when secondary markets do not exist, or are at a developmental stage (see Skinner 1999).

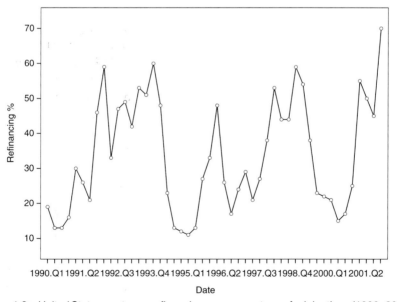

Figure 1.2   United States mortgage refinancing as a percentage of originations (1990–2001).

Source: Housing and Urban Development (1990–1997); Mortgage Bankers of America Estimates.

In summary, mortgage markets are of great economic importance for many economies. In Europe and the US mortgage markets have been becoming increasingly competitive. The growth of the secondary mortgage market has been a spur to research into those aspects of consumer decision making that impact on the cash flows to MBSs. Cost cutting, changes in funding strategies and innovative new mortgage instruments have made the consumer decision making process more complex, and even more compelling as an area for analysis and research. The impact of mortgage choices upon individual and household welfare always was an important issue; increasing competition, product heterogeneity and securitisation have merely refocused and sharpened the research agenda. Increasingly, household behaviour must be viewed in the context of the greater integration of national and international capital markets. The extent and nature of contracts and securities available to borrowers and investors reflects upon the efficiency of the housing finance system, and such choices will feature throughout this book.

The structure of the book

The book begins by looking at the theoretical and empirical basis of mortgage demand (Chapters 2 and 3). In Chapter 2 mortgage demand is presented as a core area of analysis that relates to other household mortgage choices. In the language of econometrics we find that mortgage demand is characterised by simultaneous decision making and multiple sources of selectivity bias. For example, when a household prepays a mortgage a new and larger mortgage may be raised, so that prepayment and mortgage demand can be linked. Chapter 2 considers the basic assumptions that are frequently made about the economic environment when analysing mortgage choices. The book as a whole argues that both an ideal view of the world as a competitive no arbitrage economy, and one where there are capital market imperfections, imperfect contract designs, information problems and liquidity constraints both offer important insights into mortgage choices, and mortgage market policy. Chapter 2 also offers some basic definitions, including what we mean by the value of a mortgage, which will assist understanding the more difficult arguments introduced later in the book.

The discussion in Chapter 2 presents some preliminary definitions, research questions and key perspectives on mortgage market choices surrounding such issues as the rate at which mortgages are amortised, household choice of mortgage contract design, and prepayment and default. In doing this the main themes of the book are also established. The overall aim of the book is to offer both theoretical insights and empirical evidence on the working of mortgage markets, and the importance of household decision making. For example, Chapter 3 follows up the theoretical discussion of mortgage demand presented in Chapter 2 with a review of empirical evidence on the determinants of household demand for mortgage finance, and also presents some new data.

One important theme throughout this book is the importance of the actual design of mortgage contracts for both household choices and wider economic issues. Both imperfect capital markets, and less than ideal contract design, can constrain the mortgage and housing choices of households. Chapter 4 explores this issue more fully, and notes the problems of contract design in an inflationary environment, together with the likely emphasis of many households upon affordability and cash flow. Also important are aspects of contract design that have implications for the sharing of risk between the borrower and lender, a consideration that underpins many extant mortgage instruments. The growth in so called flexible mortgages is a recent phenomenon that raises interesting questions regarding overcoming capital market imperfections or minimising mortgage costs.

Chapters 5 and 6 look at the question of credit rationing in mortgage markets. This is viewed in the wider context of how mortgage markets adjust to shifts in supply and demand, an issue raised in the discussion of the impact of securitisation. We continue with the theme of capital market imperfections, but now focus on the particularly important issues of incentives and information problems. Once again, this leads to a consideration of mortgage contract designs. Are some contracts styled to induce certain types of borrower to self-select? For example, do households with low default costs, and thus a high propensity to default, adopt larger more expensive mortgages, and does this process lead to credit rationing for those with higher default costs? Chapter 5 presents the recent theoretical developments in this area, while Chapter 6 looks at the empirical evidence.

The first half of the book (Chapters 1 to 6) is rather tantalising in its emphasis upon the importance of the design of mortgage contracts, in that there is no discussion of the fundamental question of why we observe such a variety of mortgage designs (contract heterogeneity). This is rectified in Chapter 7 and Chapter 8, which look respectively at the theoretical underpinnings of mortgage design and household choice, and the empirical evidence on the choice of mortgage instrument. In fact, Chapter 7 provides a collecting point for many of the issues raised in earlier chapters, such as the desired payment profiles of borrowers together with the links between mortgage demand, household wealth and its variance. Once again issues of information and incentives feature here with a discussion of the screening and signalling properties of mortgage instruments. Chapter 8 considers the possible simultaneity of mortgage choice and housing demand, also considering the problems that are posed by contract heterogeneity. Is there excess variety that imposes large search costs upon consumers, militating against the packaging of mortgages for securitisation? Can predatory selling (termed mis-selling in the United Kingdom), and the associated agency problems be detected as a form of classification error?

If previous chapters have been concerned with the imperfections in the operation of mortgage and other capital markets then Chapters 9 and 10 now look at the best of all possible worlds. Retaining the focus upon household behaviour and decision making, the chapters examine the view that mortgage default can be considered a put option, with prepayment looked upon as a call option. A great deal of financial economics has been about the valuation of such options, and mortgage market economics is an obvious area in which to extend this reasoning. Chapters 9 and 10 recognise that the decision to prepay a mortgage and the decision to default are not entirely separate, exposing yet another complex interaction in this fascinating marketplace.

The ideas that capital markets are imperfect, that liquidity constraints are important and that rational financial calculation is not always followed are not entirely abandoned, and re-emerge in Chapter 10. Empirical research, while generally revealing the usefulness of adopting an option theoretic approach to household decision making, has also noted that a good part of default and prepayment behaviour cannot be explained in this way. However, the jury is still out in this debate as econometric techniques become more sophisticated, and the availability and use of data becomes more refined.

The book concludes with a return to a paper published by Follain (1990); a piece of work that I would still recommend to anyone interested in the economics of mortgage markets. That paper sets out the then state of the art of mortgage market economics and points to those areas requiring further research. In returning to that piece of work we can establish a benchmark for evaluating the progress in this area over the last 12 years, and an indicator of key research areas still to be addressed. Chapter 11 also summarises the key issues explored in this book, reflects upon the main themes, and considers the future of mortgage markets and the economics of the mortgage market.

Reading the book

This book focuses upon research into the mortgage choices of households. This involves reporting and commenting on both theoretical and empirical work that has often used advanced mathematical and econometric techniques. However, the material should be of interest to both the non-technical real estate specialist who wishes to know more about mortgage market behaviour, and the real estate economist and econometrician eager to appraise the current state of the art. I have endeavoured to make the material accessible so that the mathematics does not get in the way of the broader themes, critiques and conclusions. However, it is important for more technical specialists to be aware of the techniques and mathematical reasoning adopted. Where possible, I have explained the broad nature of the econometric methods applied and the specification problems involved in empirical work.

The book is written so that particular subject areas, for example the choice of mortgage instrument, can be read alone, though I would recommend that both the theoretical and companion empirical chapters be read together. Even sections of chapters which appear mathematical and technical make some general statements regarding the key relationships, and offer intuitive glimpses of the reasoning involved. I would therefore recommend that the reader does not omit the more technical sections, and that the broader conclusions be carried forward to enhance understanding of the empirical evidence. The more difficult chapters are Chapter 7, which includes the impact of inflation on the choice of mortgage instrument, and Chapter 9 which considers the option theoretic framework that underlies rational wealth maximising prepayment and default behaviour. In these two cases I have endeavoured to make the empirical chapters more self-contained but resonant of their theoretical counterparts.

The empirical research reported in this volume largely relates to work from the US and the UK, with some research from other countries such as Canada, Australia and Japan. The dominance of work from the US, as explained elsewhere, reflects the importance of the mortgage market and its securitisation for the US and international economy. It would be a serious mistake for anyone interested in mortgage market economics to confine their interest to the research conducted within their own national boundaries. Not only have we seen the growing international nature of mortgage markets, but also there is now a large body of pertinent theory and technique that the mortgage market researcher needs to be aware of. This is not to say that the particular characteristics of housing finance systems do not impinge upon the appropriate choice of technique, modification of theory or even the behaviour of households themselves. Housing finance systems vary in their efficiency. Throughout the book there will be an emphasis upon comparisons between UK and US work and that of other countries, where possible.

Summary and conclusions

This introductory chapter has established the necessary background to the study of mortgage market economics. Mortgage markets are of obvious importance to the performance of national economies, the growth in owner occupation, and individual and household welfare. The development of the securitised mortgage market in the US has motivated an increasing amount of theoretical and empirical research into the mortgage choices of households. Though we must always keep in mind important institutional differences, variations in the efficiency of housing finance systems, and differences in mortgage contract design that obtain between countries, mortgage economics research has significantly advanced the understanding of household behaviour and mortgage choices. The choice set of mortgage contracts, and the choices made, give insight into the nature of a housing finance system, and the completeness and efficiency of capital markets. This book has these and other mortgage choices as its focus.

The major form of the empirical research discussed in this book will be cross-section studies of household decision making. Cross-section studies can give important insights into the nature of consumer behaviour and heterogeneous characteristics that are aggregated in time series studies. This book does not ignore important time series work, but does emphasise the theoretical and empirically based microeconomic foundations of mortgage market analysis. The book explores the themes of optimal mortgage contract design, rational financial calculations that impinge upon cash flows to the securitised mortgage market and the impact of capital market imperfections, liquidity constraints and information asymmetries. The reader who studies this book should gain an understanding of the importance, structure and key directions of mortgage market research, as well as a guide to research questions as yet unexplored, or in need of further investigation and analysis.

Guide to further reading

For further reading on comparative housing finance systems try Diamond, D.B. (Jnr) & M.J. Lea (1992) which offers a comprehensive overview of comparative systems. Also worthwhile for an understanding of the issues involved in comparative analysis there is Boleat (1985). Of course, some of the material in these texts is now a little dated, so for a comparatively recent update on European mortgage markets read Lea *et al.* (1997). For a continuous update on mortgage market developments across Europe keep an eye on the website of the European Mortgage Federation (**www. hypo.org**) while the Council of Mortgage Lenders website tracks UK developments (**www.cml.org.uk**). For the US the websites of government sponsored agencies such as Fannie Mae (**www.fanniemae.com**) and Freddie Mac (**www.freddiemac.com**) are prolific sources of information. The *International Housing Finance Sourcebook* is another means of keeping up to date (see Lea 2000).

Notes

1 IFC Annual report (2000).
2 Ellen P. Roche (1999) 'Loans Around the World', SMM *Online,* The author also presents an interesting Japanese character that is not reproduced here. Curious individuals are referred to the original text. www.freddiemac.com/finance/fr-smm/apr9//html-pages/loans.htm.
3 Hypostat 1988–1998, European Mortgage Federation.
4 Cited in Deng *et al.* (2000).
5 Source: Statistics Canada, Survey of Financial Security, 1999, Assets and Debts held by Family Units.
6 Source: Hicks, P. (2001) *Trends in Mortgages,* Economics, Commerce and Industrial Relations Group, Parliament of Australia, Department of the Parliamentary Library.
7 I am indebted to the insight of Professor Jim Shilling for this comment.
8 Wade, P.J. (2002) Canadian mortgage debt grows amid interest queries, Real Estate News and Advice, *Realty Times.*
9 Hicks, P. (2001) *Trends in Mortgages,* Economics, Commerce and Industrial Relations Group, Parliament of Australia, Department of the Parliamentary Library.
10 Source: Bank of England Monetary and Financial Statistics.
11 For a fuller discussion of the comparative mortgage systems in Europe and the different mortgage products available see Maclennan *et al.* (1998) and Lea *et al.* (1997).
12 Figures taken from The Bond Market Association, **www.bondmarketys.com** (Issuance of Agency Mortgage Backed Securities).

13 Figures taken from The Bond Market Association, **www.bondmarketys.com** (Outstanding Volume of Agency Mortgage Backed Securities).

14 See Tower Group Report (2002) The Canadian Mortgage Market, to be found on http://about.reuters.com/newsreleases/index2002_0.asp.

15 See O'Connell, B. and Leung, B. (1996) 'Mortgage Securitisation in Australia: Its adoption, driving forces and impediments', *Mimeo*, Syme Department of Accounting, Monash University, Australia.

16 Cooper, L. (2002) 'Mortgage Assets Expand the Market', *Risk Magazine*, November, Risk Waters Group Ltd.

17 Figures taken from The Bond Market Association, **www.bondmarketys.com** (European MBS Issuance by Country of Collateral).

18 See Schoenbeck (1999) 'ARM Borrowers Match Loans to Their Uncertainty Tolerances', *Money Market Trends*, SMM On Line, Freddie Mac.

19 Mortgage points are front loaded charges that are typically traded off against the interest rate charge. Thus a low interest rate would invite higher points. There is extensive literature on the significance of mortgage points. This will be discussed later in the book.

2

The Demand for Mortgage Finance: Theory

Introduction

The discussion in Chapter 1 demonstrated just how important the mortgage market is for national economic performance, along with its impact upon the economic welfare of individuals and households. Moreover, the burgeoning secondary mortgage market, where housing debt may be packaged into securities is a major international financial market. Of course these developments, and the scale of cash flows coursing through this marketplace, depend upon the nature and extent of the demand for mortgage debt. In this chapter we discuss the central idea of the demand for mortgage finance, and the way that it can form a focus for other issues in mortgage market economics.

That there is a link between housing demand and the demand for housing debt is stating the obvious, whether it relates to the decision to enter owner occupation, or the demand for a given level of housing services. However, the link is not always clear cut and mortgage finance might be used for a number of purposes, including the demand for non-housing assets (Jones 1993, 1994, 1995). The discussion begins by looking at formal theoretical models which do relate mortgage demand directly to decisions on housing, based upon utility maximising decisions by households. However, the second part of this chapter takes a broader view of mortgage demand, relating it to several other issues. Examples here are prepaying a mortgage, defaulting on payments, choosing a particular type of mortgage contract and more widely, examining the impact of mortgage decisions on the saving and investment portfolios of households. This approach provides a good introduction to the main topics covered in the rest of the book.

A critical factor in the discussion is the view taken of the general economic environment in which borrowers make decisions. Chapter 1 noted that in a perfectly competitive no arbitrage economy many mortgage choices would appear irrelevant, or not exist at all. For example, if different mortgage instruments are correctly priced to reflect their different risk then borrowers ought to be indifferent to which one they choose. This echoes the discussion of the efficiency of housing finance systems in Chapter 1, and the M & M proposition on the irrelevance of gearing. The contrast with approaches that stress capital market imperfections, information problems and less than fully efficient housing finance systems will be an issue raised throughout this book, with both 'world views' argued to have an important role in describing and formally analysing mortgage market behaviour.

The chapter begins with an exposition of models of mortgage demand under conditions where future incomes, interest rates and house prices are known with certainty. The discussion then moves on to examine the application of the type of models typically used in financial economics, which involve uncertainty and key portfolio choices. The chapter then adopts an overview of the interconnections between the different elements of mortgage market analysis, with mortgage demand at its core. Where relevant, reference will be made to the implications of the theory for the empirical estimation of mortgage demand equations, a matter taken up in Chapter 3. However, the discussion in this chapter is primarily theoretical, and for now ignores differences in institutional, tax and regulatory arrangements between countries, matters to be raised in the empirical implementation of mortgage demand models.

The theoretical basis of mortgage demand

Existing theoretical models of mortgage demand suggest a complex set of relationships, not least arising from the joint consumption/investment aspects of housing (see Ioannides 1989; Brueckner 1997). In fact, many of the mathematical models developed in this area do not have closed form solutions (e.g. Alm & Follain 1987). However, the formal models do offer important insights into the basis of mortgage demand, links with the demand for housing services, and other related decisions. Certainly the models are highly suggestive of the appropriate empirical specification of econometric models of the demand for housing debt. Theoretical constructions based upon uncertainty are the most complex of all, but they do give important insights into portfolio decisions, of which mortgage and housing choices are surely an important part. The discussion which follows explores mortgage demand in a world of certainty, followed by an application of the types of theoretical models involving uncertainty, typically found in financial economics textbooks.[1]

Modelling mortgage demand under conditions of certainty

Several authors have modelled mortgage demand in the context of certainty (Brueckner 1994a; Jones 1993, 1994; Follain & Dunsky 1997; Dunsky & Follain 2000). It is assumed that future interest rates, incomes, rates of return, housing and other asset prices are all known. Certainty models help to introduce the basic building blocks and common approaches to modelling mortgage demand, also providing some useful initial simplification and important results. They have also informed most econometric specifications of mortgage demand equations (Follain & Dunsky 1997; Jones 1993, 1994, 1995). A seminal paper by Brueckner (1994a) established some 'basic results' for a model of mortgage demand, and it is that model which forms the basis of the discussion presented here.

Brueckner's model of mortgage demand with certainty

The general structure of models with certainty is as follows. Typically we examine choices over two periods, or within a single period with a focus on wealth (W) at the beginning of period 2 (end of period 1). The consumer chooses between housing (H) and a non-housing composite consumption good (c). The consumer's problem is to maximise utility (U) over the two periods. This involves choosing optimum amounts of housing, non-housing consumption, and levels of mortgage debt. Of course, this maximisation is subject to the constraints set by income, prices and the rate of return r_s on any savings s used to generate wealth. So for example, the amount available for spending in the first period will be limited and the amount of potential wealth at the end of the second period will also form a constraint. Wealth in housing and mortgage demand models yields positive utility.

Intuitively, varying the amount of mortgage debt will effect final wealth via the lost opportunities from saving, and the payment of interest rate costs. The amount of debt also impacts upon the trade off between housing and non-housing consumption. Increased debt reduces the size of any required deposit on the property in the first period, and therefore facilitates increased consumption of the non-housing composite good. Thus mortgage size is linked to wealth accumulation and the determination of consumption. Mortgage demand can then be examined in a framework where the time preference ('impatience') of the borrower becomes important as well as the rate of return on savings compared to the mortgage interest rate. Given a number of other constraints on the borrower, the Brueckner model deduces the implications for mortgage demand of varying rates of impatience, and different interest rate regimes, that is the size of the mortgage rate compared to the rate of return on savings.

$$U = U(c, H + \lambda^{-1}W) \tag{2.1}$$

Formally, Brueckner presents a utility function for the household, and this is given by expression (2.1). The utility function is assumed to be strictly concave, with the utility of non-housing consumption and housing completely separable. Note that future wealth W is discounted by the discount rate λ and that this rate represents the individual/household rate of time preference. Decisions are based on the assumption that the household has already decided to enter owner occupation.

The household faces two budget constraints, one for each of the two periods. The first period budget constraint is given by expression (2.2). This simply states that the amount available for spending on non-housing consumption c, depends upon an endowment of initial wealth w, minus the amount saved s, minus the down payment on the property $(p_hH - m$, where p_h is the price per unit of housing services, H is the level of housing services and m is the size of mortgage debt).

$$c = w - s - (p_hH - m) \tag{2.2}$$

The second period budget constraint relates to the level of potential final wealth W, and is given by expression (2.3). Positive contributions to wealth emerge from several sources. Wealth is made up of income received in the second period y, the total return on the savings from the first period $(1 + r_s)s$, and housing equity. The contribution of housing equity is reduced by any interest due on the outstanding mortgage balance m, that is $(1 + r_m)m$. To simplify the analysis the mortgage is assumed to be an interest only contract, with the total amount borrowed due at the end of the second period. So we now have the problem of maximising utility given by (1), subject to the constraints on consumption and end of period wealth established by expressions (2) and (3).

$$W = y + (1 + r_s)s + p_hH - (1 + r_m)m \tag{2.3}$$

$$U = [(w - s - (p_hH - m), \ H] + \lambda^{-1}W(y + (1 + r_s)s + p_hH - (1 + r_m)m)] \tag{2.4}$$

Substituting the constraints on c and W (expressions 2.2 and 2.3) into the utility function given by (2.1) results in expression (2.4). This is now a single equation which can be maximised to select the optimum quantities of H, s, and m. However, there are some further constraints on any solutions. The loan-to-value ratio must be less than or equal to 100%. Also, in terms of the household balance sheet a negative mortgage would imply lending at the mortgage interest rate, and this is prohibited. Again thinking of a household balance sheet negative saving implies borrowing to finance non-housing consumption, and again this is not allowed within the model. This last restriction represents a liquidity constraint with borrowing restricted to financing house purchase. These constraints simplify the model and represent some important stylised features of many mortgage markets.

Brueckner (1994a) solves for mortgage demand in this model by assuming a fixed amount of housing demand H.[2] The model is also solved for two different interest rate regimes, when $r_s < r_m$ and when $r_s > r_m$. Thus, the two regimes represent the case when the rate of return on savings is greater than the mortgage interest rate, and the case where the mortgage interest rate is higher than the rate of return on savings. These inequalities are important, not only in generating different solutions to the model, but also representing different tax regimes; for example the USA compared to Canada,[3] and the recent removal of tax relief on mortgage interest payments in the UK. It may also be the case that borrowers have different opportunity costs of equity in property reflecting their different portfolio positions (Leece 1995b),[4] thus resulting in varying relationships between net of tax mortgage costs and the rate of return on savings.

The results for the mortgage demand under certainty model state that in the case where $r_s > r_m$, that is mortgage finance is comparatively cheap, then the consumer will borrow as much as possible (up to the maximum loan-to-value ratio) to finance the purchase of H.[5] The case of $r_s < r_m$, with a comparatively more expensive mortgage, is less clear cut. A corner solution of zero debt occurs if the consumer wishes to save, that is if the consumer has positive savings $s > 0$.

There is a neat intuitive argument here.[6] Clearly if a borrower could raise negative mortgage debt then they would be lending/saving at the more expensive mortgage rate r_m. If savings are positive because they are willing to save at the lower savings rate r_s, then such mortgage lending/saving at the higher rate would certainly be an attractive option. However, the borrower is precluded from lending at the mortgage rate and the nearest they can get to a negative mortgage is to hold no mortgage at all. Thus in the case of more expensive mortgage debt, and positive savings, there is a corner solution of zero borrowing. However, it is possible to have a number of intermediate positions.

The choice of mortgage size in the $r_s < r_m$ scenario can be anywhere between zero and the maximum allowed, depending upon the time preference, or degree of impatience of the borrower. For example, a very impatient borrower would wish to maximise their mortgage debt; given that they are not allowed negative savings (that is they are liquidity constrained) then they will hold zero savings. This is the opposite case to the zero mortgage borrowing/positive saving situation. A borrower who was not so impatient might desire to borrow at both the saving and the mortgage rate, while again being constrained to having zero saving and borrowing less than 100% of the value of the property. Thus when mortgages are comparatively expensive the desired level of mortgage debt depends critically upon the degree of impatience of the borrower.

Two main outcomes of the Brueckner model, under the two scenarios, are corner solutions. Jones (1994) obtains a similar result[7] as does Rothenberg (1983). It is straightforward to analyse this form of decision making in a multi-period life cycle framework, looking at lifetime wealth, and very similar results can be derived (see Ranney 1981; Jones 1993, 1994).

The analysis by Brueckner suggests the appropriate arguments for any cross-sectional empirical estimation of a mortgage demand equation guided by the certainty case. The econometric model should include initial wealth, expected future income and the borrower's discount rate. These variables may not be observable, and will require some proxy measures. Importantly, the level of housing services demanded (or an instrument for this) should also be included as this is likely to be simultaneously determined with mortgage demand.[8] For example, a household can overcome a loan-to-value constraint on borrowing by purchasing a more expensive property. The difficulty with econometric estimation is that under some conditions the predicted effects of some of these variables is zero.

The comparative static results based upon the certainty model depend upon the presumed regime. In the case where the mortgage is comparatively cheap and the maximum loan-to-value ratio binds then the marginal effects of income, initial wealth and time preference will be zero. However, due to simultaneity, the level of housing services is predicted to have a positive impact upon mortgage demand. The predictions for the regime where mortgage debt is comparatively more expensive are more satisfying, though impatient debt maximises can still exist, and estimates involving those choosing, but denied, negative mortgage borrowing will also exhibit zero coefficients. Apart from the two corner solutions the analysis predicts a positive relationship between mortgage demand and housing and between mortgage size and expected income. There is a predicted negative relationship for initial wealth and the discount rate. This is a useful model though we shall see shortly that a consideration of uncertainty also renders the expected signs on these variables ambiguous.

Observed variations in loan-to-value ratios can reflect credit market restrictions; that is prudential lending rules (mortgage underwriting criterion) that bind and differ between borrowers. Brueckner's analysis also demonstrated that when mortgage rates are comparatively high variations in borrowing can be driven by different rates of time preference. However, there is an alternative explanation for observed differences in loan-to-value ratios and this arises out of uncertainty relating to incomes, asset prices and wealth. If borrowers do not possess portfolios which are fully hedged, and they are not risk-neutral, then the choice of mortgage size will effect both potential wealth and its variance.

Modelling mortgage demand under conditions of uncertainty

Modelling mortgage demand assuming a world where the value of key economic variables is known with certainty has provided a concise modelling framework with clear predictions in some cases and sometimes involving corner solutions. A key variable in the maximisation of the consumer's utility function was the level of second period wealth W. Theoretical research has also focused upon the stochastic nature of W, an approach that invites the application of modern portfolio theory to mortgage demand.

$$E[U] = U(c, H) + F(\lambda^{-1}E(W, \sigma_W^2(W)))\qquad(2.5)$$

The modelling under certainty provides a basis for the uncertainty model. However, some new arguments are assumed to enter the household's decision-making framework. Looking at expression (2.5) we can see that the variance of wealth σ_W^2 becomes a negative argument in the utility function. This reflects the trade off between risk and return with risk yielding disutility. Uncertainty is further reflected in the use of the expectations operator $E(.)$. The borrower now has to make an optimal portfolio choice meaning that the return and risk of both housing and the alternative savings vehicle must be taken into account. It is now possible to apply the standard mean variance model, taken from financial economics, to the analysis of mortgage demand.

The decision problem for the household remains the same, that is to choose utility maximising levels of housing, non-housing consumption, savings and mortgage debt. A variety of models have been applied to this decision problem. A good representative model is that presented by Alm & Follain (1987) a version of which is discussed here (see also Follain & Dunsky 1997).

The budget constraints applied in this case are similar to those presented for the model with certainty, except considerably more complex. In the interest of exposition and comparison tax arguments (e.g. property tax) are excluded from the equation. The budget constraint for the first period of the two-period model is expressed in terms of initial wealth w, income y and the mortgage payment m; this is given by equation (2.6). The budget constraint for the second period is expressed in terms of final period wealth W and is given by equation (2.7). The novelty is the appearance of a risky financial asset A, to provide a competing investment for housing. The argument r_A is the expected return on the alternative asset, and r_y is the expected growth in income. Expression (2.8) is the variance of final wealth.

$$w + y = p_c \cdot c + p_h \cdot H - m + A \qquad (2.6)$$

Uncertainty in this modelling framework is present in all markets, save the interest rate on the mortgage debt.[9] Such a model can prove analytically intractable, and difficult to estimate. It does demonstrate that housing has a place in the consumer's savings and investment portfolio, as well as the utility function. Alm & Follain simulate the model numerically. In some cases the results of their analysis confirm the results of the certainty model, that is corner solutions emerge. However, their answers prove very sensitive to the choices of values for the cost of debt and the expected rate of return on risky assets (Follain & Dunsky 1997).

$$E(W) = [1 + E(r_p)]p_h H - (1 + r_m)m + (1 + E(r_A))A + (1 + E(r_y))y \qquad (2.7)$$

The derivation of a mortgage demand equation under uncertainty is in the rather unsatisfactory state of proving that the link between the after tax cost of mortgage debt and mortgage demand is not clear cut. The modelling does suggest that mortgage demand should be viewed in the context of a system-wide set of equations covering labour markets, the housing market, the market for non-housing consumption and the market for alternative financial assets to housing (Ling & McGill 1998).

$$\sigma^2(W) = E[W - E(W)]^2 \qquad . \qquad (2.8)$$

Either because of the worldview adopted, or analytical intractability, un-certainty models generally tend to neglect liquidity constraints, though they can be introduced as restrictions in numerical simulations. An ex-ception to this is theoretical work into variations in the rate of amortisa-tion of debt where liquidity constraints are often combined with a choice between amounts of housing and a risky asset (see Plaut 1986). Changes in the rate at which debt is repaid can help to overcome liquidity constraints or meet investment objectives, including hedging non-diversified port-folios (Plaut 1986; Goodman & Wassmer 1992). Brueckner's (1994a) sim-plified model also combines uncertainty with liquidity constraints. Despite the analytical difficulties, uncertainty models can be useful in guiding empirical work and will be alluded to again in Chapter 3.

Brueckner takes a simpler yet illuminating approach to the impact of uncertainty. Given that for the United States $r_s > r_m$ is the typical situ-ation, the certainty model predicts that existing homeowners will con-tinuously increase the size of their mortgage to extract equity from appreciating house prices. However, Brueckner notes that this is contrary to the stylised facts: US households tend to minimise their mortgage debt. The model demonstrates that with an uncertain r_s, any combination of saving and borrowing is compatible for some set of preferences. For example, when the rate of return on saving is risky, some borrowers will be reluctant to raise additional mortgage debt to facilitate increased saving in the risky investment. This can occur even though $r_s > r_m$. Brueckner notes that the household may adopt an intermediate size mortgage, combined with some non-housing investment. Thus with uncertainty the predicted signs on variables are ambiguous in the $r_s > r_m$ case.

Considering the case of $r_s < r_m$ the riskiness of returns on the savings vehicle does not alter the previously explored outcomes of the certainty model, and the role of time preference (impatience). The modelling sug-gests that empirical estimation will need to carefully control for any regime changes and variations in time preference.

The recent expansion in the use of mortgage debt to release equity to finance consumption is interesting, a phenomenon particularly facilitated in the US where mortgages are not specifically assigned to house purchase.[10] Equity extraction is also proving to be a significant phenomenon in the UK. This increased borrowing may reflect life cycle adjustments to a low interest rate environment, with a reduction in perceived uncertainty also leading to higher debt levels. So Brueckner's model is suggestive here, though the mortgage interest rate is ambiguous in sign when the loan-to-value ratio is positive, but less than the maximum allowed.[11] More theoretical research is needed into the optimality of such changes in debt levels. For example, some form of Harberger analysis might be used to demonstrate any welfare enhancing effects of tax subsidies and changes in interest rates (see Harberger 1971).

The analysis of mortgage demand under conditions of uncertainty is a complex problem. Placing mortgage demand in the setting of portfolio theory (mean variance analysis) involves adopting some strong assumptions. In particular perfect capital markets, zero transactions costs and continuous re-organisation of portfolios as a consequence of changes in the mean and standard deviation of returns on assets, including the return on housing. These complications, and difficulties in obtaining adequate data, make such models difficult to implement empirically (Ling & McGill 1998). Also, the predicted signs in an uncertainty model, when borrowing is intermediate (that is not at a maximum and greater than zero), are ambiguous (Brueckner 1994a). However, this indicates the importance of recourse to empirical analysis. The certainty model can be seen as a special case of the more general model under uncertainty (Follain & Dunsky 1997), and each of these models have guided the specification of mortgage demand equations.

Down payment constraints and mortgage demand

Housing demand has been typically analysed by treating housing as an asset (Poterba 1984). In this approach the demand for housing is based upon the user cost of owner occupation. User cost reflects the theoretical models discussed above; it is the marginal rate of substitution between housing and non-housing consumption. This measure gives the amount of non-housing consumption forgone for a one-unit increase in the consumption of housing services. The trade off reflects mortgage costs, forgone rates of return on housing equity and expected capital gains on residential property, and would also have depreciation and property taxes as arguments. Thus user cost reflects both consumption and investment aspects of housing choices.[12] The theory implies that mortgage demand equations should either have user cost arguments in the specification, or such arguments should appear in housing demand equations when housing and mortgage demand are being modelled simultaneously.

With credit constraints, user cost and the treatment of housing as an asset might be less applicable. The emphasis now shifts to housing as a consumption good rather than an investment. Given the importance of liquidity to provide down payment on a property, and the significance of housing in the net worth of households, then house prices effect liquidity and liquidity effects house prices. Stein's modelling of this process generates multiple equilibria; this offers some explanation for house price boom and bust, and therefore why house price changes have a predictable component (Case & Shiller 1989, 1990). The model suggests the importance of differences in the accumulated equity in property for the household's ability to adjust housing demand. This presents an alternative, or at least complementary, explanation for the build up of equity to that offered by Brueckner.

Early work on the impact of down payment requirements focused upon the timing of entry into owner occupation, effects upon aggregate savings, and housing as a proportion of net wealth (Slemrod 1982; Hayashi *et al.* 1988). Hayashi *et al.* (1988) extended the work of Slemrod (1982) and simulated the effects of down payment constraints in a multi-period life cycle model. Liquidity constraints were included by not allowing borrowing for non-housing purposes. The model was used to compare the Japanese and United States housing finance systems. This is an interesting comparison because unlike the US the Japanese system did not tax savings, and had no mortgage interest rate subsidy. The predictions of the model corresponded with Japanese experience and suggested that high transactions costs, relatively higher house prices and imperfect capital markets led Japanese households to defer home ownership. These general arguments are supported by later work in this area (Stein 1995; Ortalo-Magné & Rady 1998, 1999, 2002).

This concern with housing consumption and household liquidity has been further developed by Ortalo-Magné & Rady (1998, 1999, 2002). Their work focuses on explanations of house price cycles, and the co-movement of house prices and transactions, a phenomenon at odds with the idea of an efficient housing market.[13] The authors note the need for accumulated wealth to trade up the property ladder. The model investigates the transmission of income shocks in the context of a stochastic life cycle model, where heterogeneous households face credit constraints on their ability to trade up. The process is initially driven by the demand of first-time buyers for starter homes. Importantly, the model demonstrates the key role of variations in the income of young cohorts in generating house price cycles, and explaining the co-movement of house prices and housing transactions. That is, favourable income changes can overcome credit market constraints and presumably increase mortgage demand.

A key group in the Ortalo-Magné & Rady model are young homeowners who are accumulating wealth to trade up, a process facilitated by increased house prices.[14] So both income and past house price changes will drive housing/mortgage demand. These results do not require a large proportion of credit constrained households. Thus this research contrasts with that of Stein (1995) who requires an extensive distribution of liquidity constrained households, and focuses purely upon repeat buyers. This modelling has implications for the microeconomic estimation of mortgage demand. The key sources of variation in housing/mortgage demand are income and its variance, past house price changes and age.

The focus upon the home ownership decision and its timing, and the size of debt required, indicates that there are both discrete and continuous choices to be modelled. The modelling of the discrete tenure choice and mortgage demand under credit rationing will be fully explored in Chapter 6. The Ortalo-Magné & Rady model does not consider the sources of uncertainty other than income, and so an extension of this type of modelling to reflect portfolio considerations remains a significant theoretical challenge. Future modelling might also build upon the work of Rosenthal (1997) who has used simulation techniques to demonstrate the importance of housing chains, and their ability to explain the way that house price series for first time buyers leads those for former owner occupiers.

It is possible that down payment requirements and the relevance or importance of user costs as a determinant of housing/mortgage demand might vary according to the point in the housing cycle, by socio-economic group, by economy, by policy regime (say pre- and post-financial deregulation). Particularly when estimating mortgage demand equations for disaggregated groups (e.g. liquidity constrained households) then nominal changes in income and nominal rather than real interest rate variations should be tested in the econometric specification. The significance of user costs might also vary by age, perhaps by choice of mortgage instrument and according to variations in the opportunity cost of equity in property. The relevance of user costs versus affordability arguments should be addressed by empirical experimentation. The notion of down payment constraints appears throughout this book, from its obvious direct relationship with credit rationing to its role in mortgage contract design under asymmetric information. Prior to discussing these issues mortgage demand has to be positioned in relation to other mortgage choices, which will in turn raise further concerns for the estimation of housing debt equations.

Mortgage demand, other mortgage choices and the nature of the economic environment

This section of the book examines the links between mortgage demand and the other major mortgage choices. These choices include mortgage prepayment, default on mortgage debt, rates of amortisation, and choices between different mortgage instruments (contract design). The choices will in turn be influenced by the nature of the economic environment, for example the existence and extent of credit rationing, or the ability to hedge against risk and uncertainty. Although seemingly disparate topics a preliminary discussion of these issues will illustrate the complex ways in which they are related. In the language of econometrics the interactions between mortgage choices highlights the multiple sources of endogeneity and simultaneity involved in mortgage market modelling. Figure 2.1 places mortgage demand at the core of the conceptual schema, with clear links to the other choices such as prepayment.

Analytical understanding of the operation of any mortgage market must be based upon understanding the interrelationships. There are several key examples of the way in which different mortgage choices can interact. For example, it can be demonstrated theoretically that some borrowers benefit from flexibility in repaying their debt (that is flexible amortisation rates),

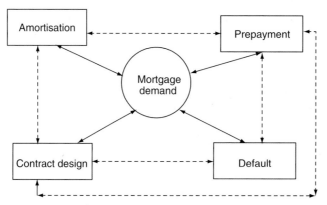

Figure 2.1 A graphical depiction of mortgage market choices and the economic environment.

but not all borrowers may be allowed full repayment flexibility. This lack may in turn result from asymmetric information in the mortgage market, which can produce contract choices that credit ration some borrowers (separating equilibrium). Thus contract design, mortgage demand and default behaviour are all interrelated under asymmetric information. Another example to be discussed in Chapter 10 is the interaction between prepayment and default, and the assumptions underpinning the analysis of the stochastic environment.

Much will depend upon the assumptions that we make about the economic environment when developing and empirically testing our models. Figure 2.1 highlights this point by implicitly distinguishing between a so called stochastic environment and one characterised by asymmetric information and credit rationing. The discussion works its way clockwise around the topics depicted in Figure 2.1. These issues will all be explored in greater detail in subsequent chapters, for now we give an overview of the implications of these various choices for the demand for mortgage debt and vice versa. The exercise is also useful in presenting some preliminary concepts, key research questions and further issues for the empirical estimation of mortgage choices.

The amortisation of mortgage debt and payment flexibility

Examining variations in the rate at which debt can, or is, repaid is important, because it has much to say about the nature of mortgage contracts, the assumed economic environment and the importance of information in mortgage markets. For example, a credit rationed household might value the ability to vary the rate at which mortgage debt is repaid, but a lender may be reluctant to offer full repayment flexibility to a borrower for whom they do not have sufficient information on credit worthiness, or the propensity to default. These factors may impact upon the choice of mortgage instrument and ultimately on mortgage demand. For example, to minimise liquidity problems an household may choose a mortgage with a teaser rate/discount (Brueckner 1993), this effects the user cost of owner occupation (Phillips & Vanderhoff 1992) which can then impact upon mortgage demand. Chapter 4 of the book deals with these features of mortgage contract design, and imperfect capital markets. Chapters 9 and 10 cover the issue of mortgage default.

Adjusting mortgage payments and the level of debt to meet life cycle spending and savings plans is an important aspect of mortgage choice. Liquidity constrained households will value repayment flexibility (Plaut

1986; Goodman & Wassmer 1992; Brueckner 1993). Households unable to borrow, or use cash to finance non-housing consumption, can use repayment flexibility on their mortgage to even out fluctuations in current income (see Leece 1995b). This raises important theoretical and empirical questions relating to optimal mortgage design, and the impact of available contract choices on mortgage and housing demand. For example, what is the impact on housing and mortgage demand of the tilting of real payments on debt towards the early years of a mortgage? Can varying the rate of amortisation ameliorate the effects of otherwise imperfect contract designs? These are interesting theoretical questions. An important yet under-researched empirical phenomenon is the emergence, spread along with the impact of mortgage instruments with more flexible payment scheduling, e.g. flexible mortgages in Australia, Canada and the UK.

The choice of amortisation rate, or indeed the very relevance of examining this decision, cannot be divorced from our view of the wider economic environment. So also under this heading we think about the stylised fact that most savings and investment portfolios in advanced economies are not fully diversified (Fratantoni 1997, 1998, 2001). Amortisation rates now become a substitute for lack of portfolio diversification, or hedging against adverse movements in mortgage interest rates (see Plaut 1986). For example, if mortgage interest rates on variable rate debt rise, then payments can be lowered. Interestingly, both Brueckner (1997) and Fratantoni (1997, 1998, 2001) have suggested that the lack of savings and investment portfolio diversification arises from housing/mortgage choices and mortgage commitments, with Brueckner formally modelling this effect. Mortgage finance could be used to correct portfolio distortions, or it may indeed create them. The link between mortgage and housing demand is therefore less direct than first anticipated (see Jones 1993, 1994, 1995).

Prepayment of mortgage debt

When a borrower chooses to refinance debt before the mortgage reaches maturity (prepayment), say by terminating a given fixed rate mortgage contract in favour of one with a lower rate of interest (coupon), then it is also likely that the level of borrowing will be adjusted. Thus we can say that mortgage demand and the prepayment of the mortgage are linked, or that mortgage demand is endogenous to the prepayment or refinancing decision (see Jones 1995). It is also important to recognise that there are other motives for prepayment with implications for mortgage demand (Brady *et al.* 2000; LaCour Little 1999). For example, households move to adjust to their desired level of housing services and so prepayment and mortgage demand is linked to household mobility (Archer *et al.* 1997; Pavlov 2001).

An important theoretical perspective on mortgage prepayment is to treat the option to prepay as a call option. In theory the mortgage holder will prepay when a fall in interest rates reduces the value of the mortgage below the current balance. The current balance is interpreted as the price at which the mortgage is bought back. The value of the mortgage is its worth at the new interest rate, and borrowers are assumed to want to minimise the burden of this debt and maximise their wealth. This is a strictly financial calculation and the subject of much theorising (see Kau & Keenan 1995) and empirical analysis (see, for example, Green & LaCour Little 1999). This kind of behaviour arises not only with fixed rate debt, but also with adjustable or variable rate mortgages which have features such as caps or collars (Cunningham & Capone 1990; Green & Shilling 1997). Later chapters will explore these valuation issues, and also consider how prepayment might vary with the choice of mortgage design.

If borrowers recognise the financial options embedded in the mortgage contract and exercise these options 'ruthlessly', then mortgage demand will be driven by the behaviour of the key variables that underpin the value of these options. Figure 2.1 shows that it is possible to characterise the economic environment as one of uncertainty, or stochastic. The key variables whose stochastic behaviour impinges upon option value are income, interest rates and house prices. Theoretical treatments assume a no arbitrage economy, with risk-neutral borrowers, and thus presents the most idealised and competitive view of the mortgage and other markets. Buist & Yang (2000) have placed mortgage demand in the context of a stochastic economic environment and established some important empirical relationships between the stochastic (state) variables, prepayment, default and mortgage demand. For example, a fall in the mortgage interest rate that places the call option to prepay 'in the money' will increase the demand for mortgage debt, as households subsequently refinance. Thus treating the choice to prepay as a financial option focuses upon some key determinants of mortgage demand.

Mortgage default and the choice of loan-to-value ratio

Working further around Figure 2.1 we arrive at mortgage default. Though the inability, or refusal, to pay back mortgage debt can clearly be influenced by affordability, it is also useful to consider the choice to default as exercising a financial option. In this case the option is a put option. If a house price falls so that the owner faces negative equity then the option to default is 'in the money', that is a borrower can increase their wealth by defaulting rather than continuing to pay off the debt and own an asset whose value has fallen (see Quercia & Stegman 1992; Quigley & Van Order 1995). The empirical question here is how ruthlessly borrowers exercise this default option? Demand for mortgage finance may increase when house prices are rising and default risk is less (Buist & Yang 2000). Default behaviour also shows the importance of differences in housing finance systems. In the UK a household defaulting and in negative equity would still be liable for the outstanding balance and so affordability issues and trigger events such as divorce or unemployment might be more important.

A complication that should be kept in mind is that default and prepayment are not entirely separate and are competing options (*competing risks*), in that exercising one of the options precludes exercising the other (Kau *et al.* 1992). This makes the link between the stochastic economic environment and mortgage demand even more complex. For example, even if the option to default is in the money, the prepayment option may still have value (say mortgage interest rates were volatile), as such default would result in the loss of this value. The effect of stochastic variables upon both prepayment and default represent potentially important drivers of the demand for housing finance.

Other links between default and mortgage demand arise where we expect liquidity constraints and/or asymmetric information to be present in the economy. A borrower who defaults may attempt to re-enter owner occupation but find that they are credit rationed, say through a reduced credit score (Bennet *et al.* 1998, 2000). Another source of credit rationing linked to default arises under asymmetric information. It can be demonstrated theoretically that if lenders have incomplete knowledge regarding the borrowers propensity to default then some borrowers will be credit rationed (see Brueckner 1994b, c). This arises from a separating equilibrium, where different mortgage contracts, defined by their combination of interest rate and loan-to-value ratio, attract borrowers with differing probabilities of defaulting. This separation of contracts leads to a group who while paying lower interest rates are not allowed to borrow as much as they would wish, that is they are credit rationed. Credit rationing in the mortgage market is an important phenomenon, both theoretically and empirically, and forms the main focus of Chapters 5 and 6 of this book.

Mortgage contract design

Differences in mortgage contract design extend beyond the mortgage size/ interest rate combinations that might form the basis of a separating equilibrium. In the United States the combination of up-front payments (points) and interest rate is another key form of variation (see Dunn & Spatt 1988; Yang 1992; Stanton & Wallace 1998). A further source of heterogeneity is the degree of risk sharing between lenders and borrowers (Arvan & Brueckner 1986; Brueckner 1986), with adjustable rate debt (variable rate in the United Kingdom) argued to place the burden of interest rate risk on the borrower, while fixed rate debt poses potential problems for the lender (Baesel & Biger 1980). Clearly there are important issues relating to why we observe such a variety of mortgage designs, and the impact of choices on mortgage/housing demand.

Once again the answers to why we observe heterogeneity of mortgage contracts depend upon how we view the economic environment, and the efficiency of the housing finance system. In the no arbitrage economy with efficiently priced debt there is no justification for the different forms of mortgage contract, and they should certainly not impact upon mortgage/ housing demand. Explanations for the observed variety of contracts include myopic behaviour, heterogeneous interest rate expectations and desired payment profiles. Different contracts including the size of debt may have the role of signalling the characteristics of borrowers and providing important information to lenders. For now we take it that contract design and mortgage demand are not entirely separate issues.

The nature of the economic environment

The discussion of the theoretical basis of mortgage demand, and the general discussion of issues, has highlighted the importance of the assumptions that we make about the competitive environment in which mortgage borrowing and lending takes place. For example, in the presence of asymmetric information, different combinations of interest rates and loan size could attract borrowers with differing risks of default, and lead to credit rationing. A more fundamental distinction was apparent in the discussion of the formal modelling. Models assuming that borrowers knew their economic environment and its future states with certainty were more readily reconciled with liquidity constraints. Models relying upon uncertainty were less tractable but also explained variations in loan-to-value ratios that deviated from the corner solutions of zero or 100% gearing.

The approach adopted in this book is eclectic in that the author believes that each of these modelling approaches can offer important insights into the actual operation of mortgage markets, and inform the empirical speci-fication of mortgage demand equations. For example, empirical evidence does suggest that the option theoretic framework is a useful way of viewing prepayment and default behaviour (Green & Shoven 1986; Schwartz & Torous 1989a, b, 1992, 1993); given this, then the assumption of a no arbitrage economy with risk-neutral borrowers is a useful one. On the other hand, important insights can be gained empirically if we admit the possibility of liquidity constraints, asymmetric information and capital market imperfections. These different perspectives also raise questions regarding the appropriate way to value mortgage-backed securities. Though techniques of mortgage valuation are not a major focus of this book, under-standing the basis upon which cash flows are generated and sustained in the mortgage market is clearly central to these valuation issues.

How we view the economic environment has important implications for the empirical specification of mortgage demand equations. Chapter 4 will demonstrate how in a world of imperfect capital markets and sub-optimal mortgage designs, cash flow considerations may influence the choice of debt levels. In these circumstances a mortgage demand equation would require the inclusion of the nominal net of tax mortgage interest rate, rather than the real rate of interest (Meen, 1990; Leece 1995a; Muellbauer & Murphy 1997).[15] The user costs measure may be less relevant, or require some modification. Assuming the prevalence of binding prudential lend-ing rules also leads to the simultaneous determination of the demand for housing services and mortgage size (Brueckner 1994a). However, binding down payment constraints might ration entry to owner occupation and both discrete and continuous housing choices need to be jointly modelled, allowing for this rationing. These and other specification issues will be discussed more fully in subsequent chapters of the book.

Though the focus of analysis in this chapter has been on credit demand there is clearly a role for the analysis of lending behaviour. This has been recognised in the literature on discrimination in lending markets. How-ever, it is difficult to ascertain if there is racial or any other form of discrimination evident in the mortgage market unless there is some con-trol for differences in credit demand between groups (LaCour Little 2001). The analysis of disaggregated forms of credit demand is therefore import-ant. However, lender behaviour will feature in later chapters, in risk sharing, assumptions regarding the degree of competition, rationing and agency problems.

Summary and conclusions

This chapter has examined the theoretical basis of mortgage demand. The literature has seen the development of theoretical models under conditions of certainty and uncertainty. The certainty models have the added feature of incorporating liquidity constraints together with binding prudential lending rules. While corner solutions of maximum and minimum borrowing were predicted by these models there where circumstances where the loan-to-value ratio might vary between zero and its maximum. However, observed loan-to-value ratios may also be explained by the presence of uncertainty that can be nicely treated in a standard mean variance framework adopted from financial economics (Follain 1990). The development of secondary mortgage markets along with the growth in securitisation have led to models taken from financial economics becoming increasingly important. Both certainty and uncertainty models have contributed to the empirical specification of mortgage demand equations.

Investment and consumption can drive the demand for housing. The imposition of binding down payment constraints can impact upon the timing of entry into owner occupation and housing demand. A significant body of research had analysed the impact of this liquidity constraint on entry into owner occupation, aggregate savings, and the behaviour of house prices and housing transactions. There are clear implications here for mortgage demand. In particular, consumption-driven models of housing demand suggest a lesser role for the user cost of owner occupation in demand estimates. Mortgage demand equations need to test alternative specifications of the relevant costs of housing, and also test for binding loan-to-value ratios, with the simultaneity of housing and mortgage demand.

The discussion in this chapter has suggested that a focus upon mortgage demand can be a convenient focal point for a consideration of mortgage market economics and analysis. There are a large number of sources of simultaneity, and mortgage demand may be endogenous to many other mortgage market choices, including prepayment, default and the choice of mortgage instrument. The formal modelling indicates the direct link between housing and mortgage demand, though at times we have questioned this relationship. The chapter which follows examines these and other issues involved in estimating mortgage demand equations for households, and reports the results of econometric research in this area.

Guide to further reading

For more detailed reading the student can do no better than read the seminal paper by Brueckner (1994a). The paper outlines the basic results of a mortgage demand model under certainty with some extensions to cover the uncertainty case. Jones (1993, 1994, 1995) offers an alternative, but highly complementary, approach to modelling mortgage demand under certainty, with the empirical extension to uncertainty. Plaut (1986) presents an interesting two-period model that allows risky asset prices, including the price of housing and also focuses upon the issues of liquidity constraints and incomplete portfolios.

Good reviews of both the theoretical and empirical literature on mortgage demand can be found in Ling & McGill (1998) and Follain & Dunsky (1997).

The reader will note that a lot of the work in this area concerns housing from which the implications of mortgage demand must be drawn. There is still much work to be done in the theoretical study of mortgage demand *per se*.

Notes

1 See for example, Elton, J.E. & M.J. Gruber (1991) *Modern Portfolio Theory and Investment Analysis*, John Wiley & Sons Inc., New York, Chichester, 4th edition, chapters 2 and 3, pp. 15–64.
2 The first order conditions, not reported here, are derived using the Kuhn Tucker theorem.
3 See Brueckner (1994a, p. 255).
4 In theory the appropriate opportunity cost of equity in a property is an asset with the same risk return characteristics. In the model under certainty we can assume such problems of asset choice away and merely focus upon savings rates. Savings deposits may be an appropriate choice of alternative asset for many liquidity constrained borrowers. Several authors have noted how user costs can vary according to differences in household portfolios (Hendershott & Hu 1981, 1983; Leece 1995b).
5 Under these circumstances consumers can always substitute the cheaper mortgage for the more expensive debt. This will not effect non-housing consumption but it will increase wealth. Also, as long as consumers are not too impatient then they can combine the maximal borrowing with some saving so that borrowing and saving are jointly observed in this case – a result generated by the difference between the rate of return on saving and the mortgage rate (see Brueckner (1994a, p. 255).
6 See Brueckner (1994a, p. 256) for his exposition of this intuition.

7 Jones (1993) uses a slightly more elaborate utility function, that is an instantaneous utility function defined with respect to time t.

8 Brueckner (1994a, pp. 259–60).

9 Theoretical modelling in the United States has tended to reflect the predominance of fixed rate mortgage contracts, which underpin this convenient assumption of a non-stochastic mortgage interest rate.

10 See 'The Housing Market: From Boom to Bust', Dresdner Bank, USA. Update on **http://group-economics.dresdner-bank.com**.

11 See Brueckner (1994a), footnote 14, p. 261.

12 More formally, user cost of owner occupation can be represented by the following ratio. This indicates that the ratio of utility gained from housing and non-housing consumption is equal to the ratio of costs to price of housing services where expected capital gains on the property are negative in effect and reduce user cost.

$$\frac{U_h}{U_c} = p_h \frac{[r_m + d - \Delta P_t]}{p_c} = p_h[r_m + d - \Delta P_t]$$

13 This analysis parallels explanations of stock market efficiency where the size of transactions in a stock should not impact upon price, that is, securities with the same risk return characteristics are viewed as perfect substitutes.

14 This raises an interesting point for the interpretation of past house price changes in the empirical estimation of mortgage demand. On the one hand significant lagged values could represent an adaptive expectations mechanism consistent with user cost arguments. On the other hand this could represent overcoming liquidity constraints on trading up.

15 The typical test for user costs is to test the restriction that the coefficients on the nominal interest rate and expected house price inflation are equal with equality, implying the validity of the user cost explanation.

3

The Demand for Mortgage Finance: Empirical Evidence

Introduction

Chapter 2 presented a number of theoretical models of mortgage demand and placed the demand for housing finance in the broader context of other mortgage choices. This chapter discusses the empirical estimation of mortgage demand equations. The main empirical evidence reviewed is drawn from work in the US, Canada and the UK. Though the discussion in Chapter 2 suggested that a fully specified system of equations, covering the markets for all assets and liabilities, labour, housing and non-housing debt were difficult to implement, the theoretical work did point to the main influences on the demand for mortgage credit. Given the ambiguity in the theoretical models regarding the expected influence of variables, then recourse to empirical evidence is particularly important.

The discussion in Chapter 1 highlighted the aggregate importance of the mortgage market in several countries. There are also significant variations in household gearing (loan-to-value ratios) across countries, time and households. The main focus of this chapter is cross-section studies of variations in household behaviour, with respect to mortgage demand. When relevant reference will be made to time series work. Knowledge of the determinants of the demand for housing debt can provide useful information to MBS investors and issuers. The results of empirical analysis will also reflect upon important policy areas. Mortgage interest payments have been subjected to taxation policies that vary between countries, and over time. These fiscal policies have important implications for the saving and consumption decisions of households, the housing market and national resource allocation.

The chapter begins with a consideration of some of the main issues involved in estimating mortgage demand equations. For example, mortgage debt is observed to be zero when households have paid off their debt, or finance housing transactions with 100% equity, and these zero values have important implications for choosing the appropriate estimation technique. There are also other significant estimation issues that arise from placing mortgage demand at the centre of mortgage market analysis, as we did in Figure 2.1. For example, dealing with liquidity constraints, or credit rationing? It is also important to recognise the selectivity issues involved relating to other mortgage choices, for example via the choice of mortgage instrument?

Having considered the main issues and problems in estimating mortgage demand equations the chapter moves on to look at the actual empirical evidence and an estimate of mortgage demand using UK data. This leads naturally to a comparison of the UK and US research, and an evaluation of how far the different systems of housing finance impinge upon the results of studies in the two economies. For example, the elasticity of mortgage demand with respect to the net of tax mortgage interest rate is found to be considerably smaller in UK research. The chapter concludes with a critical review of work to date in the estimation of mortgage demand equations, and offers suggestions for further research.

Some general issues encountered in estimating mortgage demand equations

Recent North American and UK research into the demand for mortgage finance has raised and accommodated several important estimation issues and measurement problems. These can be listed as follows:

- The censoring of data (for example zero mortgage holdings by some owner occupiers).

- The truncation of the distribution of observed mortgage balances under credit rationing (that is some borrowers obtain less than their desired amounts of debt).

- The simultaneous determination of mortgage and housing demand.

- The choice of an appropriate measure of mortgage debt.

- The choice between reduced form models and complex structural equations.

- The use of housing finance for non-housing investments and/or consumption.

The above list is by no means exhaustive of issues and problems encountered in the econometric estimation of mortgage demand equations, and neither are all of the issues considered in all studies. For example, there is the possibility that just using a sample of owner occupiers is dealing with a self-selected population, with the associated statistical biases. In addition there may be a number of simultaneous choices including the prepayment of debt. However, the issues listed above do follow from some of the important theoretical approaches examined in the previous chapter.

The theoretical discussion in Chapter 2 focused mostly upon the loan-to-value ratio. Thus there was the important question of whether borrowers would adopt corner solutions of zero or 100% debt. Brueckner (1994a) noted that in the US many households endeavoured to reduce their mortgage debt *in situ*. This was surprising given that the net of tax mortgage rate was below the net of tax rate of return on savings. The model of mortgage demand under uncertainty suggested that this behaviour was consistent with that of a rational utility maximising household. However, debt minimisation also leads to the problem that samples of owner occupiers may contain many households with a zero value on the dependent variable, that is no mortgage debt.

Recent studies of mortgage demand have dealt with the problem of zero observations in the data by using a Tobit estimator that corrects for the censoring (see Ling & McGill 1998; Follain & Dunsky 1997). The Tobit combines discrete and continuous choices, which in this case is the decision to incur a positive quantity of debt, and the decision on the size of that debt. The Tobit assumes that the estimated coefficients on the discrete choice will equal those for the continuous choice. This implies that the decision to have zero borrowing is an equilibrium choice. By combining the discrete and continuous choices in this way the censoring (selectivity bias) of observations that equal zero is controlled for.[1] The mathematical form of the Tobit, and associated techniques, will be discussed in Chapter 6.

A related estimation problem occurs when households are not allowed to borrow their desired amounts, or face binding down payment constraints (Ortalo-Magné & Rady 1998, 1999, 2002). In this case the observed values of mortgage debt do not represent equilibrium values. We say that the distribution is truncated. This situation arises under credit rationing and Leece (1995a, 2000b) has demonstrated that using a truncated regression is a more appropriate technique in this case. The continuous choice is modelled independently of the discrete choice, there is no assumption that the estimated coefficients on both choices will be the same. Some borrowers may have zero mortgages because they were credit rationed and could not enter owner occupation. The discussion of estimation under credit rationing is also deferred until Chapter 6, but it is raised here to demonstrate the several sources of selection bias that estimating mortgage demand can be subject to.

A very important result, arising out of the theory, was the possible simultaneous determination of housing and mortgage demand. This question has been addressed by both Follain & Dunsky (1997) and Ling & McGill (1998). Follain & Dunsky estimate both reduced form and structural equations. The reduced form equations exclude any endogenous variables, in this case net worth and housing value. Thus structural equations are those estimated for both the level of mortgage debt and the level of housing services, where housing expenditure (or an instrument) appears as an argument in the demand for mortgage finance. The estimates are derived from a simultaneous Tobit model, which is capable of estimating these structural equations, and this is the procedure also adopted by Ling & McGill. These studies find for the simultaneous relationship between mortgage and housing demand.

Estimating a structural equation for mortgage demand which recognises the endogeneity of the level of expenditure on housing services requires the use of instrumental variables. The instruments can be arguments from the user cost of owner occupation, or a predicted value from an housing expenditure equation that has elements of user costs as explanatory variables. User costs arguments, such as a measure of the expected rate of house price inflation, or real mortgage interest rates have not always proved to be statistically significant in UK mortgage demand equations (Leece 1995a). This does suggest that in many cases the nominal mortgage interest rate is the correct empirical specification of mortgage costs. However, this is not always true of US research (see Brueckner & Follain 1989).

The theoretical discussion in Chapter 2 suggested that the number of structural equations should extend beyond housing and mortgage choices. That is we need a general model covering the labour market, housing, non-housing consumption, asset choices and the choice of liabilities generally. Such a model poses immense data demands and might well be analytically intractable. For example, the simultaneous decisions might be subject to non-linearity. Empirical research has had to be satisfied with adopting general pointers from the theoretical modelling. Typically just a single or two equations are estimated, though Cho *et al.* (1995) does estimate a four equation model that also involves the choice of mortgage instrument.

An important issue is the actual measure of mortgage size used as the dependent variable in these estimations. For example, a measure of mortgage debt that will feature in the analysis of prepayment and default behaviour is the market value of the debt. This is measured by the present value of all future payments on the mortgage, discounted at the prevailing mortgage rate. For the US and Canada, Jones (1993, 1994, 1995) and Ling & McGill (1998) have used market values, while Follain & Dunsky (1997) experimented with both book and market values. When the mortgage is a fixed rate instrument then market value can better represent the real debt burden of the household.

UK research has typically taken the form of pooled cross-section/time series studies. The dependent variable has been the loan-to-value ratio (Leece 2001b), the real mortgage balance at the point of house purchase (Leece 2000b) or the proportion of income used for mortgage payments (Devereaux & Lanot 2003). The discouragement of prepayment of mortgages by redemption penalties has meant that market values can diverge significantly from the book values of mortgages. Any divergence between market and book values is likely to be at a minimum at the point of house purchase. Thus UK pooled time series/cross-section studies have focused upon new mortgages. US estimates can, and tend to, involve both new and 'seasoned'[2] mortgage contracts. It is probably advisable in any study of mortgage demand to estimate using a variety of measures of the mortgage liability. This issue highlights the significance of differences in the housing finance systems of the UK and the US, here impacting upon the appropriate selection of the dependent variable.

Even at the point of house purchase the mortgage may be raised to finance non-housing expenditure or other investments. Jones (1993, 1994, 1995) has argued that households engage in arbitrage by raising housing finance to purchase non-housing assets. This involves the concept of excess debt. Excess debt arises when borrowing exceeds that which is optimal to purchase a property. Jones uses a life cycle based model of mortgage demand to estimate the optimal size of debt; the study then attempts to explain variations in the demand for non-housing assets to account for uncertainty. This again raises the point that mortgage demand is complex and is best viewed in a general portfolio setting.

For younger borrowers, whose role in determining aggregate housing and mortgage demand has already been emphasised (Ortalo-Magné & Rady 1998, 1999, 2002), there is the issue of family networks, and gifts and transfers to facilitate home ownership. Such transfers can minimise the distortions in consumption, and corresponding utility losses, arising from forced saving for a deposit early in the life cycle (Artle & Varaya 1978), and perhaps generally overcome credit market imperfections. This is interesting because such assistance can vary across housing finance systems. For example, family support systems are particularly important in southern Europe (Forrest & Murie 1995; Holdsworth & Solda 2002).

Though decision making in the US and the UK is viewed in a more individualistic way, wealth transfers may still be of significance (Mayer & Engelhardt 1996; Engelhardt & Mayer 1996; Guiso & Jappelli 2002). Mayer & Engelhardt utilised survey data and found that financial constraints have led to an increased reliance upon gifts. Larger incomes and higher median house prices lead to a higher proportion of savings being used to finance the deposit on a house, implying an increased reliance on gifts by more constrained households. However, Engelhardt (1996) suggested that intergenerational transfers are not sufficient to overcome credit market constraints, at least in the US.

Guiso & Jappelli (2002), used Italian data, and also found that gifts were not significant enough to generally overcome credit market imperfections. The apparent lack of general impact of intergenerational transfers is not an argument for ignoring their possible effects in cross-section studies of mortgage demand. Clearly the likelihood of observing a young individual or household in owner occupation may *ceterus paribus* be conditional upon such gifts. Gifts and bequests can be incorporated into theoretical models, though econometrically the data requirements might be quite demanding. However, it is a relevant criticism of extant mortgage demand equations that they have not at least purposely proxied these effects, or interpreted some results in the light of the possibility of this type of transfer. Clearly, the specification of mortgage demand equations must consider the cultural context and the nature of the housing finance system in which the estimates are being made.

The general findings of United States research

Having seen the general direction in which empirical research, and econometric estimation has gone, we can now consider the general 'fit' of theory and empirical evidence in the area of mortgage demand. For example, theoretical analysis points to the importance of initial wealth, income, the gap between mortgage interest rates and saving and expected wealth and its variance, etc. It is generally considered that the net of tax mortgage interest rate in the US is less than the forgone rate of return on savings. Brueckner (1994a) notes that in the certainty case, under such a regime, borrowers will maximise their debt. In the uncertainty case the expected signs on the key theoretical variables are ambiguous (Brueckner 1994a). Given that US borrowers face uncertain rates of return on their savings, and appear to behave accordingly, then it is necessary to have recourse to the econometric evidence.

Several important cross-section studies have been conducted using US data. Follain & Dunsky (1997) estimate a series of structural and reduced form models. They use the 1983 and 1989 Surveys of Consumer Finance (SCF). A major motivation is to evaluate the impact of federal income tax policy on the demand for housing debt. They note the importance of the elasticity of demand for mortgage debt with respect to tax policy changes and the effects of this on potential revenue gains for the federal government. The results of this research are therefore of interest to the UK, where tax benefits on mortgage interest payments have recently been removed (in April 2000).

Follain and Dunsky found that the estimated coefficient on a tax price variable is positive and statistically significant. The tax price variable is measured by the difference between the after tax cost of equity in a property and the after tax cost of mortgage debt. Thus we are looking at the gap between the mortgage interest rate and the rate of return on savings discussed in Chapter 2, modified for taxation treatment and subsidies. The tax price result was robust to several different measures of the dependent variable (that is mortgage book value, mortgage market value, and loan-to-value ratio). Interestingly, the elasticity of demand of mortgage debt with respect to the tax price of debt was very high and estimated to be about -1.5.[3]

The Follain and Dunsky research was extended (Dunsky & Follain 2000) by utilising the panel nature of the SCF. The negative impact of the after tax cost of mortgage debt on mortgage demand was confirmed, and gave an elasticity of about -1. The dependent variable in this case was the net change in mortgage borrowing. Both Follain & Dunsky (1997) and Dunsky & Follain (2000) identified the importance of variations in the parameters of mortgage demand equations by income groups. Low-income groups exhibit a positive sign on income, but for high-income groups it is negative. These results are consistent with the presence of liquidity constraints. Liquidity constraints might also be apparent in the negative relationship found between net worth and mortgage demand, though higher wealth might also provide a substitute for mortgage finance.

Ling & McGill (1998) presented another important estimate of a mortgage demand equation. Like Follain & Dunsky (1997) they include households with zero debt in the sample, and estimated a Tobit model. Their dependent variable was the market value of mortgage debt. They found a positive relationship between housing demand and the size of mortgage, thus confirming the results of Follain & Dunsky, and emphasising the need to account for the simultaneous determination of housing and mortgage choices. Ling & McGill also found a positive sign on earned income, a result consistent with the presence of liquidity constraints, though it might also have been a proxy for differences in marginal taxation rates.

The previous chapter noted that the link between mortgage and housing demand may not always be so mechanical, as is often assumed. The work of Jones in particular stressed the importance of non-housing portfolio objectives. Jones has established the empirical significance of this proposition for both the United States using SCF (Survey of Consumer Finances) data (Jones 1993, 1994), and for Canada using the Canadian SCF (1995). The focus of the estimation was the noted demand for excess mortgage debt. Jones focused upon the link between mortgage finance and the acquisition of specific forms of non-housing asset. The research suggested that excess mortgage debt was used to finance business or additional real estate assets. Mortgage finance was not used to acquire financial assets, and households showed little inclination to use non-mortgage finance to purchase a property.

The discussion in Chapter 2 indicated the possible links between mortgage demand and prepayment and default behaviour, both of which had the features of options. Given the importance of the stochastic behaviour of variables in the option theoretic approach then these relationships are perhaps best explored through time series estimates. Buist & Yang (2000) confirm the positive impact of house prices and incomes on aggregate mortgage demand. Rising incomes increase the likelihood of prepaying, and reduce the expectation of default, the combined effect of which is an increase in demand. The study found the predicted negative sign on the mortgage interest rate. Jones (1994) noted that mortgage choices are likely to be endogenous to prepayment where prepayment is a call option. The issues of default and prepayment will be considered more fully in Chapters 9 and 10. The research of Buist & Yang, and the other studies reported here, highlight the usefulness of adopting the different perspectives on the economic environment outlined in Chapter 2.

North American studies have confirmed the importance of some of the key variables and relationships highlighted in the theoretical discussion in Chapter 2. For example, housing and mortgage demand were found to be simultaneously determined. Wealth (net worth) has been found to have a negative impact upon mortgage demand (Follain & Dunsky 1997), but not always (Jones 1995; Cho *et al*. 1995). Some of the limitations of empirical analysis, such as the difficulty of testing a comprehensive structural model, remain. In this sense most theoretical models remain broadly indicative. There has been some evidence of liquidity constraints, usually detected by dissagregating the estimation by wealth and/or age, or other characteristics (Linneman & Wachter 1989; Follain & Dunsky 1997).

Empirical research in the United Kingdom

The background to United Kingdom research

The theoretical discussion in Chapter 2 noted the importance of the difference between the net of tax mortgage interest rate, and the rate of return on equity in a property. Muellbeur & Murphy (1997) argued that the rate of return on a building society share account seems the most appropriate forgone rate of return for the UK. Research in the US presumed that the net of tax mortgage rate was lower than the savings rate. In the UK net of tax mortgage rates tend to be higher than savings rates on basic cash accounts. This is indicated by Figure 3.1, which shows differences in gross rates, which are broadly commensurate with net of tax differences. It has generally been unlikely that a borrower would get a higher rate of return on an investment than the interest cost on borrowing (Spero 1993). However, the net of tax picture becomes increasingly complicated with the introduction of tax-free savings/investment products, and the gradual diminution and final demise of tax relief on mortgage interest rates.[4] It is also complicated for earlier periods when, at least up to 1991, interest on savings accounts was taxed at a lower rate (composite tax) than earned income. So the difference in mortgage and savings rates in the UK has been subject to some instability over time.

It is possible that for some UK borrowers there was a fairly consistent expectation that the rate of return on the forgone investment would be higher than the net mortgage interest rate costs. This was possibly so for the UK endowment mortgage choice, a case to be analysed below. Choosing the appropriate opportunity cost of equity in property can be critical to expected mortgage choices, either directly or indirectly through the

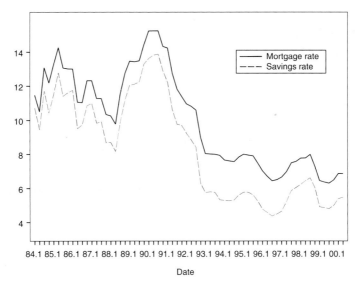

Figure 3.1   United Kingdom, Mortgage and Savings Rates (1984 to 2000).

Source: Economic Trends.

effects upon housing demand. For example, Miles (1992) notes that using an historical mean return of 8% on equities as the opportunity cost of equity can lead to negative user costs of owner occupation. Understanding differences in household behaviour in the mortgage market requires a careful consideration of the appropriate opportunity cost of equity in a property. The mortgage choices facing UK households (that is the endowment) provides a unique opportunity to identify a group of borrowers for whom the opportunity cost of equity can be broadly identified.

Much empirical research in the UK has been time series based, and often primarily interested in the impact of mortgage market rationing on the demand for housing, and the implications of the amelioration or removal of credit rationing. Thus mortgage demand has been represented directly in housing demand equations, usually in the form of a stock measure (aggregate number of mortgages) or a net change in the stock of debt (Hendry 1984; Wilcox 1985; Dicks 1989, 1990; Hall & Urwin 1989; Meen 1990). Leece (1995a) estimated a cross-section analysis of mortgage demand under credit rationing and financial deregulation. More recent research has used pooled cross-section/time series data and has disaggregated mortgage demand by mortgage type, that is by the endowment/ repayment mortgage choice (Leece 2000b; Devereaux & Lanot 2003). Pooled cross-section/time series data allows the analysis of both interest cost effects and variations in household behaviour.

One important feature of the UK mortgage market has been the co-existance of two mortgage instruments, each with different taxation implications (see Devereaux & Lanot 2003). These are the standard annuity (repayment) mortgage and the endowment. The endowment is a saving scheme based on an interest only mortgage. Tax relief on the interest only payments means that the endowment would secure the greatest tax benefits over time. Also, under favourable interest rate regimes there can be an investment surplus in excess of the outstanding mortgage balance. The choice of an endowment provides a convenient backdrop to understanding mortgage demand in the UK economy. In particular, Leece (2000b) has used this choice to suggest a separating equilibrium in the mortgage market, a concept to be introduced in Chapter 4. Meanwhile, the UK data provides an excellent opportunity to estimate the Brueckner model of mortgage demand presented in Chapter 2.

An estimation of Brueckner's basic results of mortgage demand

There are few studies of mortgage demand for the UK. This section presents the estimates for a basic mortgage demand equation, with expectations based upon the uncertainty case, reflecting the theoretical arguments presented by Brueckner (1994a). The key variables discussed in Chapter 2 were the discrepancy between savings and borrowing rates, the level of housing expenditure, income and initial wealth. The theory also indicated the importance of time preference and attitudes to risk. The latter factors proved to be influential arguments when the net of tax mortgage interest rate was greater than the net of tax savings rate, or when there was uncertainty and the rate of return on savings was higher than the net of tax mortgage rate. In these cases households would not necessarily attempt to maximise their mortgage debt, but would limit the extent of their gearing according to their individual preferences. In this estimation it is argued that the mortgage interest rate was lower than the expected forgone rate of return on savings/investment.[5]

Empirical counterparts to the key theoretical variables are not always available, and must be proxied by other measures. In the case of this study we have no data on initial wealth. The analysis adopts the usual practice of using personal and household characteristics to represent time preference and attitudes to risk. The empirical specification controls for the endogeneity of housing expenditure by estimating a two stage least squares model. The sample is pooled cross-section and time series data (1991–1994), and is drawn from the British Household Panel Survey (BHPS). There is a sample of 508 borrowers, all of whom are endowment mortgage holders. This latter feature is important because the choice of an interest only endowment mortgage implies an expectation that the rate of return on the endowment fund will exceed the net of tax mortgage interest rate[6] (see Leece 1995b).

The choice of time period in this study is important. This is a period of comparative accessibility for the investigator. Subsequently, the mortgage market became more complex with an increasing variety of mortgage choices, and more and more heavy discounting of mortgage debt. Savings and investment opportunities also became increasingly differentiated, with tax free savings products. Tax relief on mortgage interest payments was gradually removed, finally disappearing in April 2000. Switching between providers became a major portion of new mortgage demand. Though these facets of UK financial markets are of interest in themselves, the period 1991 to 1994 is a comparatively less problematic one in which to test a basic mortgage demand model, and to include a variable representing the cost of different mortgage instruments (variable versus fixed rate).

The house price equation, estimating the instrument for housing demand, was identified by using dummy variables for regional location, and lagged values of house price inflation as a dimension of user costs. Interestingly, the measure of user cost was not statistically significant, this may not be too surprising given a period of nominal and real house price declines and the dominance of affordability considerations. Though the theoretical work on housing cycles suggested that lagged house price changes would facilitate overcoming down payment constraints (Stein 1995; Ortalo-Magné & Rady 1998, 1999, 2002), this may also be difficult to detect given the short and particular sample period.

The model does not use the Tobit for censored data that has featured in recent US work. The main reason for this is that endowment balances are typically held to maturity, thus there are likely to be fewer observed zero balances among owner occupiers. In addition, house movers can transfer their endowment. In any case it is not possible to create a consistent sample containing zero debt observations for endowment mortgage holders having paid off their debt, that is we do not know exactly what type of mortgages they used to hold. Also, the theoretical expectation here is that endowment mortgage holders will not be debt minimisers *per se*. The use of a sample of endowment mortgage holders only can introduce selectivity problems, but statistical testing suggested that this was not the case. This corresponds with Devereaux & Lanot (2003) who find no evidence of this particular selectivity problem in their analysis of mortgage demand by mortgage type.

The results of estimating a basic mortgage demand equation for the UK are presented in Tables 3.1. and 3.2. The estimates are indicated for both the log of the real mortgage balance (Table 3.1) and the log of the loan-to-value ratio (Table 3.2). The focus of analysis is the demand for mortgage debt at the point of house purchase. The instrument representing the real house price at the time of purchase is seen to be statistically significant in both sets of results. Housing expenditure appears to be endogenous to decisions on mortgage size. Interestingly the sign on this variable differs according to whether the loan-to-value ratio (negative sign), or the real mortgage balance (positive sign) is used. This is consistent with the findings of US research (Ling & McGill 1998; Cho *et al.* 1995).

It is not absolutely clear why there should be a negative sign on the real house price in the loan-to-value ratio equation. Possibly, high levels of housing expenditure raise the risk profile of household portfolios (see Brueckner 1997) and this is compensated for by lower gearing.

Table 3.1   Mortgage demand: two stage least squares (dependent variable: log of loan-to-value ratio)

Variable	Coefficient	t-value
Constant	0.7971	1.375
Log (age of reference person)	−0.0553	−0.993
Log (variable rate)	−0.2451	−2.002
Log (weighted premium on FRM)	−0.0001	−1.896
Log (savings rate − variable mortgage rate)	−0.2017	−1.292
Log (household income)	0.0457	1.368
Log (real house price)	−0.0456	−2.243
Children present under 5 years of age	0.0480	0.980
Male head of household	0.0155	0.526
Marital status of reference person	−0.1098	−3.470

($R^2 = 0.1808$)

Table 3.2   Mortgage demand: two stage least squares (dependent variable: real mortgage balance)

Constant	−3.8081	−6.567
Log (age of reference person)	−0.0553	−0.993
Log (variable rate)	−0.2451	−2.002
Log (weighted premium on FRM)	−0.0001	−1.896
Log (savings rate − variable mortgage interest rate)	−0.2017	−1.292
Log (household income)	0.0457	1.368
Log (real house price)	0.8440	12.133
Children present under 5 years of age	0.0480	0.980
Male head of household	0.0155	0.526
Marital status of reference person	−0.1098	−3.470

($R^2 = 0.6128$)

Alternatively, if housing wealth proxies high levels of non-housing wealth then there might be some substitution of non-housing wealth for mortgage debt (see Hendershott & Lemmon 1975; Jaffee & Rosen 1979; Ioannides 1989); though some researchers have found a positive relationship between non-housing wealth and mortgage debt (Jones 1994; Jones 1995; Cho *et al.* 1995). However, the elasticity of demand of gearing with respect to housing expenditure, in the UK study, is small with an elasticity of just −0.0456. So any wealth effect may not be large for this sample of mortgage holders.

Given the expectation that endowment mortgage holders have a comparatively high cost of equity then it may appear superfluous to include the discrepancy between the rate of interest on cash savings and the net of tax mortgage interest rate. Though statistically insignificant results cannot be interpreted as establishing any specific hypothesis the result is of interest. The lack of statistical significance of the savings rate variable may suggest that this is not the appropriate opportunity cost of equity, and that the expectation of a persistently high rate of return on investment, compared to the mortgage interest rate, is incorporated in the selectivity of the sample.

Though the lack of statistical significance of income is disappointing, interest rate effects are significant. Higher net of tax mortgage interest rates reduce mortgage demand.[7] The elasticity of demand with respect to the net of tax mortgage interest rate is not high in either set of results, being 0.2451 with respect to both dependent variables. Brueckner's theoretical analysis suggests that when the discrepancy between the rate of return on investment and the net of tax mortgage interest rate is high then the elasticity of demand for mortgage debt with respect to the net of tax mortgage interest rate will be low. Thus this result also lends some confirmation to the assumption that the expected forgone return on equity in property, for interest only mortgage holders, was comparatively high. Interestingly, Devereaux & Lanot find an elasticity of 0.20 for the mortgage demand of endowment mortgage holders covering a slightly earlier period of time (1985 to 1989).[8]

The model also includes a measure of the premium paid by fixed rate mortgage holders, and this is statistically significant with a negative sign. The interpretation here is that households choose between fixed rate and variable rate debt on the basis of comparative costs. The modelling of the simultaneous choice of mortgage instrument and mortgage demand will be discussed in Chapter 8. For now, note that this study found these costs to be exogenously determined. The premium used is that on five-year fixed rate debt. However, a large number of borrowers would pay smaller premiums not identified by the data (that is one-, two- and three-year fixed rates). In this case multiplying the five-year premium by the probability of take up, estimated by a discrete choice model, gives a proxy for actual costs paid. Thus borrowers with a high likelihood of take up are assumed to be willing to pay more.[9]

In the uncertainty case the borrower's degree of impatience and attitudes to risk can influence mortgage demand and so estimates of the impact of borrower characteristics become important. Only one such characteristic, marital status, is statistically significant. US research has taken this variable to represent impatience and attitudes to risk. Thus the negative sign here can be interpreted as indicating that married households consist of a more patient and more risk averse group of individuals, the usual expectation with this variable. Other factors proxied by marital status, such as the presence of a second earner, are not consistent with the negative sign. Thus this estimate, added to the other results, provides an indication of the efficacy of Brueckner's mortgage demand model in guiding empirical specifications.

A comparison of United States and United Kingdom research

The UK mortgage market context is important when comparing US and UK research. For example, the UK has a system of variable rate mortgages with fixed rate debt typically being fixed for short periods of 1 to 5 years. Thus reactions to changes in the current mortgage interest rate could differ in elasticity, as most contracts reverted eventually to the variable rate. Also, unlike US research (Brueckner & Follain 1989), there is no evidence of simultaneity in the choice of mortgage instrument and housing/mortgage demand for the UK (see Leece 2000b, 2001b). Given these differences then we might predict significantly different elasticities of mortgage/housing demand with respect to the net of tax mortgage interest rate. Of course, this is what we find with US estimates of 1.00 or 1.5 and UK elasticities of 0.24 and 0.20. Differences might also reflect the perceived gap between mortgage rates and the relevant rate of return on the alternative investment to housing.

Tax benefits on UK mortgage interest rates were automatically calculated at source under a scheme called MIRAS (mortgage interest relief at source), while in the US, households are responsible for claiming relief through self-assessment. Some UK borrowers could separately claim tax relief at the higher rate of tax up to 1991 when mortgage interest relief was reduced to the standard rate. Whether tax deductions have, or have not, been claimed has proven to be a significant impact upon mortgage demand in US research (Ling & McGill 1998; Dunsky & Follain 2000). With automatic deduction this is clearly less the case for the UK; as noted, the tax relief on mortgage interest payments in the UK was finally abolished in April 2000.

Ling & McGill (1998) suggest that in the US the general belief is that the after tax cost of equity exceeds the net of tax mortgage interest rate. This is also the position adopted by Brueckner (1994a). A criticism here might be that with imperfect capital markets, and less than complete portfolio diversification, the opportunity cost of equity in property might vary between households. The borrower's actual perception of the relevant opportunity cost of equity in a residence is an area that merits further research. Estimating the cost of equity for owner occupied property is a topic where a number of different techniques have been applied, and a variety of estimates made (see Gillingham 1983; Miles 1992; and Leece 2000b). The advantage of the UK study reported above is that we can be fairly certain that the mortgage rate is perceived to be lower than the forgone return on investment.

A direct comparison of parameter estimates obtained in US and UK research are difficult, and may not be very meaningful. However, there are a number of general lessons to be drawn from such a comparison. The importance of locating the appropriate opportunity cost of equity in property has been noted. The elasticity of demand for mortgage debt with respect to the mortgage interest rate may vary according to the discrepancy between net of tax mortgage rates and the appropriate forgone rate of return. Key characteristics of the system of housing finance, including prevalent mortgage designs might also influence these relationships. For example, the short periods for which mortgage rates are fixed on fixed rate debt in the UK may have resulted in a more short-term perspective on movements in interest rates, and a focus upon comparative costs of mortgage instruments (Leece 2001a). Later chapters will provide further comparisons between US and UK decisions on mortgage size, in particular the simultaneity of mortgage demand and choice of mortgage contract design.

Summary and conclusions

The discussion in this chapter has highlighted some of the issues involved in the econometric estimation of mortgage demand, and the main empirical findings. A key finding throughout has been the simultaneous determination of expenditure on housing services/house value and mort-gage demand. This theoretical point, elaborated upon by Brueckner (1994a), has been largely vindicated by empirical studies. That model also indicated that the elasticities of demand for mortgage credit varied according to the size and sign of any discrepancy between the mortgage interest rate and the rate of return on any alternative investment to housing. This result has been generally vindicated though more research is needed. Both US and UK work has suggested that existing theoretical models provide good guides for the econometric specification of mortgage demand equations.

An empirical implementation of a basic mortgage demand model using UK data highlighted the importance of the housing finance system under which mortgage demand equations were estimated. Interest only mortgage holders may have perceived a significant gap between the rate of return on the alternative investment and the net of tax mortgage interest rate. This would produce a lower elasticity of demand with respect to the mortgage interest rate. This was certainly significantly lower than that found in US research. Other differences between the housing finance systems may have produced this result. The tendency of UK fixed rate debt to be fixed for short periods of time is another possible explanation for lower interest rate elasticity. How the elasticity of demand for mortgage debt might have changed given the general demise of the endowment mortgage is a matter for further research.

Differences in mortgage contract designs are a key feature in the selection of econometric techniques. Research in the US had used the Tobit model which allows for censoring of the data, in this case deriving from those households with no mortgage balances. In the UK interest only mortgages meant that the balance was typically carried to maturity. The choice of mortgage instrument (e.g. fixed rate debt) could also impact upon mortgage demand, and this was indicated in the UK research. A further complication is the possibility that some households are credit rationed, and this might also be reflected in the choice of mortgage instrument. Subsequent chapters will have much more to say about the importance of mortgage con-tract design and credit rationing. There is clearly substantial scope for further experimentation in the mortgage demand estimation literature.

Other criticisms of the existing estimates of mortgage demand concern the need to estimate structural equations, representing not only the housing and mortgage markets but also the markets for labour and for financial assets. This would be a formidable task both in terms of data and efficient and consistent estimation; progress is eagerly awaited in this area.

Certainly the potentially complex relationships between different mortgage choices, as depicted in Figure 2.1, is indicative of a number of sources of endogeneity and selectivity bias. For example, the demand for mortgage finance is clearly endogenous to the refinancing of mortgage debt. Not all the interrelationships between different dimensions of mortgage choice have been theoretically explored or empirically investigated in the research reported in this chapter.

The chapter which follows looks at the rate of amortisation of debt as a key mortgage choice. Amortisation is a further aspect of mortgage demand, for example there may be a trade off between maturity and the size of debt. The chapter will also further develop ideas of how contract designs emerge from, and interact with, capital market imperfections. The theory of mortgage demand discussed in Chapter 2 adopted a utility maximisation approach that could be extended to optimum life cycle choices, while the empirics discussed here have noted the need to allow for liquidity constraints and credit rationing. It is interesting then to see how far varying the amortisation of debt can overcome capital market imperfections, and imperfections in prevalent mortgage designs.

Guide to further reading

This chapter has reviewed the empirical literature on mortgage demand and discussed its links with the theoretical propositions outlined in Chapter 1. There are clearly gaps in the translation of theory into empirical estimation that can inform policy and practice. In particular, the modelling of mortgage demand under uncertainty has yet to be fully empirically implemented, and forms one of the greatest challenges to applied mortgage market research. An excellent discussion of the state of the art, which still largely applies, can be found in Follain (1990).

The papers which review the theoretical work also provide good reviews of econometric estimates of mortgage demand, at least for the US. Thus Follain & Dunsky (1997) and Ling & McGill (1998) provide extensive reviews of US work. It would also pay the researcher/student to return to Brueckner's (1994a) theoretical paper on mortgage demand, which has a lucid and interesting concluding section on some of the issues involved in the empirical estimation of mortgage demand equations.

UK research is sparse, but a brief review of the issues involved in econometric estimation of UK mortgage demand equations can be found in Leece (2000b).

Notes

1 For further reading on the Tobit model see W.H. Greene (1993), Econometric Analysis, 3rd edition, chapter 20, Section 20.3, pp. 959–72.

2 'Seasoned mortgages' is a term meaning mortgages of some age. Thus they are not mortgages at the point of house purchase.

3 The estimated structural equations suggested two separate effects on mortgage demand arising from the reduction of tax benefits. More expensive debt leads to the greater use of savings to finance house purchase and the reduction in the size of debt is added to by the fall in housing demand.

4 The persistence of comparatively high mortgage interest rates is indicated by the tendency of lenders in this period to place increasing emphasis upon offering repayment flexibility that facilitates early repayment of debt and generates significant savings in interest payments over the life of the mortgage.

5 Brueckner models a risky rate of return to saving with a fixed mortgage rate. In the UK rates of return on variable rate debt is risky and fixed rate debt has rates fixed mostly for short periods. This should not fundamentally alter the analysis. Interestingly, given the confidence placed in endowments it might be argued that they were falsely perceived as having a riskless rate of return. Thus the situation might be considered symmetrical to that obtaining in the US.

6 The issue of mis-selling is relevant here. The point is, however, that those households sold endowment mortgages believed (possibly with certainty) that the expected rate of return on the endowment would exceed the mortgage interest rate.

7 Dunsky & Follain (2000) also suggest including the cost of consumer credit in mortgage demand equations exhibiting liquidity constraints. This is less relevant in this case as the focus is on mortgage finance to purchase a property only. It is worth noting that US mortgages are not specifically tied to the purchase of the property.

8 Devereaux & Lanot (2003) use the percentage of income spent on mortgage payments as their dependent variable, though we would expect the results to be fairly commensurate with estimations using other measures of mortgage demand.

9 This proxy measure is only feasible because the premium was not a significant explanatory variable in a mortgage instrument choice equation (see Leece 2001b).

4

The 'Tilt', Mortgage Design and the Amortisation of Debt

Introduction

This chapter begins with an examination of the so called 'tilt' – the tilting of the real value of mortgage payments towards the early life of a mortgage. This is an important concept that informs the discussion of some alternative mortgage designs, and the specification and interpretation of mortgage demand equations, for example, the need to use nominal rather than real mortgage interest rates. The discussion then moves on to the optimum rate of amortisation of debt. Amortisation behaviour is relevant to the design and choice of flexible mortgage instruments and is implicit in the household's choice of mortgage maturity. The focus of the chapter is on the importance of repayment flexibility, particularly in the presence of imperfect capital markets and can liquidity constraints.

Flexible payment scheduling is one way of overcoming the tilt, and can also be used to hedge portfolios and achieve the same results as a perfect capital market (Brueckner 1984; Plaut 1986; Goodman & Wassmer 1992). The chapter looks at both the theoretical issues surrounding the tilt and flexible amortisation, plus empirical evidence on household behaviour in these respects. Mortgage design and the tilting of real payments can have significant effects on the relative price of housing and housing demand (Kearl 1978), and can create liquidity squeezes at times of high interest rates (Chinloy 1995).

While the theoretical importance of flexible amortisation has been known for some time (see Brueckner 1984; Plaut 1986; Goodman & Wassmer 1992), flexible mortgage instruments have recently emerged as an increasingly important phenomenon. In the UK the flexible mortgage has become more popular since its introduction in 1995. By the first quarter of 2000 flexible mortgages accounted for 12.4% (£3.8 billion) of gross lending. This mortgage instrument is evident internationally, having originated in Australia, and is now important in Canada in the form of the 'open' mortgage. The UK flexible mortgage design facilitates cost minimisation by charging interest daily and thus crediting partial prepayments with immediate interest rate savings.[1] These mortgage instruments are often combined with a cash account that facilitates under- and over-payment, as in Canada.

Flexible mortgages, in the sense of significant control over the rate of amortisation, are significantly less apparent in the US. However, there are mortgage instruments that attempt to accommodate differences in required payment profiles, such as graduated payment mortgages, balloon mortgages and teaser rates on adjustable rate debt that result in lower initial mortgage costs. This involves a choice between discrete payment schedules rather than complete flexibility. No matter how defined and accommodated the issue of flexibility in the choice of payment scheduling is of growing practical importance, and is a key issue in mortgage design. Again the rationale of flexibility could be overcoming liquidity constraints, or cost minimisation over the life of the debt.

It would be surprising if at some point the US mortgage market does not follow the trend towards flexible amortisation scheduling. Witness the prediction by Roche (1999) that conventional mortgage debt will be replaced by a universal account combining all forms of borrowing, liquidity and investment needs. Increased payment flexibility may ultimately impact upon default probabilities and prepayment behaviour, with implications for both MBS valuation and social and economic welfare. Whether the standardisation of contracts to facilitate securitisation, and uncertainty over default and partial prepayment patterns on flexible debt, has inhibited its spread is an interesting research question.[2] Brueckner (1984) notes that with asymmetric information adopting a level payment mortgage does signal the borrower's ability to pay. The theory and empirics of payment scheduling discussed in this chapter offer an important first step in analysing and understanding this key aspect of mortgage design.

Liquidity constrained households will be concerned with the tilt and cash flow squeezes that can arise from unexpected changes in the mortgage interest rate. When capital markets are imperfect households with high discount rates and rising income streams will value the ability to defer mortgage payments. However, there will be some households for whom prudential lending rules (underwriting criteria) are not binding. Such households will possess some latitude in their choice of the rate of amortisation and may look more to cost minimisation over the life of the mortgage. This raises interesting questions regarding the choice of mortgage maturity, with its implied rate of amortisation; or if the household holds a flexible instrument, how this will be used. Ultimately these considerations cannot be separated from the question of the risks that face borrowers and lenders when they issue/take up different mortgage instruments. Risk and mortgage design will feature more explicitly in later chapters of the book but must also be noted in this chapter as an important dimension of affordability problems and cost minimisation behaviour.

The tilt and cash constraints

The discussion of mortgage demand presented in Chapter 2 and Chapter 3 briefly noted the importance of the so called tilt, that is the tilting of the real value of mortgage payments towards the early years of the debt. The presence of the tilt meant that borrowers might experience cash flow problems, and a case was made for using the nominal, rather than the real mortgage interest rate when estimating mortgage demand equations. The tilt is likely to be particularly problematic at times of high and volatile inflation when borrowers using variable rate debt are exposed to adverse interest rate risk, that is, sudden unanticipated increases in their mortgage costs. Existing fixed rate mortgage holders face the risk of a fall in the prevailing inflation rate which front loads real payments even more, though the eventual impact of this depends very much on the ease of refinancing.

Though house price inflation can reduce user costs by generating capital gains on residential property, the tilt may offset any such benefit. A number of alternative mortgage designs have been suggested to overcome, or to minimise this problem; for example the graduated payment mortgage or GPM. The tilt owes its importance to other capital market imperfections, such as liquidity constraints that prohibit borrowers taking out additional loans to overcome their temporary cash flow difficulties. This has led to suggestions that mortgage payments should be indexed, so they remain equal in real rather than nominal terms over time (Friedman 1980; McCulloch 1982; Houston 1988, Buckley *et al.* 1993). These arguments and the proposed alternative mortgage instruments are discussed below, but firstly it is important to understand exactly what the tilt is, and when it is a significant problem.

The basic annuity formulae determines a constant mortgage payment, at a given interest rate, that is just sufficient to pay off the principal sum borrowed plus all interest due by the end of a given term. This is the standard formula used in mortgage repayment calculation.[3] The annuity formulae front loads, or tilts, the real value of payments towards the early life of the loan. This is the inevitable result of keeping payments constant in nominal terms. In a static economy with a constant and fully predicted inflation rate, constant nominal payments will fall in value in real terms over time. So the tilt occurs even with steady state inflation. Now, if the inflation rate, increases, the aim of the lender will be to preserve the present value of the cash flows attached to a mortgage. If interest rates rise to match new inflation expectations then the mortgage payments in the early years will have to increase more than proportionately to compensate for the higher rate at which payments fall in value in future years. Of course, the increase in the inflation rate must be unanticipated or it would be priced into the original mortgage contract, a further obstacle to affordability. Thus the tilt is exacerbated when inflation is not in a steady state and unexpectedly increases.

Figure 4.1 illustrates the tilt problem from the lenders' point of view, and is based upon an illustrative method used by Brueggeman & Fisher (1997).[4] The line labelled NVP represents the nominal value of payments on a 25-year term, £50,000 mortgage (that is £263.90 per month). The interest rate generating these payments is 4%. The line labelled NVP assumes that inflation is zero, so that the 4% is the real rate of return to the lender. Now consider the effect of the rather dramatic occurrence of inflation at a rate of 6%. Assuming that the lender wishes to earn the same real rate of return

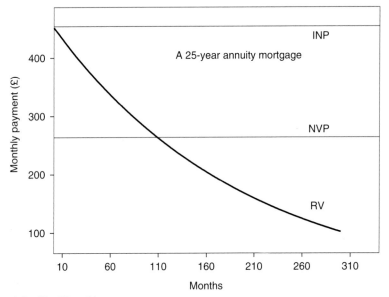

Figure 4.1   The tilt problem.

(4%), then the nominal interest rate charged on the mortgage must be approximately 10% (that is roughly 4% real rate plus 6% inflation). The line INP represents constant nominal payments after including the compensation for the 6% inflation rate, that is £454.40 per month. It is worth noting the effect of the additional 4% here, which is to raise payments by 72%, from £263.90 to £454.40 per month. Though for heuristic reasons the example is rather extreme, it is clear that the cash constrained household is vulnerable to mortgage interest rate changes (Kearl 1978; Friedman 1980; McCulloch 1982; Houston 1988; Buckley *et al.* 1993).

Figure 4.1 includes a third curve (RV) representing the real value to the lender of the constant monthly payments that they will receive after charging the 10%. Not surprisingly the payments fall in real terms over time, reflecting their constant nominal value. In the early years the deflated payments are above the 4% real payment line, in the later years they are below. The objective of the lender is to sustain the real rate of return of 4% over the life of the loan. To offset the declining real value of the nominal payments, the real payments must be front loaded. This front loading applies to any mortgage instrument where payments are constant in nominal terms.[5] From the borrower's point of view nominal incomes may be growing with inflation, but they are unlikely to offset higher real mortgage payments. Equally, younger households who might anticipate rising incomes are disadvantaged by high initial and constant payments rather than facing a gradually increasing payments' profile.

Kearl (1978) presented another interesting way of viewing the tilt that represents this bunching up of real payments in time. He used a measure of duration typically applied to evaluating and immunising bond portfolios. This formula emphasises the weighting given to early years of debt repayment.[6] Duration is time weighted (multiplied) by the present value of the debt repayment due at that time. So the maturity or life of the debt is not viewed in calendar years, but according to the significance of these years in terms of the present value of the cash flows associated with them. The upshot of this calculation is that when the nominal mortgage interest rate rises then the duration of the debt falls (future payments are discounted more heavily). This means that in real terms more of the debt is paid off more quickly. Duration changes though the contractual time to maturity of debt payments remains the same.

Miles (1994) utilises a comprehensive calculation to demonstrate and contextualise the tilt, and to demonstrate the effects of various levels of inflation and corresponding nominal interest rates on the mortgage payment burden that a household faces. A slightly modified version of this equation, presented below (4.1), highlights the characteristics of mortgage contracts which impact upon the debt service burden facing the borrower. For clarity the subscript for time period t, is generally suppressed.

The arguments are the loan-to-value ratio lv, the house price-to-income ratio hi, the rate of growth in income g, and the rate of price inflation π. The burden of debt is measured by m / y where m is a period t mortgage payment and y is the value of disposable income at t. The formula is based upon the assumption of a constant nominal interest rate r. This formulation places the tilt in a wider economic context, for example by including rates of income growth and the chosen loan-to-value ratio. The intuitive picture here is that the mortgage burden increases with gearing, inflation (including house price inflation), and the interest rate, but falls with rising incomes.

$$m/y = \left(\frac{r}{1+r}\right)(lv)(hi)[(1 + \pi)(1 + g_y]^{-t}/[1 - (1/(1 + r)^{T+1})] \qquad (4.1)^7$$

Using typical UK values to parameterise the equation, simulations by Miles for various rates of inflation (maintaining a constant real interest rate) indicate that even at low rates of inflation the proportion of income taken up by mortgage payments is significant. Thus at 2% inflation the debt burden was over 14.5%, falling to 10% of income after nine years. Miles notes that the greatest difficulties for borrowers arise when there is both high inflation and a policy response by the monetary authorities involving raising the real rate of interest. However, the tilt and affordability problems can be important even at low mortgage interest rates. Low inflation and corresponding low interest rates slow the erosion of the real value of mortgage payments and expose the borrower to interest rate and credit risk for a longer period of time. Also at low interest rates rapid house price inflation could impose stresses on affordability, and ration entry into owner occupation.

There can be confusion when reading the literature regarding whether the tilt refers to the level payments determined at the outset of a mortgage contract (a steady state model), or to the effects of changes in the mortgage interest rate on the profile of the real payment burden (unexpected changes in inflation). In fact, as suggested above, it relates to both of these considerations. US books and papers typically associate the tilt with the fixed rate mortgage, where payments are fixed in nominal terms for the period of the contract. Clearly, adjustable or variable rate debt can see a fall in the immediate payment burden if interest rates fall. However, mortgages with adjustable or variable rates of interest do face interest rate risk, and potential cash flow problems. Prospective homeowners might also face difficulties in entering owner occupation as a result of adverse changes in the mortgage interest rate and its effect on the real burden of debt repayment (Brueckner 1984). Fixed rate debt holders also face the risk of a fall in inflation and interest rates which will bring real payments forward in time (see Miles 1994), a significant effect in the UK where prepayment can be attended by penalties.

Why does the tilting of mortgage debt emerge as such a problem? With perfect capital markets consumers would be able to borrow more money to offset any increased real debt burden. Alternatively, a mortgage instrument could be designed that allowed consumers to pay off their debt at a constant level in real rather than nominal terms. There have, in fact, been a number of mortgage designs that have been introduced to overcome this difficulty. These range from graduated payments giving first time buyers lower initial outlays, to actual price level adjusted mortgages. However, these mortgages have not always been prevalent, and the cash flow problems remain for some households. In periods of low inflation affordability problems can still arise if house price inflation is not neutral in its effects on the value of the asset (the property) and the burden of the liability (the mortgage).

So what are the effects of the tilt on economic welfare? House price inflation, leading to capital gains on property, can lead to falling user costs of owner occupation, even at times of rising nominal interest rates (Diamond 1980). Tax subsidies on mortgage interest rates also add to this effect (Rosen 1979). However, increasing mortgage interest payments exacerbate cash flow difficulties arising from the tilt. This raises the interesting question of which has the greater effect on consumer welfare, reductions in user costs or the negative impact of the tilt?

Alm & Follain (1984) presented a model of constrained lifetime utility maximisation using a constant elasticity of substitution (CES) utility function, with housing and non-housing consumption as arguments. Simulations were used to evaluate the impact of the tilt. They also assessed the efficacy of various forms of mortgage design. Three types of mortgage were considered – the graduated payment mortgage (GAP), the shared appreciation mortgage (SAM) and the price level adjusted mortgage (PLAM). They concluded that at high rates of inflation the negative impact of liquidity constraints offsets the lower user costs. The three alternative mortgage instruments did confer significant benefits to consumers, but these might have been overstated by using a model based upon certainty.

Mortgage instruments for dealing with the tilt

There are a number of mortgage instruments that can assist in overcoming capital market imperfections and replace mortgage contract designs that suffer from the tilt. Mortgage contracts vary in the manner and extent to which risk is shared between the borrower and the lender. For example, the variable rate mortgage places the adverse effects of unanticipated inflation with the borrower. The borrower takes the full burden of the tilting of mortgage payments. In contrast the fixed rate mortgage potentially places the risk of a fall in interest rates on the lender, though this is typically priced into the mortgage in the form of a correction for expected inflation, and a premium to cover the risk of unexpected inflation. Thus mortgage design is essentially about risk sharing, a topic to be developed further in chapter eight. However, who takes the burden in sharing interest rate risk cannot be separated from susceptibility to the tilt, a factor that we will see in the mortgage contract designs discussed here.

One candidate for overcoming the tilt problem is the price level adjusted mortgage (PLAM). In this design the real payments on the mortgage are indexed to a price, or other suitable index (Friedman 1980; McCulloch 1982; Houston 1988, Buckley *et al.* 1993). The main design feature is that the real mortgage payments are evenly spread up to maturity, and the front-loaded burden (the tilt) is removed. Of course, unexpected increases in the rate of inflation will cause a real increase in mortgage payments for prospective mortgage holders and those facing a variable rate of interest, but these rises are significantly less than the disproportionate changes in real payments resulting from the tilt.

Not surprisingly, the use of price indexed mortgage designs has predominated in developing economies where inflation rates can be very high. However, this system is not without its problems; for example Chile abandoned indexed mortgages in 1982, while some countries such as the Philippines and Ecuador had to halt mortgage lending or obtain government funding (Buckley *et al.* 1993). The problem here for households is one of affordability if real wages decline. This is evident from the important role of income growth in equation (4.1), which places the payment burden in the wider macroeconomic setting.

One argued solution to the indexing problem is to index mortgage payments to the average wage. This would suit households because it is now possible to ensure that nominal mortgage payments always form a constant proportion of income.[8] However, if the general rate of inflation is in excess of the rate of increase in wages, problems now emerge for the lender. The lender would be facing reductions in real mortgage payments and this can cause problems of sustainable funding. One possible solution is the use of a duel index (Buckley *et al.* 1993). Payments are indexed to the average wage and the mortgage balance is indexed to the general level of prices. Payments are a constant proportion of income, and the lender retrieves the real mortgage balance. Shortfalls in real payments are added to the mortgage balance outstanding. Extending the mortgage term further accommodates this.[9] Lea & Bernstein (1996) argue that the duel index mortgage (DIM) was effective in Mexico during the 1980s, but had its efficacy blunted by government policies and bank reactions during the 1990s.

The tilt creates problems of affordability. One way of overcoming this is to offer lower nominal payments to the borrower in the early years of the mortgage. This might take the form of a graduated payment mortgage where later payments are higher to compensate for initially lower payments. Alternatively, temporary discounts or teaser rates can be offered to borrowers, which lower their initial payments (Phillips & Vanderhoff 1992). In some countries these approaches may also create funding problems for lenders (Buckley *et al.* 1993). A further problem is the increased risk of default if lower initial payments are amortised (Brueckner 1984). GPMs are not widespread in the US, comprising only 9.3% of households' primary mortgages reported in the 1999 American Housing Survey. This is also true of the UK where, like the US, teaser rates are more popular. However, GPMs might be expected to become more prevalent during periods with high rates of inflation (Brueckner 1984).

One further means of overcoming the tilt and achieving an optimum mortgage design is to allow borrowers to have autonomous control over their payment scheduling. That is to have a fully flexible mortgage that facilitates the smoothing of lifetime consumption. Brueckner (1984) noted that flexible scheduling can create the conditions characteristic of a perfect capital market, achieved through the ability to borrow and lend by varying the amortisation rate. Households who have a discount rate higher than the mortgage rate, and who expect increased incomes, can vary mortgage payments to bring non-housing consumption forward in time. This is not possible with level payment scheduling.

Brueckner pointed out that even with flexible amortisation the exact conditions for optimal spending and saving over time may not be achieved due to a default constraint. This is the condition that the total debt does not exceed the value of the property, that is there should be no negative equity. With sufficient build up of deferred payments the lender could face the risk of ruthless default. However, if the major cause of default originates with affordability and fluctuations in income, then flexible amortisation scheduling might minimise this risk. Brueckner's analysis offers some important results, including the possibility that the introduction of flexible amortisation might lower rather than increase housing demand.[10] More generally, the impacts of flexible amortisation are best considered in a portfolio context with uncertainty, a perspective to be explored more fully below.

In the UK borrowers may be more wary of fully flexible amortisation because default on negative equity does not relinquish obligations to pay off the mortgage. Payment flexibility that allows an increase in the rate of amortisation, generating savings in interest cost over the life of a mortgage, might be more favoured, and competition in the UK market has made this option generally available. One outcome might be that lenders place constraints on flexibility that favour over-rather than under-payment. In fact, Brueckner's model suggests the asymmetric treatment of faster and slower rates of amortisation. The optimum payment profile in the Brueckner model is flat while the default constraint binds (that is, too low payments build up too much future debt and risk default), followed by a gradually increasing size of payment to reflect rising incomes.

There is some casual but suggestive empirical evidence from the United Kingdom for the presence of asymmetry in payment flexibility.[11] Most so called flexible mortgages emphasise the facility to increase the rate of debt amortisation rather than reduce it, though payment holidays are often provided. First Active Financial PLC, in the United Kingdom, conducted a survey of flexible mortgages and their characteristics. First Active established a benchmark of characteristics to determine what can correctly be described as a flexible mortgage product. The required features include full flexibility for under- and over-payment, with daily calculation of interest and no redemption fees for early repayment. Only four products achieved all of these characteristics by October 2000.[12] United Kingdom mortgage providers place a clear marketing emphasis upon potential cost savings over the life of a mortgage.

The time profile of real mortgage payments is an important consideration of optimum mortgage design. A second linked design focus is the sharing of inflation risk between borrowers and lenders. The conventional FRM imposes the tilt on the borrower and inflation risk on the lender. The fully indexed mortgage imposes the tilt on the lender and inflation risk on the borrower. Thus these two mortgage instruments represent extremes in the sharing of different risks. Scott *et al.* (1993) introduced the idea of the partially indexed affordable mortgage. The design is based on a trade-off between the lender and borrower with respect to risk sharing and affordability (that is the tilt). This suggests that the borrower and the lender might wish to compromise on the extent to which they adopt these varying risk positions. Put another way, the consumer's demand for indexed debt may be less than 100%.

Scott *et al.* argued that it would be optimal for borrowers to have a hybrid price level adjusted mortgage (PLAM) that consists of a mix of FRM and PLAM.[13] Though this mortgage instrument is not evident in the major economies there is a tendency towards hybrid debt; for example 'pick and mix' mortgages in the UK, and combinations of fixed and adjustable rate debt in the US.[14] With this framework in place a more inflationary environment might well lead to the emergence of the partially indexed affordable mortgage. The tendency towards facilitating consumer choice is most apparent with the flexible mortgage which can help overcome many of the problems emerging from capital market imperfections and less than optimal mortgage designs. The discussion which follows considers the theoretical and empirical importance of flexible payment scheduling.

The role of the flexible amortisation of mortgage debt

The previous discussion noted how liquidity constrained borrowers will be concerned with the tilting of real mortgage payments towards the early years of the mortgage. Other households may not be so constrained by considerations of affordability, and be more concerned with cost minimisation over the life of the debt (Breslaw *et al.* 1996). Both of these choice dimensions involve the rate at which debt can be, or actually is, amortised, an important aspect of mortgage design. This still involves a discussion of imperfect capital markets because even for borrowers for whom the underwriting criteria do not bind, variations in the amortisation rate can be used to hedge portfolios. In a perfectly competitive no arbitrage economy the rate of amortisation would be of little interest. There is now a body of literature on this topic, involving both theoretical and empirical work (Brueckner 1984; Plaut 1986; Goodman & Wassmer 1992; Leece 1997).

How fast, in theory, can we expect borrowers to repay their mortgage debt and accumulate equity in their property? In a sense this is a return to the theory of mortgage demand. The discussion in Chapter 2 demonstrated the critical relationship between net of tax mortgage rates and the net return on savings, in addition to the risk characteristics of these costs and returns. The US typically has a net of tax mortgage rate lower than the rate of return on savings. This implies that mortgage debt will be maximised. However, Brueckner (1994a) has theoretically demonstrated how the riskiness of the rate of return to savings might explain the observed rapid accumulation of equity in a property, that is mortgage demand *in situ*. The Canadian and now the UK cases are different, with no tax subsidy to mortgage borrowing in the former case and its recent removal in the latter. When the mortgage rate is comparatively expensive we would definitely expect an emphasis upon faster rates of amortisation. The discussion which follows considers two major theoretical models that offer insights into both the implications of flexible amortisation, and the key influences upon amortisation behaviour.

The Plaut model

Seminal work by Plaut (1986) has indicated the importance of the ability to vary the rate of amortisation for liquidity constrained households. With constant payment scheduling, and no access to non-mortgage finance, increases in interest rates require a cut in consumption. An equivalent to this restriction is created by tax subsidies on mortgage interest payments that encourage the use of mortgage debt rather than consumer credit. Flexible amortisation scheduling could facilitate the smoothing of consumption over time. Variations in the rate of amortisation also assist hedging against house price falls, and adverse interest rate movements. If households are given flexibility then liquidity constrained consumers choose the rate of amortisation according to the mortgage interest rate, the opportunity cost of equity in property, house prices, and the risk attached to housing and non-housing assets. The actual structure of the model very closely follows mortgage demand under uncertainty presented in Chapter 2, but the amortisation rate is now identified as the dependent variable. Also, the modelling explicitly covers two periods, so for example c_1 and c_2 are non-housing consumption in periods 1 and 2 respectively. A bar, as in $\bar{c}_1$, represents expected consumption.

Equations (4.2) and (4.3) correspond to equations (2.5) and (2.7), which were presented as the general form of the demand for mortgage finance under uncertainty. The equations follow Plaut, but the notation is changed to be commensurate with that used elsewhere in this book. Equation (4.2) is the utility function and equation (4.3) is the expression for expected wealth from which a budget constraint can be derived. The interest lies in the use of the additional arguments z and lv, which are the payment in the first period (the rate of amortisation) and the chosen loan-to-value ratio respectively. Also, note that expression (4.3) contains the argument $(1 + E(r_h)^2)H$ which represents the expected increase in the price of housing, and A is the alternative risky asset to housing. The decision problem for the borrower is the choice of z, given optimum values of other variables. The modelling assumes that a prior decision has been made on the desired quantity of housing services to be consumed.

$$E[U] = U(c_1, \ c_2, \ H) + U_2(E(W_2), \ \sigma^2_{W_2}(W_2)) \qquad (4.2)$$

$$\begin{aligned} E(W_2) &= A(1 + E(r_A))^2 + (y_1 - \bar{c}_1 - z)(1 + E(r_A)) \\ &+ y_2 - \bar{c}_2 - (1 - Iv)M(1 + r)^2 + (1 + E(r_h)^2)H \end{aligned} \qquad (4.3)$$

Table 4.1 shows the first order comparative static results for the Plaut model with respect to the rate of amortisation. The results indicate that a household with higher income, facing a risky alternative investment to housing, and not subject to mortgage rationing is likely to choose a large direct investment in their property, i.e. a high rate of amortisation in the first period of the two-period model. Plaut has an interesting note on the implications of varying amortisation rates for housing demand. The impact of a change in the amortisation rate depends upon the covariance between house price and the price of the alternative asset. If the covariance is positive then an increase in amortisation reduces the hedging possibilities

Table 4.1   The predicted signs on key variables from the Plaut model[1]

Income	+ An increase (decrease) in first period income increases (decreases) amortisation. A change in second period (forward looking or expected income) has no effect. An increase in first period income lowers the likelihood of a binding liquidity constraint.
Wealth	$(+, \ -)^2$ Changes in initial wealth have an ambiguous effect.
Variance	+ Increases (decreases) in the riskiness of the alternative asset to housing increase (decrease) amortisation. The increased riskiness of savings favours the build up of housing equity.
Mortgage interest	+ An increase (decrease) in the mortgage interest rate increases (decreases) the rate of amortisation. Costly mortgages are repaid more quickly.
Expected return on the alternative asset to housing	− An increase in the alternative rate of return (ceterus paribus) renders the alternative asset more attractive and reduces the accumulation of equity in the property.
Expected return on housing	− If the return on the asset has a negative covariance with housing then an increase (decrease) in the rate of return on housing will lower (increase) the amortisation rate. With negative covariance, changes in housing effect the variance of wealth. The effect is ambiguous if covariance is positive.

Notes
[1] Plaut also considers the effects of price covariance, changes in mortgage limits and risk aversion. See Plaut (1986, p. 236).
[2] $(+, \ -)$ indicates ambiguity of expected sign.

of the consumer and housing demand falls. Negative covariance is ambiguous in its effects, higher amortisation can reduce housing demand because the borrower wishes to reduce the risk of a cash flow squeeze. Alternatively, housing demand can increase with increased amortisation due to the reduction in portfolio variance. The links between the choice of mortgage design, the tilt and housing demand will be discussed further in Chapters 7 and 8 where a number of key covariances will also be seen to be critical.

Plaut's model has an interesting focus on the circumstances under which a balloon payment would be considered optimal. A balloon payment is a one-off payment of the mortgage debt on the date of maturity, and corresponds with an interest only mortgage. This can be formally represented in a two-period model by determining when zero amortisation would be optimal for the first period. The model predicts that this option will be preferred when the household has a small mortgage, and when there is little risk attached to the mortgage interest rate, or the rate of return on the alternative asset to housing.

One strongly intuitive result is that a balloon payment will be preferred when there is a comparatively large rate of return on the non-housing asset, and the mortgage interest rate is comparatively low. This corresponds nicely with the case of the UK endowment mortgage where there have been periods of time when the expected rate of return on the endowment was higher than the net of tax mortgage interest rate (Lamb 1987, 1989). This was the basis of the mortgage demand estimates for endowment mortgage holders presented in Chapter 2. In the US, balloon mortgages may have maturities of 30 years but the final payment can be due after 3, 5 or 7 years. Thus these mortgages match the needs of mobile households and provide another interesting perspective on amortisation.

The Goodman & Wassmer model

The work of Plaut has been significantly extended by Goodman & Wassmer (1992). This is a multi-period model that demonstrates the advantages of a fully flexible mortgage instrument. That is the contribution to the economic welfare of the borrower deriving from the ability to vary the rate of amortisation of debt period by period. Optimum life cycle decision making requires that the marginal utility of income is equalised between periods. Liquidity constrained households will have difficulty in achieving this equality because of restrictions on their borrowing, and because conventional mortgage designs require constant payment scheduling. Flexible amortisation is one way of overcoming liquidity constraints and smoothing expenditure and saving between periods. This differs from the work of Plaut in that it is a model based upon certainty, and does not incorporate an alternative risky asset to housing, but it does offer important insights into mortgage design and life cycle planning. The discussion here is a broad brush presentation of what is a rather complex model.

Goodman and Wassmer formulated both a multi-period and a two-period model. The multi-period model is less tractable, hence the alternative formulation, but an inspection of the conditions for multi-period optimality where variable repayment is allowed, and where it is not, is instructive. Following Goodman & Wassmer, equation (4.4) gives the consumers' optimal decision with a constant repayment schedule. Expression (4.5) gives the consumers' multi-period optimal conditions when variable payments are allowed. The expression MU_{inc}^t is the marginal utility of income in each period (t), MRS_t is the marginal rate of substitution between housing and a composite consumption good per period, p is the price of housing relative to the price of consumption with the latter used as a numeraire, and F is the discount factor.

$$\sum_{t=1}^{t=\tau} MU_{inc}^t[MRS_t - p^*/F] = 0 \tag{4.4}$$

$$\sum_{t=1}^{t=\tau} MU_{inc}^t[MRS_t - p_t] = 0 \tag{4.5}$$

Both expression (4.4) and expression (4.5) aggregate the period by period conditions over time periods. Both represent the equality of the price ratio with the marginal rate of substitution, multiplied by the marginal utility of income. The key difference is that the non-variable payment requires this equality to be achieved on average, that is with respect to an average price over all periods p^*, while the variable payment mortgage allows period-by-period equality by equating the marginal rate of substitution multiplied by the marginal utility of income to the current price ratio p_t. Removing the constant payment constraint increases the borrower's utility, with the size of this effect depending upon the form of utility function, prices and incomes (Goodman & Wassmer 1992).

Summary of the theoretical models of amortisation behaviour

The above discussion of the Plaut and Goodman & Wassmer models demonstrates the optimality of being able to vary the rate of amortisation of debt. Though this perspective on mortgage design does not directly address the tilt, it does indicate the importance of repayment flexibility for overcoming constraints on the ability to borrow to finance non-housing consumption (or the effects of a tax subsidy on mortgage interest rates), a factor that adds to the impact of the tilt. The theoretical work of Plaut in particular emphasises the link between amortisation and the theory of mortgage demand under conditions of uncertainty. For example, the role of portfolio characteristics and key covariances such as that between the house price and the price of the alternative asset.

Goodman & Wassmer's model also has implications for housing, and thus mortgage demand. Simulations were carried out to assess the potential effect of a variable payment mortgage (VPM)[15] compared to an FRM on housing demand in the US. Not only was there a significant positive impact upon housing demand, but there was also substantial capacity for a lender to charge insurance to cover the risk of attracting borrowers with an high propensity to default (adverse selection). These offer interesting perspectives on the recent growth of more flexible mortgage instruments. Whether VPMs can and do boost UK housing demand, reduce sensitivity to changes in the mortgage interest rate, or lengthen the planning horizons of borrowers are interesting questions for further research.

Perspectives on the maturity of mortgage debt

The maturity of mortgage debt, as a contractual feature and a household choice, has played a variety of roles in the mortgage economics literature. For example, the analysis of mortgage credit rationing by Kent (1980) focuses upon maturity as an element of the mortgage contract that can be varied to clear the mortgage market when it is in temporary disequilib-rium. Moreover, the maturity of debt can be used as an indicator of mortgage credit rationing. This view should be qualified to the extent that choice of maturity reflects cost minimisation behaviour. It is also possible that choice of maturity can signal a borrower's credit risk charac-teristics (Harrison *et al.* 2004, Ben-Shahar & Feldman 2003). That is, if shorter maturities carry lower risk premiums then more creditworthy borrowers may choose shorter-term contracts.

The effects on the probability of default of increasing maturity are ambigu-ous (Ben-Shahar & Feldman 2003). Long maturities lower the risk of a liquidity squeeze via lower periodic payments, but also increase the number of periods over which a problem can arise. The net effect will depend upon actual contract terms and arguments such as the variance of the borrower's income and the variance of house prices. Interestingly, the balloon payment with its zero amortisation also increases the risk of default at the point at which repayment is required (see Noordewier *et al.* 2001). Thus both the choice or contractual restriction of maturity has relevance to mortgage/housing demand, default probabilities and the signalling of credit worthiness.

It is also worth noting that changes in maturity are one reaction, or strategy, for borrowers to avoid impending default, as well as a means of lowering its risk. Lenders will also prefer this as otherwise there are time and costs associated with default imposed on the lender (Harding & Sirmans 2002). There is now a literature on the renegotiation of debt to ease problems facing borrowers involving the choice between discounting the principle sum owed, or renegotiation of the term (Riddiough & Wyatt 1994; Anderson & Sundaresan 1996; Mella-Barral & Perraudin 1997). Though most of this work is applied to the commercial mortgage market it is clearly applicable to residential mortgages.

In the US maturity renegotiation is the more common form of dealing with 'troubled debt' than discounting the outstanding principal (Harding & Sirmans 2002). The preference for this strategy has been explained in terms of the fewer agency problems facing lenders. For example, borrowers for whom discounting of debt is a possibility may be tempted to divert cash flows from a property or take on more risk (Harding & Sirmans 2002). Residential borrowers facing risks of default may not maintain the value of the collateral for the loan by carrying out repairs and maintenance. Harding and Sirmans note the existence of a 'mortgage externality' where the limitation of the liability of the owner occupier to mortgage debt reduces maintenance and investment in property. This would not be less true of the UK where the mortgage liability remains after default.

So the maturity of mortgage debt is a complex variable to interpret and supplies yet another potential source of endogeneity and selectivity in mortgage demand equations. It can signal default risk, reflect the management of financial distress, be a means of minimising the impact of payment tilting or correspond with desired rates of amortisation. Given the likely endogeneity of choice of maturity in mortgage demand equations then reduced form equations in past research may have proxied this choice by the choice of mortgage instrument, personal characteristics, income, etc. The choice of mortgage maturity is an area that deserves more attention in empirical research. The empirical literature has largely focused upon the choice of debt maturity and its relation to amortisation.

Empirical studies of amortisation behaviour

Empirical studies have been concerned with the choice of maturity of a mortgage and thus implicitly consider the rate of amortisation. This research has covered mortgage choices in the US (Dhillon *et al.* 1990), Canada (Breslaw *et al.* 1996) and the UK (Leece 1997). For example, Dhillon *et al.* (1990) evaluated the choice between a 15- and a 30-year fixed rate mortgage and estimated a simple probit to represent this choice. The empirical results stress the importance of affordability and tax subsidies. For example, the demand for contracts with short maturities was likely to be less when interest rates were high. Wealthier households, more able to adopt higher rates of amortisation of debt, were more likely to choose the shorter maturities. An interesting result was that liquidity constrained households maximised gearing, and consequently chose mortgages of a long duration. However, affordability has not been the major finding in all of the studies and cost minimising behaviour over the life of the mortgage is also apparent (see Breslaw *et al.* 1996).[16]

Breslaw *et al.* (1996) reported research on the Canadian mortgage market. The authors made an important distinction between the term and the maturity of the mortgage debt. The term is the time period for which the interest rate is fixed on the FRM. The maturity is the usual life of the mortgage over which payments are calculated, and implicitly represents the rate of amortisation. It is worth remembering that Canadian fixed rate mortgages are similar to those obtaining in the UK, that is rates of interest are typically fixed for between 1 and 5 years. The choice between this term and the maturity of the debt (that is the rate of amortisation) was modelled simultaneously. The estimation involved the use of an ordered bivariate probit model and covered the period 1980 to 1988.

Breslaw *et al.* identified different consumer strategies in the joint choice of mortgage instrument and mortgage term. The results indicated the importance of risk aversion, and mortgage cost minimising behaviour. For example, risk averse households facing a comparatively high mortgage cost adopted fixed rate debt and repaid quickly. This result depends upon the absence of a binding borrowing constraint. Such a constraint would encourage risk averse borrowers to cover the higher cost of fixed rate debt by lower payments, through an extension of maturity. Interestingly, there is a stream of largely normative literature that examines the implications of the choice of mortgage instrument from a cost minimisation point of view (Milevsky 2001; Tucker 1991; Sprecher & Willman 1993; Templeton *et al.* 1996). This literature examines lifetime costs over the given maturity of a mortgage, generally finding against the FRM. This research will be discussed in Chapter 7 of the book.

Zorn & Lea (1989) considered a range of possible payment behaviour for Canadian ARM holders. This included an analysis of partial prepayment and thus implicitly amortisation rates. Zorn & Lea found partial prepayment to be sensitive to the opportunity cost of equity in a property and the mortgage interest rate. The elasticity of partial repayment with respect to the opportunity cost of equity was negative, so that low opportunity cost increased repayment; a result compatible with theoretical predictions of Plaut. Higher incomes led to lower amortisation, a result that might be a proxy for the impact of wealth. Wealthy individuals might have a higher opportunity cost of equity that reflects more sophisticated portfolios. It might be worthwhile examining the behaviour of low and high income groups separately as in the mortgage demand models of Follain & Dunsky (1997).

Leece (1997) estimated a multinomial logit model of choice of debt maturity, using UK data. Three discrete choices were modelled: a standard 25-year contract, contracts greater than 25 years, contracts of less than 25 years. The study used a sample of 2033 mortgage holders taken from the British Household Panel Survey (BHPS) for 1991. The empirical analysis used personal characteristics (age, education, marital status) and income from both employment and investments. A unique aspect of the specification was a qualitative variable indicating that a household was experiencing problems meeting their housing costs. The results of the research suggested the importance of a household's perception that it faced financial problems – leading to longer maturities. Overall the results emphasised affordability, perhaps not surprising given the recession of the 1990s.

The Plaut model suggested the basis upon which a borrower would prefer a balloon mortgage, that is zero amortisation of debt. The balloon mortgage is not widespread in the US forming only 7.7% of the primary mortgages of households in the 1999 American Housing Survey. For the UK this choice corresponds to the endowment mortgage. The endowment represents a corner solution, that is when the preferred rate of amortisation is zero an endowment is optimal.[17] Though some research suggests the dominance of affordability in driving endowment choice (Leece 1995b), there is also indicative evidence that the perceived rate of return on the endowment was a determinant of choice, offering some confirmation of the insights of the Plaut model (Leece 2000b).

The theoretical predictions of the Plaut model are not always confirmed by empirical work. For example, Dhillon *et al.* (1990) found a negative rather than a positive sign on the mortgage interest rate with respect to the choice of mortgage maturity. There may be some difficulties in translating the theoretical restrictions of the Plaut model directly into empirical practice. Actual mortgage choices may reflect constant repayment scheduling which in a two-period model would set an absolute constraint on amortisation. It might also be advantageous to identify constrained and unconstrained borrowers. Cost minimisation may be more important for some households. Amortisation is a part of a complex picture of multiple mortgage choices including the level of housing demand, gearing, portfolio choices and choice of mortgage instrument. The increase in the availability of flexible mortgages may ultimately generate the necessary data for more detailed study of amortisation behaviour.

Ultimately the prevalence of a truly flexible mortgage instrument may assist in overcoming liquidity problems and facilitating optimum life cycle and portfolio planning. Other issues would also arise, including the possibility and limitations of flexible scheduling being used to minimise default risk. Behavioural finance offers an interesting perspective on repayment flexibility that suggests that this facility may not be unproblematic. Thaler & Shefrin (1981), and Shefrin & Thaler (1988) argue that individuals struggle between impulse and planning and that some regular savings contracts represent commitments that discipline economic agents. This was an often-used rationale for the sale of the rather inflexible endowment mortgages in the UK. Commitment and fulfilment of regular savings contracts may also have information content for the lender. Thus, whether truly flexible amortisation schedules reduce or add to default risk, due to the removal of this financial discipline, might be a further interesting research question. For the UK recent evidence suggests it is the wealthier and more sophisticated borrowers that are taking advantage of increased payment flexibility.[18]

Summary and conclusions

This chapter has examined a key issue in mortgage design. That is, the ability to alter the payment scheduling of mortgage debt. The discussion began with the tilting of real payments towards the early life of the mortgage, and the cash flow problems that can arise for borrowers, particularly those choosing mortgage instruments which expose them to interest rate risk. There are a number of alternative mortgage designs that can and have been used to overcome the tilt, particularly at times when the rate of inflation is high. The tilt is important if capital markets are imperfect and liquidity constrained borrowers are not be able to achieve their optimum life cycle plans, a feature that might be mitigated by the ability to vary the rate of payments on a debt.

A number of theoretical studies had been undertaken which emphasised the importance of flexible amortisation and different payment schedules. In particular, the models of Plaut and Goodman & Wassmer which demonstrated how flexible amortisation can be used to hedge portfolios (Plaut 1986) and achieve an optimum life cycle consumption plan (Goodman & Wassmer 1992). This research was apt given the recent growth in flexible mortgage instruments. Compatible with these models, and in the absence of a binding constraint on non-housing consumption, households could minimise their mortgage cost over the life of the debt. There had been some empirical work on the choice of mortgage maturity, and on consumers' strategies in fixing their interest payments and choosing their rate of amortisation.

There are a number of reasons why further theoretical and empirical work on amortisation behaviour would be of benefit. There is the issue of the optimal mortgage contract designs that lenders should offer and the risk sharing arrangements between borrowers and lenders. Amortisation is implicitly about mortgage demand *in situ*, and has effects upon the demand for housing. The build up of housing equity by some groups of borrowers, and the extension of mortgage maturity by others, has implications for the form and distribution of wealth for households in later life, and even across generations (e.g. inherited wealth). Housing equity may be increasingly called upon to finance retirement. A study of the implications of partial prepayment, that is facilitated by flexible mortgage instruments, for cash flows to the secondary mortgage market and MBS valuation, would be useful. How far the requirements of the secondary mortgage market and information problems have inhibited the spread of flexible amortisation scheduling is another interesting research question.

The theoretical and empirical modelling presented in this chapter has been both explicitly and implicitly based upon capital market imperfections. Liquidity constraints have created affordability problems and incomplete portfolios have emphasised the need to vary amortisation to exploit hedging opportunities provided by an alternative asset to housing. The chapter which follows will take the issue of credit market imperfections further by examining the role of information problems and rationing in mortgage markets. The recurring theme of optimal mortgage design will arise again in the next chapter as we are introduced for the first time to the signalling capabilities of the various features of a mortgage contract, an issue to be developed even further in Chapters 7 and 8.

Guide to further reading

The original article by Plaut (1986) is well worth detailed study. The paper presents an accessible two-period model of housing demand, which incorporates the demand for mortgage finance in a novel and fundamental way. This chapter has noted the importance of varying the rate of amortisation to overcome liquidity constraints, or minimise lifetime mortgage costs. Empirical work has tended to focus upon the choice of mortgage maturity. There are, in fact, limits to which changes in maturity at the margin can ease liquidity constraints, etc. Miles (1994) provides some interesting simulations of the consequences of inflation for mortgage payment patterns and the impact or lack of impact of marginal changes in the maturity of debt. This book is also recommended for an understanding of the role of the mortgage market in the wider economy and appreciating the tilt and the mortgage design issues involved.

Notes

1 The more typical procedure would be to wait until the year end before reducing the capital sum, though money for partial prepayment could be placed on deposit this might typically be at a lower rate than that charged on the mortgage debt.
2 Interesting would be the possibility that flexible amortisation itself generates a new option that enhanced the value of the prepayment option, thus discouraging prepayment. For example, if interest rates fall it would no longer be necessary to fully prepay debt and lose this option.
3 The basic annuity formulae is $R = r^*M/(1 - (1+r)^{-n}/r)$ where R is the level repayment, M is the principal sum borrowed, r is the mortgage interest rate and n is the number of payment periods to maturity.
4 A more extensive treatment of the impact of the tilt can be found in William B. Brueggeman & Jefry D. Fisher, *Real Estate Finance and Investment* (10th edition, Irwin 1997), Chapter 4, pp. 112–18.
5 Though the tilt is typically discussed in terms of the annuity mortgage, it emerges for any mortgage that involves a constant nominal, rather than a constant real payment schedule. Leece (1995b) demonstrates how the tilt applies to both the repayment and the interest only endowment mortgage, both offered in the United Kingdom.
6 Kearl (1978) notes that there is no unambiguous measure of the tilt but suggests the following Macaulay measure of 'duration' of a stream of quarterly mortgage payments. Taking M as the present value of mortgage payments then the

elasticity of this present value with respect to the discount (mortgage) rate is given by $\hat{T} = \sum_t^T tQP(t)d^t / \sum_t^T QP(t)d^t$ where QP are quarterly payments and d is the appropriate discount rate. The formulae are discussed in footnote 5 on page 1121 of Kearl's (1978) paper.

7 The derivation of this formulae can be found in Miles (1994, pp. 189–90). Interestingly, the derivation begins with the standard annuity formulae which is then expressed as a ratio to household income, and then substitutes growth rates for house prices and income and inflation in this ratio. So we have a more dynamic view of the tilt incorporating income growth and house price inflation.

8 Indexation also has the advantage of allowing the borrower to hedge internally against inflation risk. This means that the value of an asset (the house price) will offset the fall in the value of the liability (the mortgage debt). However, this only works with neutral inflation.

9 Of course, the difficulty with the duel index system arises when the mortgage term is at its maximum. This has led advocates of duel indexing to suggest that the initial term on debt be set short of the maximum as a kind of insurance policy against large discrepancies between the two indices. This argument is interesting in highlighting the importance of the ability to vary the term of a mortgage.

10 This result is sensitive to the choice of utility function. So, for example, in the case of a Cobb Douglas utility function a flexible mortgage instrument increases housing demand compared with a level payment design, but an alternative specification does not (see Brueckner 1984, p. 149).

11 The flexible mortgage is less evident in the United States; this may be due more to servicing and accounting issues than lack of demand from borrowers.

12 **www.firstactive.co.uk** offers a web-based publication, 'The First Active Flexible Mortgage Index' though a recent visit to this site suggested that the survey had been discontinued.

13 Scott *et al.* (1993) note that the tilt is at its maximum for the lender when a fully indexed mortgage is introduced. Thus they note the value of a tilt parameter equal to 1. It should be noted that this is an arbitrary but practically based limit to the tilt in that graduated payment streams with negative amortisation are considered impractical (e.g. too much default risk). They point this out in a footnote (Scott *et al.* 1993, fn. 1, p. 2).

14 See Simon, R. 'Hybrid Mortgages Offer The Best of Two Worlds', *Real Estate Journal*, Wall Street Journal Online, 15 January 2002.

15 Author's abbreviation not used in the original paper.

16 Of course, there is a limit to which changing maturities can significantly lower or higher payments and the effects may be small when the existing maturity is long. Differences will be more significant, say, when comparing 10- or 15-year choice with a 25- or 30-year choice.

17 The main fault with this apparent correspondence between the Plaut model and endowment choice is that only the corner solution of zero amortisation is compatible with the endowment choice. The inflexibility of the endowment prevents intermediate levels of amortisation.

18 Cited in Parliamentary Hansard 24 July 2002.

5

Rationing, Mortgage Market Adjustment and Separating Equilibrium

Introduction

This chapter examines the process of mortgage market adjustment, and equilibrium in the market for housing debt. The possibility that some households could be credit rationed has been an enduring concern in the mortgage economics literature. Though many economies have experienced financial deregulation, and correspondingly more competitive markets for housing finance, the possibility of credit rationing is still an important issue to address. At a minimum the deregulation of financial markets facilitates a comparison of household behaviour under different credit regimes.

Despite financial deregulation recent work has attested to the relevance of mortgage credit rationing in the US (Duca & Rosenthal 1991; Linnemann *et al.* 1997; Ambrose *et al.* 2002). Mortgage markets in other economies may also experience mortgage market regulation and credit rationing (Deutsche & Tomann 1995). Theoretical work discussed in Chapter 2 suggested that liquidity constraints need not be widespread to have a significant impact upon housing and mortgage demand (Ortalo-Magné & Rady 1998, 1999, 2002). The securitisation of mortgage finance and the growth of the sub-prime lending also raises the question of the current extent and importance of credit rationing.

Previous chapters referred to prudential lending rules, or mortgage underwriting criterion. Mortgage lenders in most economies have rules which limit the amount of individual mortgage borrowing that is allowed, though there have been times, in the UK at least, when these have been criticised as imprudent and lax.[1] The extent to which these rules bind or vary in application between borrowers, possibly leading to some individuals consuming a smaller amount of housing services than they desire, or renting rather than owning, is an important question. There may also be effects on the distribution of wealth, as it is the poorer members of the community who will be most subjected to rationing constraints (Hendershott & Hu 1983; Meen 1990). It is the prime purpose of this chapter to explore the circumstances under which credit rationing arises in the market for housing finance, and its relevance to mortgage demand and contract design. Such a discussion also provides the opportunity to raise some issues in mortgage pricing and mortgage market adjustment.

Any discussion of credit rationing cannot be divorced from the nature of mortgage market adjustment. For example, dynamic rationing occurs as a result of lags in the upward adjustment of the mortgage interest rate to its long-run equilibrium value. This form of rationing needs to be distinguished from the notion of equilibrium rationing. Equilibrium rationing occurs when lenders face hidden (asymmetric) information, for example data on the default and prepayment probabilities of borrowers. Equilibrium credit rationing can persist even in a deregulated economy, and can be contrasted with the more widespread mortgage rationing that occurred in the UK, and possibly in the US, during the 1970s.

The chapter begins with a classification of the main sources of credit rationing. The discussion is divided into disequilibrium rationing that focuses upon the situation prior to financial deregulation, dynamic rationing which incorporates issues in mortgage pricing and market adjustment; and equilibrium rationing with its basis in asymmetric information. Where relevant the impact of the MBS market on credit rationing and market adjustment will also be discussed. We find that the most relevant contemporary source of credit rationing in the mortgage market is equilibrium rationing. This and other concepts also provide a foundation for the discussion of mortgage designs in Chapter 7, along with the valuation of mortgages discussed in Chapters 9 and 10.

A classification of credit rationing in the mortgage market

This section explores the various conditions under which credit rationing can occur. Rationing arises when the effective demand for funds exceeds the supply, with the observed amount of mortgage debt being equivalent to the short side of the market. Some writers have defined mortgage market rationing in terms of the use of non-price features of mortgage contracts, for example the loan-to-value ratio, to decide the allocation of credit when mortgage markets are in disequilibrium (Kent 1987). For the purposes of this chapter it is useful to identify three sources of credit rationing (equilibrium, disequilibrium and dynamic). These can be generally described and considered as follows:

- *Disequilibrium rationing* occurs when the interest rate is maintained at its current level due to an imperfect market structure (e.g. an interest rate cartel), or due to government regulations or usury laws. In the United States a ceiling on deposit rates when retail funds were used to finance mortgage loans had a similar effect. Non-price terms such as the loan-to-value ratio or mortgage maturity are not adjusted sufficiently to clear the market. Criterion for granting loans may then involve a queuing system, the need for a savings record with the lender, etc.

- *Dynamic rationing* occurs when the mortgage market adjusts slowly so that excess demand persists until the long-run equilibrium mortgage interest rate is achieved. Explanations for the slow adjustment of interest rates vary from the menu costs of price changes to imperfect market structures, and theories of asymmetric information and adverse selection. Some authors argue for a temporary equilibrium through changes in loan-to-value ratio and maturity (Kent 1980; Ostas & Zahn 1975), though this can be shown to be problematic (Nellis & Thom 1983). For example, interest rates and desired loan-to-value ratios are not entirely independent of each other.

- *Equilibrium rationing* is where non-price loan terms and the mortgage interest rate adjusts to achieve a new market equilibrium. However, if lenders face default risk, asymmetric information on the extent of this risk, and costs against which they are not insured, then rationing can persist for some households. Interest rates and loan-to-value ratios can be varied to accommodate the needs of some borrowers but there may still be unsatisfied demand. This may lead to some potential borrowers being excluded from owner occupation, or having less than their desired level of mortgage debt. This gives a key role to mortgage contract design (e.g. loan size/interest rate combinations) in signalling and screening credit risk and bringing about credit market rationing.

The categories of credit rationing described above are not unambiguous. For example, Kent (1987) adopts a wide ranging definition of dynamic rationing that incorporates disequilibrium rationing. Indeed there are overlaps, market imperfections can be common to both explanations. It is also true that asymmetric information and adverse selection can lead to slow market adjustments (Stiglitz & Weiss 1981) thus further confounding

these distinctions. However, for heuristic purposes the distinction between disequilibrium, dynamic rationing and equilibrium rationing is
maintained. This allows a consideration of mortgage price behaviour (dynamic rationing), the type of economy-wide rationing existing in the UK,
and possibly the US, during the 1970s (disequilibrium rationing), and the
role of default costs, information and mortgage contract design in credit
rationing (equilibrium rationing).

Disequilibrium rationing

The most clear cut example of disequilibrium rationing is the UK mortgage market in the 1970s and early 1980s. Up to 1983 UK mortgage finance
was controlled by a cartel of building societies (mutual organisations). The
existence of disequilibrium rationing in the United States is more contro-
versial (Meltzer 1974; Hendershott 1981; Jaffee & Rosen 1979), though
Kent (1987) cites 1966, 1969–70 and 1974–75 as periods when disequilibrium credit rationing might have been evident in the US economy. In the
US a range of factors have been cited to explain the possibility of disequilibrium rationing. These include usury laws in some states (Ostas 1976),
ceilings on pass book accounts-regulation Q (Swan 1973), and upper limits
on mortgage interest rates set by the Federal Housing Association (Jaffee &
Rosen 1978, 1979).

Kent (1980) presented a model of credit rationing in the US under imperfect competition. Equilibrium stopped short of the competitive outcome
because of the rising marginal cost of financing mortgages from retail
deposits, as total lending expanded. With fixed rate mortgages an increase
in interest rates is only paid by new borrowers, but all depositors received
interest rate increases. Thus lending stops short of competitive equilibrium when the supply of funds and mortgages have different elasticities.
This was treated as dynamic rationing because the imperfect competition
emerged out of temporary disequilibrium. In the UK, building societies
also depended upon financing from retail deposits though debt was typically variable rate. Credit rationing occurred because the mutuals acted as a
cartel with the objective of keeping mortgage interest rates low, thus
generating excess demand.

Excess demand and disequilibrium credit rationing requires a means of
allocating credit, either access via a mortgage queue and/or binding constraints on those that borrow. Dougherty & Van Order (1982) consider the
case of an absolute constraint on the amount that an individual can
borrow. In this case the user cost of owner occupation has an additional

argument, the ratio of the shadow price of the borrowing constraint to the marginal utility of non-housing consumption. Thus the extra cost reflects the departure from optimality at the margin. It is also the case that if a maximum payment to income ratio forces a borrower into a corner solution then changes in real interest rates will not effect housing/mortgage demand, but changes in nominal rates will ease or tighten this constraint (Muellbauer & Murphy 1997). Thus mortgage credit rationing also argues for the use of nominal rather than real interest rates in mortgage demand equations.

Rationing raises the user cost of owner occupation and reduces housing/absolute mortgage demand. Dougherty & Van Order also note that in the case of a binding loan-to-value constraint then the interest rate term in the user cost equation should be a weighted average of the mortgage interest rate and opportunity cost of equity in the property. This forgone rate of return reflects the marginal cost of mortgage finance, which is not likely to be effected by the household chosen loan-to-value ratio. This means that lenders cannot remove excess demand for mortgage credit by changing their underwriting rules (Nellis & Thom 1983). The marginal cost of mortgage debt remains constant and credit rationing will persist. Financial deregulation should ease or remove credit rationing, and the user costs of owner occupation, and real interest rates, become a more applicable specification in housing/mortgage demand equations.

Ortalo-Magné & Rady (1999, 2002) demonstrate theoretically how relaxing loan-to-value ratio requirements predicts the observed post-deregulation increases in house prices observed in the UK. Thus the research offers an explanation for the increase in borrowing post-financial deregulation and its subsequent fall, in addition to the co-movement in housing transactions and prices. As previously noted, a key feature in Ortalo-Magné & Rady compared to Stein (1995), is that they do not require liquidity constraints to be widely spread, so that in theory liquidity constraints persisting in a deregulated environment, for some borrowers, could still generate the noted effects.

Market adjustment and dynamic rationing

Dynamic rationing occurs when the mortgage interest rate is slow in adjusting to its long-run market equilibrium. There are several reasons why mortgage interest rates might be sticky. Lagged adjustments can arise from menu costs, convex cost functions and via imperfect competition (Heffernan 1997). Tacit collusion and second-guessing who will make the first interest rate move can all slow down the adjustment of mortgage interest rates to their long-run equilibrium. Brueckner & Arvan (1986) have noted the possibility of risk sharing between borrower and lender that results in less than full adjustment to interest rate changes, though this could result in an equilibrium state.

The usual approach to mortgage pricing/valuation is to posit that the mortgage is a combination of a non-callable bond plus the value of the options to prepay and default (Kau & Keenan 1995; Vandell 1995). These values are all determined in a perfectly competitive no arbitrage economy. Thus, there should be no credit rationing due to inappropriate pricing. Another argument against dynamic rationing is that mortgages exhibit a menu of features that can be traded-off against price, allowing the borrower to achieve equilibrium. The ARM bundles caps, frequency of the adjustment, the choice of index to which the rate is tied, fees, etc. How these features are combined effects the price of the ARM (see SA-Aadu & Sirmans 1989). Consumers may choose combinations of features of the mortgage contract that do not leave them with excess demand for mortgage debt.

Securitisation may also impact upon the prevalence of dynamic credit rationing. The tendency to standardise mortgages, for the purposes of bundling into mortgage-backed securities, may lead to an increasing uniformity of contracts. Some households might then continue to be credit rationed if their individual credit risk is not correctly priced, though this is a form of equilibrium credit rationing. However, the speed of adjustment of mortgage interest rates to exogenous shocks might be increased by securitisation. Lenders who rely on secondary market funding are obliged to pass interest rate changes to security holders quickly and not to smooth changes. Heuson *et al.* (2001) demonstrated how securitisation can exacerbate fluctuations in the mortgage rate. There may be less risk sharing with borrowers, but also less dynamic credit rationing.

Stiglitz & Weiss (1981) argued that lenders would be reluctant to raise interest rates if it resulted in adverse selection, that is, attracted borrowers with a high risk of default. The first lender to raise interest rates on loans might also find that the 'safer' borrowers leave first. Stiglitz & Weiss show that banks are reluctant to increase rates but readily lower them, therefore excess demand and credit rationing can arise. Thus dynamic credit rationing can emerge out of information asymmetry, and adverse selection. This emphasises that the distinction between disequilibrium and dynamic credit rationing can be arbitrary. Empirically, much depends upon the nature and speed of price adjustment Chapter 6 discusses the integration of mortgage markets with other capital markets, and the effects of this on the speed of mortgage market adjustment.

The theoretical work on the impact of down payment constraints (Stein 1995; Lamont & Stein 1999; Ortalo-Magné & Rady 1998, 1999, 2002) is difficult to place in our categorisation of credit market rationing. This is because the theories are concerned with the consequences of binding liquidity constraints rather than their cause. The theories do have implications for housing and therefore mortgage market adjustment. They predict housing booms and slumps, and over- and under-reaction to exogenous shocks such as changes in income levels. It can be shown that credit constraints amplify the effects of income shocks on the housing market, and significantly effect the timing of housing moves. Thus initial liquidity constraints may generate cycles in which the market is significantly, if temporarily, out of equilibrium, exhibiting an excess demand for mortgage credit. Insofar as house price increases facilitate meeting down payment requirements then credit rationing is endogenous to such models. Of course, any existing and binding loan-to-value ratios might reflect equilibrium rationing.

Asymmetric information and equilibrium credit market rationing

Information asymmetry

The discussion in this section of the book examines how equilibrium credit rationing can arise in situations of asymmetric information. A good example of information asymmetry between the borrower and the lender is the borrower's propensity to default on mortgage payments. In particular the likelihood of default may relate to the psychic costs of default, which are essentially unobservable (Brueckner 2000). Under certain conditions heterogeneous mortgage contracts and information asymmetry may result in a separating equilibrium, with at least one of the contracts leading to the rationing of mortgage credit. That is, under some circumstances borrowers self-select in their choice of contracts. Rationing in this case is a form of externality arising out of the imbalance of information.

Information asymmetry raises important questions. Offering a single contract to all borrowers is termed pooling. Does pooling form a stable equilibrium? Is it possible to design mortgage contracts that appeal to different risk categories, and will these risk categories self-select and form separating equilibrium? Does such a separating equilibrium still contain a rationing dimension? Can the separating equilibrium form a stable equilibrium, or will there be an unstable dynamic process featuring lenders switching between pooled and separating equilibrium? The answers to these questions impinge not only on an understanding of mortgage market rationing, but explain the existence and role of non-price contract features and the nature and persistence of the menu of mortgage contracts available to the consumer. Information asymmetry reflects upon the issues of mortgage demand and contract design.

Recent work has applied models of asymmetric information to mortgage markets (Brueckner 1994b, c, 2000; Harrison *et al.* 2004; Ben Shahar & Feldman 2003). Research suggests the possibility that different mortgage contracts might highlight characteristics of borrowers that impinge on the profitability of the lending process, for example default probabilities. Mortgage choices have been viewed as signalling both the mobility of borrowers (Dunn & Spatt 1985; Chari & Jagannathan 1989); and their propensity to default (Brueckner 1994c, 2000; Harrison *et al.* 2004; Ben Shahar & Feldman 2003). These models have been used to explain variations in loan-to-value ratios, the existence of mortgage points (Brueckner 1994c; Stanton & Wallace 1998), and the screening potential of fixed and adjustable rate mortgage contracts (Posey & Yavas 2001). The work of Brueckner (1994c, 2000) has particular applicability to the issue of mortgage rationing.

Prior to examining the particular mortgage market applications we recall an earlier model of credit rationing under imperfect information developed by Jaffee & Russell (1976). This model, hitherto referred to as the J & R model, significantly extends the notion of supply and demand for credit by considering imperfect information. There are a large number of significant papers on asymmetric information and credit rationing. Most mortgage market applications of asymmetric information models refer to Rothschild & Stiglitz (1976). However, the J & R model presents some useful insights into mortgage market behaviour. The J & R model is also reviewed here as a useful prelude to the application of some important ideas to rationing in mortgage markets.

A first look at pooling and separating equilibrium

The J & R model helps to introduce some of the fundamental concepts used in the analysis of credit markets with asymmetric information. The model considers honest and dishonest borrowers, with dishonest individuals intending to default on debt repayment in the second period of a two-period model. The asymmetric information arises because lenders cannot discriminate between the two types of borrower. A diagrammatic treatment of the J & R model is presented in Figure 5.1 and is adapted from their original paper. Referring to Figure 5.1, equilibrium occurs in the aggregate mortgage market where supply (*TS*) equals demand (*DD*).

Various combinations of the interest rate and the size of loan represent different loan contracts. For rationing to occur there must be a loan contract (for example *E*) lying on the supply curve below market equilibrium (that is with excess demand), and this must be the preferred choice of some individuals. It must also be 'profitable' for lenders to offer such a contract. The loan market is assumed to be perfectly competitive. Lenders' profits are constrained to be zero, as any positive profit is quickly competed away. An alternative term for this relationship is the incentive compatibility constraint. The constraint is embodied in the supply curve for loans.

The truncation of the supply curve at market equilibrium (*S*) reflects the zero profit constraint. That is excess supply is not allowed, as it violates the incentive compatibility constraint; there would be negative profits. The model assumes that lenders face a constant cost of funds (*I* to *T*). However, the supply curve rises from point *T*, reflecting an increase in the probability of default by dishonest borrowers as interest rates increase; reflecting the higher return required by lenders to compensate for this greater risk. Below a minimum cost of funds (mortgage interest rate)

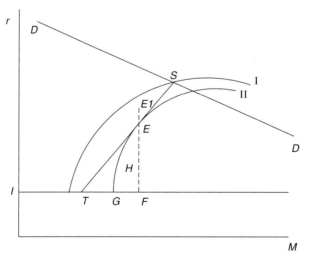

Figure 5.1   Pooling and separating equilibrium in credit markets: the Jaffee and Russell model.

Source: Jaffe, D. M. & Russell (1976) Imperfect information, uncertainty, and credit rationing.

I, the probability of default is zero, and therefore requires no compensation.

The demand curve (*DD*) is derived from a set of iso utility curves (I and II) representing a trade off between loan size and the interest rate. Lower curves (further to the *S.E*) represent higher utility. Lower interest rates and higher loans are considered 'goods'. Higher interest rates and smaller loans are 'bads'. For a rationing contract to be favoured over the market equilibrium then this contract must lie on a higher utility curve (that is further to the *S.E*). In Figure 5.1 this condition holds at point *E*. This contract will appeal to honest borrowers who experience lower interest rates, reflecting their lower default risk. Rationing occurs because there is evident excess demand for credit when this contract is chosen.

Some loan contracts like *E*1 lie at points higher than *E*, and below the utility curve I, are more profitable (that is they are above the incentive compatibility constraint). However, competition between lenders will drive contract rates down to the zero profit line, back to point *E*. Thus rationing appears in this loan market as a result of the competitive process, under conditions of imperfect information. If this was the only contract available then it could be described as a pooling equilibrium exhibiting credit rationing. But just how stable is this position?

What does the J & R model indicate regarding the possibility of a separating equilibrium? This would consist of one contract that attracts honest borrowers and another contract that attracts dishonest borrowers. Certainly, it is possible to have a loan contract that lies on a higher utility curve that will be more attractive than contract *E* to honest borrowers. Such a contract can be found at *H*. Honest borrowers face a lower interest rate at *H*, that is they are not paying such a large premium to compensate for the dishonesty of less virtuous customers. The existing contract at *E* will remain attractive to dishonest individuals. The reason that the dishonest (risky) borrowers stick with loan contract *E* is that they always prefer a larger loan. But is this situation stable?

There is no stable separating equilibrium in this case, despite the relative attractions of the two contracts. The problem is that the movement of honest borrowers to contract *H* denudes contract *E* of the more trustworthy and more profitable individuals. The emergence of the new contract at *H* was an attempt to 'cream off' the more profitable customers. Eventually, losses on contract *E* will lead to its withdrawal. Consequently, the undesirable borrowers seek out *H* and make that unprofitable. The fate of this process is now uncertain with either a continuously repeating sequence, or a total meltdown of the competitive process. But is this what we observe in practice? Is the theory directed at an observable phenomenon? The answer is certainly no, we do not observe this instability.[2] The mortgage market is certainly dynamic and contracts appear and disappear as a part of the competitive process, but this is not necessarily the same phenomenon.

The J & R model is useful because it points to the role of information and also suggests the importance of a variety of non-price terms and institutional arrangements that might prevent the instability arising from the dynamic between pooling and separating equilibrium. There is also an implication here that empirically we may have to detect any separating equilibrium in terms of contract features other than just loan size and the interest rate. So a broader notion of the price vector might also add to the understanding of the form of any separating equilibrium in advanced systems of housing finance.

The J & R analysis is placed in interest rate/loan size space, and this facilitates a comparison with the application of other models to the mortgage market. The model is based upon particular assumptions regarding the behaviour of defaulters. Note that the dishonest borrowers take out loans with every intention of defaulting. Such borrowers cannot be identified by their revealed mortgage demand. Both honest and dishonest borrowers have the same utility functions, and make up the same demand curve for debt. This is a useful simplifying assumption when examining how information asymmetry can produce credit rationing, but it militates against the emergence of a separating equilibrium.

It may not be the case that borrowers take out a loan with the intention of defaulting. If default is expressed as a risk of incurring default costs, and enters as a negative argument in the borrower's expected utility function, then variations in default costs between borrowers will result in different slopes in their indifference curves. In terms of Figure 5.2 the indifference curves of borrowers could even cross. In this case separating equilibrium contracts might well arise, and rationing might be an enduring characteristic of a particular groups mortgage demand.

Specific applications of pooling and separating equilibrium to the mortgage market

Though the J & R model highlights potential credit rationing, arising out of asymmetric information in credit markets, the more common point of departure in the mortgage literature is the work of Rothschild & Stiglitz

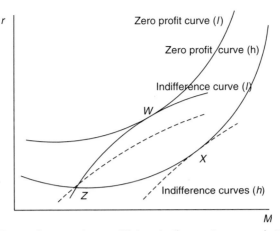

Figure 5.2 Pooling and separating equilibrium in the mortgage market: the Brueckner model.

Source: Brueckner, J. K. (2000) Mortgage default and asymmetric information, *Journal of Real Estate Finance and Economics*, 20(3): 251–74.

(R & S) (1976). The R & S model deals with high and low risk customers in the insurance market. The asymmetric information in this case is the probability of having an accident. An example for the mortgage market is the propensity to default on mortgage debt. Consumers may vary significantly in the financial and psychic costs of default which are likely to remain hidden from the lender (Brueckner 1994c, 2000). So called ruthless default occurs when the option to default is 'in the money', that is the value of a property is less than the market value of the mortgage. However, hidden costs may explain why this default option is not always exercised. Moreover, this information asymmetry can lead to the emergence of separating equilibrium with credit rationing.

A significant result of the R & S model is that it demonstrates that a pooling equilibrium in the insurance market is not likely to emerge, or persist. The simple reason is that it would always pay another insurer to supply a more favourable contract that would 'cream off' the more profitable low risk clients, an effect observed above. The model demonstrates that equilibrium emerges when there is a menu of insurance contracts that separately appeal to individuals with high and low accident probabilities. This is the Nash equilibrium, that is, there is no possibility of a new more profitable contract being introduced. It seems reasonable to presume that different loan size/interest rate combinations might perform the same task in the mortgage market, that is, a separating equilibrium emerges.

Though the idea of a separating equilibrium in mortgage markets had been applied by other authors (Dunn & Spatt 1985; Chari & Jagannathan 1989;

Yang 1992), it was Brueckner (1994c) who first rigorously analysed the implications for loan size (loan-to-value ratio). Implicitly this is also an analysis of mortgage demand, and also presents an approach to mortgage pricing that is not derived from an option theoretic framework. The research consists of two pieces of work (Brueckner 1994c, 2000). The earlier piece developed the analysis in loan/interest rate space in a manner compatible with the other models presented in this chapter. The second model used loan/balance space with the interest rate implicit in loan/balance combinations. The reason for the second choice was the mathematical instability of analysis using loan size, interest rate choices.[3]

The exposition that follows mainly uses the analysis in interest rate/loan size space (Brueckner 1994c). This is done merely to facilitate continuity with the graphical approach adopted so far. The essential features of the model suggested by Brueckner are represented by Figure 5.2.[4] Compared to the J & R model there are now two types of indifference curve, and two zero profit curves. The possibility of default and different levels of default costs are now incorporated into the incentive compatibility constraints facing lenders and the indifference curves of the two types of borrower.

With full information lenders would offer two separate contracts representing the equilibrium choices of two types of borrower (at W and X). So, for example, those borrowers with high default costs (type h) would be offered/take up bigger loans at a lower interest rate (at X), reflecting their lower likelihood of defaulting on the mortgage debt. Borrowers with low default costs (type l) and a greater propensity to default would be offered smaller loans at a higher interest rate (at W). As with Figure 5.2 indifference curves lying to the south east represent higher levels of utility. Like the J & R model solutions must lie on appropriate zero profit curves.

However, what happens when lenders cannot observe default costs? If W and X are offered under conditions of asymmetric information then the low cost (high risk of default) borrowers would find contract X very attractive. They would obtain a larger loan at lower interest rate. The high risk individuals would impose losses on contract X. But there may be contracts which can encourage borrowers with a high risk of default to reveal themselves. Two contracts that work in this way are contract W and contract Z, with high risk individuals choosing contract W. Note that if contract X is not available then those who face a high cost of default will now choose a smaller loan at a higher rate of interest than would have been chosen under full information. So imperfect information has led to rationing for this group. The model follows a usual assumption that high risk individuals though actually indifferent between W and Z will make a choice consistent with a separating equilibrium.[5]

Brueckner (2000) further develops this approach to mortgage contracts and asymmetric information by applying a similar model in loan size/loan balance space. In this case the consumer trades off between a good (the loan size) and a bad (the balance to be repaid in the second period of a two-period model). The outcome of this model is also a separating equilibrium, with the rationing of borrowers who have a low risk of default. If a 'fair price' price contract were offered to safe borrowers then risky borrowers would also be attracted to such a contract. A pooling contract is unstable because it will always pay some lenders to offer contracts that 'cream off' the safe borrowers. Thus competitive forces produce a separating equilibrium with self-selection, and credit rationing for at least one group of borrowers.

Alternative perspectives on separating equilibrium in the mortgage market

In the Brueckner model less risky borrowers signal their default risk by selecting smaller balances at low interest rates. They bear the cost of the signalling of high risk borrowers by being credit rationed. Now consider the symmetrical and completely opposite case where low risk borrowers bear the cost of signalling by borrowing more than they would under full information equilibrium. Low risk borrowers now use this additional borrowing to signal their credit worthiness. This is the outcome of a model recently developed by Harrison *et al.* (2004) which contradicts what has become the conventional wisdom that risky borrowers borrow more. The model emphasises the impact of income variability, that is, it takes an approach to mortgage default based upon affordability.

The analysis now shifts to loan balance/loan size space where L is the initial loan and the balance B is the amount due plus interest at the end of the second period of a two-period model. Implicitly the balance-to-loan ratio defines the fixed interest rate. From the borrower's perspective a higher balance due is a poor attribute whereas loan size is a desirable attribute. The Brueckner (2000) and the Harrison *et al.* (2004) models are presented by equations (5.1) to (5.4). Both models assume risk-neutral borrowers and risk-neutral lenders. Though emanating from a common analytical framework, a brief overview and comparison of these two models highlights significantly different perspectives on the causes of mortgage default, and their impact upon credit rationing.

The Brueckner (1994c) model discussed above, and its counterpart in loan/balance space (Brueckner 2000) focused upon the stochastic variation in house prices. Using the same modelling framework and allowing income to vary stochastically, but not the price of the property, can produce very different results. The intuition is that a lack of variation in property prices gives the borrower a form of limited liability with respect to default. The most that they can loose is the known value of the asset (the house) and the given cost of default (C). Borrowing more allows an increase in consumption in the first period of the two-period model, but beyond the default point this has no effect on the marginal cost of default. For example, lower default costs encourage greater borrowing by low risk borrowers who are less likely to face such costs. Low risk borrowers indicate their credit worthiness by borrowing more, and they are not subject to credit rationing.

The utility functions that form the basis of two models are represented by equation (5.1) (Brueckner) and equation (5.3) (Harrison *et al.*). The common notation includes P_0 for the first period house price, y for income, C is default costs and λ represents the borrower's discount rate, while B and M are as previously defined. The utility functions in both models begin with the loan size and first period income as positive arguments, with the expenditure on housing P_0 as a negative argument. Both expressions are made up of probability distributions defined over ranges in which default will or will not arise. Clearly the borrower's utility depends on whether default occurs or not. The key difference between the two models is the stochastic variable which generates default, that is house prices in the Brueckner model and income in the Harrison *et al.* model.

In equation (5.1), $\lambda \int_{\underline{P}}^{B-C} Cf(\mathbf{P})dP$ is the default cost defined over a probability distribution for house prices (P) bounded by a minimum house price $\underline{P}$, and the mortgage balance less the default costs $(B - C)$. The second integral represents the borrower's utility if the revealed house price is above this range, but below the maximum house price $(\overline{P})$. In the Harrison model, equation (5.3), the focus is on income ranges and $\lambda q_i \int_0^{B-P} (y - C)f(y)dy$ is the discounted utility if default occurs. This would happen if income in the second period was not sufficient to cover any positive difference between the house price and the mortgage balance $(B - P)$.

$$u(M, B) = Y + M - P_0 - \lambda \int_{\underline{P}}^{B-C} Cf(\mathrm{P})dP + \lambda \int_{B-C}^{\overline{P}} (P - B)f(P)dP \qquad (5.1)$$

$$\Pi(M, B) = -M + \eta \int_{\underline{P}}^{B-C} Pf(P)dP + \eta \int_{B-C}^{\overline{P}} Bf(P)dP \qquad (5.2)$$

The different sources of default risk are further reflected in the arguments determining lenders' expected profits, being equation (5.2) (Brueckner) and equation (5.4) (Harrison *et al.*). Both expressions have the loan size M as a negative argument, and profits are discounted by the lenders discount rate η. In the case of default the lender receives the house price, while if default does not occur the lender receives the loan balance. Comparing the two models the default outcome depends upon the revealed outcome of house price variation (Brueckner), or the revealed outcome of stochastic variations in income (Harrison *et al.*). The utility functions and their corresponding zero profit constraints set up the constrained maximisation problems.

Separating equilibrium occurs when the marginal rate of substitution of loan for balance differs between high and low risk borrowers. The basis of the slopes of the indifference curves are variations in default costs (Brueckner), or the risk of an income fall defined as q_j in the Harrison *et al.* model, where j is the type of borrower. Separating equilibrium based upon risky income, when the risks are not known to the lender, are shown in Figure 5.3. In this model both indifference curves and zero profit curves are convex, and equilibrium is possible because of the different degrees of convexity of the curves. Defining risk as the probability of a fall in income, then the diagram illustrates the case where the less risky borrower has a larger loan and a larger balance (N) than the risky borrower who chooses (M). Note that M is the full information equilibrium for the risky borrower, but for the safe borrower the full information equilibrium

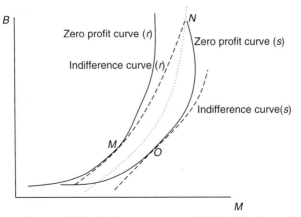

Figure 5.3 Separating equilibrium in the mortgage market: the Harrison *et al.* model.

would be a smaller loan and balance (O). So the less risky borrower signals their credit worthiness with a larger loan.

$$U(M, B_i q_i) = Y + M - P_0 + \lambda q_i \int_0^{B-P} (y - C) f(y) dy + \lambda q_i$$

$$\int_{B-P}^y (y + P - B) f(y) dy + \lambda (1 - q_i)(Y + P - B) \qquad (5.3)$$

$$\Pi(M_j B_j; q_j) = -M + \eta q_j \int_0^{B-P} P f(y) dy + \eta q_j \int_{B-P}^y B(f(y)) dy + \eta (1 - q_j) B = 0$$

$$(5.4)$$

It is important to note that both a credit constrained outcome and a pooling equilibrium can be derived from a model with stochastic variation in income as the determinant of default (Harrison *et al.* 2004). A separating equilibrium with low risk borrowers borrowing more than high risk borrowers occurs when the costs of default are high. A separating equilibrium with low risk borrowers' credit constrained occurs when default costs are low. In all cases high risk borrowers achieve the same loan size as under a full information equilibrium, it is the low risk borrowers who incur the cost of signalling. The key discriminator between these two theories must be empirical analysis.

If less risky borrowers do borrow more, then a potentially important source of credit rationing in the mortgage market disappears. The debate over whether mortgage market rationing actually exists, or is an important phenomenon is now reinvigorated. Paradoxically, housing finance systems where default costs are high are likely to experience less rationing. Interesting for the US and the UK is the growth in sub-prime lending which may lower default costs for some groups, that is there is 'forgiveness' for bankruptcy, or other events triggering previous defaults. Thus credit rationing should increase. However, sub-prime lenders may have significant information on the credit riskiness of borrowers. Information and default costs may be negatively correlated so that improved information systems, efficient pricing, and more complete markets lower equilibrium credit rationing. If rationing of some borrowers generates house price cycles (e.g. Stein 1995) then these considerations are of critical importance for housing market behaviour and macroeconomic policy.

Given the focus of the above modelling upon income variations then this does raise the question of the role of credit records and credit rating in signalling a borrower's likelihood of default. Ben-Shahar & Feldman (2003) argue that credit ratings offer important, but incomplete signals of a borrower's default probability. In this case borrowers may be segmented by credit rating, and then offered a menu of mortgage contracts which screen out the higher risk borrowers within each group. Theoretical results demonstrate that for a given class of credit score, safer borrowers have shorter maturities and pay lower risk premiums. A key feature of the Ben-Shahar & Feldman paper is the combination of both signalling and screening, and the possibility that such a combination is Pareto efficient. Borrowers acquire credit records to signal their standing while lenders screen by offering mortgage menus that lead to self-selection.

The Ben-Shahar & Feldman model is consistent with the previously discussed theories in that only risky borrowers obtain their equilibrium full information contract, but now this occurs within each subset of credit scores. Moreover, because of improved signalling via credit scores other borrowers move closer to their full information equilibrium. Again there are some implications for the impact of the sub-prime lending market here. Sub-prime borrowers can be considered as a subset of households who signal poor credit records. However, some information asymmetry may persist and there may be a screening menu of contracts and credit rationing for some households who demand sub-prime loans. Once again there is a clear agenda here for empirical, in addition to more theoretical, research.

Automatic underwriting and credit scoring also has implications for the impact of securitisation on the availability of mortgage credit. Lenders have more local knowledge about the quality of loans that they pass on to mortgage securitisors so that they can effectively 'cherry pick'. Increased credit scoring information reduces this problem as securitisors can demand a threshold credit score, but lenders still retain first mover advantage, and some asymmetric information is likely to persist. The implications for the availability of mortgage credit are a complex outcome of the interactions between lenders likelihood of rejecting loans and the pricing and other strategies of securitisors. Heuson *et al.* (2001) models strategic games between securitisors and lenders and conclude that credit availability is unaffected when demand is high, and is actually increased by securitisation when credit demand is low. So securitisation may also generally increase credit availability and reduce credit rationing.

Though the Brueckner and Harrison models, and to some extent the Ben-Shahar & Feldman model, emanate from a common analytical framework, they have a very different focus. Brueckner's model is not an option theoretic model of default of the kind to be discussed in Chapters 9 and 10, because it does not extend stochastic variations in house prices beyond a single period. However, the approach is based upon so called ruthless default where the wealth maximising borrower defaults if the house price is less than the mortgage balance plus default costs. In contrast the Harrison *et al.* and Ben-Shahar & Feldman models raise the issue of affordability and have implications for the debate upon the relative importance of affordability and option theoretic arguments, that will be picked up on again in later chapters. Even more critically they implicitly raise the question of just how prevalent credit rationing is in the advanced mortgage markets such as those of the US and the UK?

The significance of models of asymmetric information and credit rationing

The asymmetric information models modify the usual supply and demand framework in a fundamental way. In the models with imperfect information lenders fix both quantity and price rather than just one of these variables. The purpose, of course, is to allow borrowers to self-select and reveal their default risk. A question arises with respect to the ability of lenders to charge differential interest rates on mortgages, based on personal characteristics. In the US this would be an illegal practice.[6] Consequently, lenders will need to encourage borrowers to self-select. Brueckner (2000) notes that price discrimination might arise by charging higher insurance premiums on larger mortgage contracts. This form of price discrimination is also applicable to UK mortgages.

It is also worth noting that the Brueckner (2000) model in particular yields interesting comparative static properties in relation to borrower characteristics, other than the propensity to default. For example, separating equilibrium can occur as a consequence of differences in the patience of borrowers, as reflected in their respective discount rates. Here, the case of heterogeneity of borrower characteristics involving both default costs and differences in their degrees of patience is interest. Both higher default costs and higher level of patience lead to flatter indifference curves. Thus a borrower who was very patient and had a low likelihood of default would face even more severe credit rationing.

An important implication of the asymmetric information models involves the impact of this market imperfection on mortgage demand. Under certain conditions low risk individuals will obtain smaller mortgages than high risk borrowers. The econometric specification of a mortgage demand equation for this group of borrowers must allow for this truncation of the distribution of observed mortgages. Alternatively, the asymmetric information model of Harrison *et al.* demonstrated that when affordability was the main consideration less risky borrowers may bear the cost of signalling by borrowing more than high risk borrowers. Thus mortgage demand may be a negative function of income variability and the costs of default, or those variables which proxy these arguments. In this case there is no truncation of the distribution of observed mortgage balances.

The asymmetric information models do suggest that chosen loan size (mortgage demand) is endogenous to the likelihood of default decision and vice versa. This is a point noted by Yezer *et al.* (1994). The merit of Brueckner's work is that considering the microeconomic decision making of individuals highlights this simultaneity. This and the truncation of the observed distribution of mortgages, for rationed households, has potentially important implications for the econometric specification of mortgage demand equations, an issue to be explored more fully in Chapter 6.

Summary and conclusions

The chapter began with a classification of credit rationing into disequilibrium, equilibrium and dynamic rationing. Though the distinctions were somewhat arbitrary, and often have asymmetric information has a common causal factor, they do provide a useful way of viewing credit rationing in mortgage markets. The categories will also guide our review of empirical material. Disequilibrium rationing focuses upon the possible impact of financial deregulation and household behaviour, pre- and post-economy-wide rationing. Dynamic rationing focuses upon the process of mortgage market adjustment, the impact of securitisation and the integration of mortgage markets with other capital markets. Equilibrium rationing highlights the continuing possibility of credit rationing in a post-financial deregulation environment.

The non-price characteristics of any mortgage contract can be used to bring about equilibrium in the loan market. This was seen as problematic for the loan-to-value ratio, and mortgage maturity, but can be usefully applied to caps, collars and other contractual features. However, a range of non-price features, including the loan-to-value ratio, can be set to ensure a separating equilibrium. Information asymmetry changes the role of these non-price characteristics. Credit rationing, and separating equilibrium, can arise when expected default costs vary by individuals, and when such costs enter their utility functions. However, it is also possible that a separating equilibrium can arise without credit rationing and involve more borrowing by less risky households signalling their credit worthiness.

Securitisation and the growth in sub-prime lending had potentially important implications for the existence and extent of credit rationing. In theory, securitisation facilitates mortgage market adjustment and increases the supply of credit. Sub-prime lending did not mean that credit rationing was removed, as information problems might still persist. The persistence of information problems and mortgage credit rationing has important implications for the estimation of mortgage demand equations. For example, the truncation of the distribution of observed mortgage choices, and the simultaneous estimation of mortgage demand and default. The chapter which follows, examines the empirical methodologies and main findings relating to the existence, extent and influence of credit rationing in the US, UK and other economies.

Guide to further reading

Readers are recommended to read the original Brueckner (2000) article on asymmetric information and credit rationing in mortgage markets. The paper conducts a large number of interesting and relevant comparative static exercises. Of particular interest are those exploring variations in default costs and time preference. The original Jaffee & Russell (1976) paper is also very accessible, with strong intuitive and clear graphical expositions. An excellent introduction to issues of asymmetric information and credit rationing is the text by B. Hillier (1997).

Notes

1 See *Daily Mail*, headlines, 1 August 2001.
2 Jaffee & Russell (1976) note that one way of overcoming any inherent instability in loan markets is to establish monopoly powers (or a cartel). In theory a pure monopoly will not produce rationing, but if monopoly power is established by governments facilitating a cartel then rationing may well be a rational outcome.
3 See Brueckner (2000, endnote 17).
4 The diagram is adapted from Brueckner (1994c, p. 220).
5 Borrowers are also assumed to be risk-neutral and so utility maximisation can be expressed as a simple function of terminal wealth.
6 Until 1983 it was possible to charge a higher interest rate on endowment mortgages.

6

Credit Rationing, Mortgage Market Adjustment and Separating Equilibrium: Empirical Evidence

Introduction

A study of credit rationing is important because such rationing can impact upon household behaviour and welfare. Credit rationing can effect tenure choice, levels of housing consumption and life cycle planning. Similarly financial deregulation which reduces credit rationing can exacerbate the tendency for boom and bust cycles in the housing market (Dale-Johnson 1995; Ortalo-Magné & Rady 1998, 1999, 2002). In some economies the extent of credit rationing reflects, and is effected by, the institutional structure of housing finance. For example, in the US studies have shown that the Federal Housing Association can absorb borrowers from the conventional mortgage sector who would otherwise be credit rationed (see Duca & Rosenthal 1991; Ambrose *et al.* 2002). This institutional structure can actually be used to identify the presence of mortgage rationing. Deutsch & Tomann (1995) find that the risk sharing and institutional arrangements in Austria and Germany lead to mortgage credit rationing and disadvantage poorer sections of society.

The chapter begins with the empirical analysis of disequilibrium rationing. That is economy-wide credit rationing that emerges from regulation, usury laws or interest rate cartels. This phenomenon is not purely of historical interest. It both points to lessons for other economies where regulation may remain in place and reflects upon household behaviour in the mortgage market. Financial deregulation should have facilitated mortgage market adjustment and efficient pricing. However, market adjustment can be sluggish with interest rates sticky (Allen *et al.* 1999; Heffernan 2002). This chapter briefly discusses the empirical evidence on mortgage price behaviour, together with the degree of integration of the mortgage market with other capital markets. In theory the increased securitisation of mortgages and the growth in sub-prime lending should have led to the greater integration of capital markets, with more flexible and efficient pricing of mortgage debt. Mortgage credit rationing should be significantly less.

Some mortgage credit rationing is likely to persist, even in a financially deregulated environment (Stiglitz & Weiss 1981). This chapter considers the use of non-price terms to ration credit in the presence of default risk, that is equilibrium rationing. Mortgage underwriting criterion can be varied to reflect different degrees of default risk. Under conditions of asymmetric information price and loan sizes might be combined to produce a separating equilibrium (Brueckner 1994c, 2000). The discussion in this chapter considers the evidence for screening in the mortgage market. The implications for the estimation of mortgage demand equations will be explored throughout the discussion.

United Kingdom (disequilibrium) mortgage credit rationing research

Chapter 5 cited the UK mortgage market in the 1970s, and early 1980s, as a prime example of disequilibrium rationing. The existence of a mortgage cartel until 1983, and periods of negative real interest rates, led to mortgage queues and the use of non-price rationing mechanisms. These are the results we would expect if non-price terms of mortgage contracts were not being adjusted to clear the market (Drake & Holmes 1997). Thus the UK provides an ideal setting for the study of disequilibrium rationing, and financial deregulation and its effects.

Early UK research used time series data and generally incorporated dummy variables to represent regime changes, or variations in the severity of credit rationing (Nellis & Longbottom 1981; O'herlihy & Spencer 1972; Hendry & Anderson 1977). Some work used continuous proxy measures of the extent of rationing, such as the mean loan-to-value ratio (Ostas & Zahn 1975; Wilcox 1985), or the loan-to-income ratio (Nellis & Thom 1983). Studies using such continuous measures test for the presence of equilibrium rationing (see Holmes 1993). Rationing variables were typically statistically significant, and possessed the expected signs.[1] However, Nellis & Thom (1983) and Holmes (1993) did not find any evidence of disequilibrium rationing. For example, coefficients on differences in the loan-to-value ratio between periods where not significantly different from zero.

One problem with most of the early studies of mortgage rationing was their inability to incorporate a major shift in regime, such as financial deregulation (Meen 1990). Meen (1989, 1990) follows some previous authors (Wilcox 1985; Hall & Urwin 1989) in using a direct measure of rationing where the demand function is implied by the structural equations of a supply and demand model. The extent of rationing was found by deducting estimated mortgage demand from observed supply. The empirical estimates indicated that mortgage rationing ceased to be a major problem for the UK after the middle of 1980, a result consistent with the findings of Wilcox (1985), and Hall & Urwin (1989). Excess demand and rationing was certainly apparent for earlier periods.

Meen found a large and statistically significant coefficient on the nominal mortgage interest rate in housing/mortgage demand equations. It is also possible to test for the appropriateness of a specification incorporating the user costs of owner occupation, and therefore the relevant interest rate specification (real or nominal) by introducing the nominal mortgage interest rate with some measure of expected house price inflation as separate variables. If the user cost is the appropriate specification then there should be no statistically significant difference between the coefficients on the interest rate and expected house price inflation, that is, they can reasonably be combined. A variety of tests of expectation formation mechanisms suggested that housing demand equations should not purely rely upon a real interest rate or user cost specification (Meen 1990). This issue concerned the tilting of mortgage payments discussed in Chapter 4. However, the tilt is not entirely separate from mortgage credit rationing. Restrictions on mortgage lending can exacerbate the tilt, also mortgage maximising households who are rationed will respond to nominal interest rate changes.

Muellbauer & Murphy (1997) estimated housing demand equations for the UK covering the period 1957 to 1994 and found that real interest rates were more relevant after financial deregulation. If households are at a corner solution with their demand for housing/mortgage debt then real interest rates will not be relevant. Muellbauer & Murphy also argued that expected income growth would reduce housing/mortgage demand under rationing as this was used to finance increases in non-housing consumption, a result borne out by the econometric estimation. The role of the nominal mortgage interest rate in econometric estimation of mortgage demand was also reinforced by the results of pooled time series/cross-section research (Leece 1995a, b, and 2000a). The tilting of mortgage payments, liquidity constraints and other capital market imperfections mean that nominal cash flows are an important consideration for some borrowers. This finding was seen to apply even in a financially deregulated environment, where mortgage contract design may still not be optimal (Leece 2000a).

The work of Ortalo-Magné & Rady (1998, 1999, 2002) demonstrated a correspondence between the outcomes of their consumption driven theory of housing demand and the aggregate behaviour of the UK housing market, pre- and post-financial deregulation. Ortalo-Magné & Rady (1999) estimate the relative contributions of income shocks or financial deregulation to the housing boom (1982 to 1989) and the bust (1990 to 1993). Their theoretical model, discussed in Chapter 2, indicated that rising income caused increases in house prices, with owner occupation among young households falling during the transition to equilibrium. However, this is not what occurred during the 1980s when owner occupancy rates among young households increased. Thus, the authors deduce that financial liberalisation allowed more young households to enter owner occupation.

United States (disequilibrium) mortgage credit rationing research

The research reported here concerns studies the span both pre- and post-financial deregulation in the US. That is, they can be used to detect the impact of financial deregulation or assess the extent of credit rationing during regulated periods. Before 1983 there were restrictions on the rates charged on savings deposits. This meant that during periods when the maximum deposit rates were binding, lenders were short of funds with mortgages rationed, a process known as disintermediation. It has been argued that the disappearance of disintermediation together with mortgage securitisation removed an important source of mortgage credit rationing. Indeed some US studies found little evidence of such rationing, even in regulated periods (see Hendershott 1981; Jaffee & Rosen 1979). Much work in the US has been concerned with the existence of mortgage credit rationing post-financial deregulation.

An important study with a methodology that has been mimicked by researchers in other countries (Leece 2000a; Moriizumi 2000; Bourassa 1995) is research by Linnemann & Wachter (1989). Linnemann & Wachter used two periods of time, 1975–77 and 1981–83 and divided their sample into constrained and unconstrained borrowers.[2] The binding constraint was either an income constraint (loan-to-income ratio), or a wealth constraint (loan-to-value ratio, or down payment requirement). Rationed households were detected by comparing an estimate of their housing demand, derived from choices of non-constrained households, with the actual size of property they purchase.

A probit model was used to estimate the likelihood of home ownership, including a measure of the degree of mortgage rationing.[3] Separate probit estimates were made for each sample period. A comparison of the two periods implicitly allowed for the securitisation of mortgages, and innovations such as the emergence of adjustable rate mortgages. It is important to note in the US context that income underwriting criteria were less stringent for adjustable rate debt. This is also true of government guaranteed mortgage loans. For example, Phillips & Vanderhoff (1994) show that government guaranteed loans increase housing demand via more relaxed loan-to-value ratios.

Linneman & Wachter (1989) found that the impact of income and other control variables fell when a measure of the degree of rationing was included; and the overall fit of the model improved substantially. Thus, tenure choice models that do not control for rationing are subject to omitted variable bias. The impact of rationing was found to be less during the 1981–83 period, a result attributed to securitisation and the emergence of the ARM, though it was not possible to attribute the results to any particular cause. Linnemann *et al.* (1997) update their empirical analysis by applying their model to the 1989 Survey of Consumer Finances. They found that borrowing constraints had continued to impact upon the probability of home ownership. Following their previous work they distinguished between the income and wealth constraints on mortgage borrowing. Their main finding was that wealth constraints (operating via the deposit requirement) was the main limitation on tenure choice.

The work of Linneman & Wachter and Linneman *et al.* was important in estimating the degree to which mortgage credit rationing could bind. However, there are a number of qualifications that should be made to the results. The choice of sample period is obviously important. For example, Zorn (1989), assesses the impact of mortgage market qualification constraints on the entry into owner occupation in the US during 1986, finding that these constraints did not significantly bind. Technically, there are also likely to be a number of sources of sample selection bias in the estimation. For example, the error terms in the estimation of the choice of level of housing services and the tenure choices might be correlated. Also, it is not clear why rationing constraints actually bind. For example, is this equilibrium rationing? Should we explain some of the cross-sectional variation in housing demand by measures of the likelihood of default (or measure of default costs). However, this study offers the main approach to date to controlling for credit market constraints. The 1997 study using the 1989 Survey of Consumer Finances also suggested that some form of rationing persisted post-financial deregulation.

More recent US research has concentrated upon default driven or equilibrium mortgage credit rationing and this has become the main focus of debates on the extent of rationing in the US mortgage market (Duca & Rosenthal 1991; Ambrose *et al.* 2002, Harrison *et al.* 2004). This work will be considered in some detail below. Certainly, a characteristic of most US research, old and new, has been a focus upon access to home ownership. This is clearly an important policy consideration. However, constraints on the level of housing services available to households also has important implications for economic welfare. Thus an important but comparatively neglected aspect of credit rationing research is the link between the continuous choice of housing/mortgage size and the discrete choice of tenure. The section which follows presents one way of dealing with this link highlighting some key issues for the estimation of mortgage demand equations with the presence of credit rationing.

Modelling mortgage demand under credit rationing

Most (pooled) cross-section research has used a simple discrete choice model such as a probit or logit specification to model the mortgage/housing choices of constrained and non-constrained households. Also, most of the research has been concerned with the impact of mortgage underwriting criterion on the probability of home ownership. A comparatively neglected consideration is the nature of the interdependence of the discrete and continuous choices. That is the decision to take out mortgage debt (that is enter or renew owner occupation) together with the decision on the size of debt or gearing. Theoretical work on mortgage demand typically takes the tenure choice decision as given. This issue can be usefully explored via the so called double hurdle model (Cragg 1971; Leece 1995a, 2000b). The discussion of this model also provides a framework for a consideration of approaches to estimation.

If a household makes an equilibrium decision then any choices involving zero debt (including renting rather than owning) will also be equilibrium choices. Also, the influences upon the discrete and continuous choice will be the same. This can be modelled using a Tobit. The Tobit model is based upon a latent unobservable demand for mortgage debt M^* generated by the index $M^* = \beta_i x_j + u_i$, where x_j is a set of independent variables, β_i are parameter estimates and u_i is an error term. The observable mortgage demand M equals M^* if $M^* > 0$. That is, the underlying demand in terms of the size of mortgage is only observed when $M^* > 0$. The expected value of a mortgage is the expected mean value conditional upon $M^* > 0$, multiplied by the probability of observing a positive value (described as a non-limit observation). This can be taken as the probability of entering owner occupation financed by a mortgage. Thus the general form of a mortgage demand equation (a Tobit) that contains zero values is given by expression (6.1).

$$E[M] = 0^* \, Probability[M = 0] + E[M|M^* > 0]^* \, Probability[M^* > 0] \quad (6.1)$$

In the case of Tobit estimation zero values are not discarded and aspects of both discrete and continuous choice are retained in the estimation. This further assumes that any household with non-zero mortgage demand will always obtain a loan. This is a restrictive assumption when applied to mortgage markets because some zero observations could represent households which had a positive demand for M but were precluded from obtaining one, that is they were rationed. Households might also be rationed in the size of loan available and decide not to enter owner occupation (Ortalo-Magné & Rady 1998, 1999, 2002). This relates to some degree to the discussion of estimation of mortgage demand functions in Chapter 2. Zero values occurred where households had paid off their mortgage debt, but the household owned their home. It may be more valid in that case to assume that zero observations are equilibrium choices, compared to, say, those arising out of credit rationing. The general form of a truncated regression used to estimate mortgage demand where credit rationing may be present is given by equation (6.2). Note that zero values are discarded and that there is a correction for the truncation of the observed distribution of choices $\sigma\lambda_i$.

$$E[M|M^* > 0] = \beta_i x_i + \sigma\lambda_i \quad (6.2)$$

In summary, most analysis of mortgage demand under credit rationing has been concerned with discrete choice models that estimate the likelihood of home ownership. It could be argued that the estimation of mortgage demand under credit rationing is of equal interest. This raises the question of how best to estimate such demand. The model suggested here is a double hurdle model. The double hurdle model estimates a probit for the discrete choice and a truncated regression on the non-zero observations. This allows for the possibility that not all mortgage demands will be met and that different parameter estimates and even variables apply to the discrete and continuos choices. Though there are other approaches to modelling the selectivity issues involved with credit rationing, the discussion highlights the possibility of complex relationships between the discrete and continuous choices. These can be modelled in other ways, and at times selectivity problems are just not evident (Leece 1995b). There are other forms of the double hurdle model (e.g. with correlated error terms, or Box & Cox specifications), mainly applied to discrete and continuos choices in markets other than that for mortgage debt (see Burton *et al.* 1994, 2000; De Sarbo & Choi 1999). There is considerable scope for further applications of these models in this area of research.

An example of estimation of mortgage demand under mortgage credit rationing

This section presents an example of a mortgage demand equation estimated using a basic double hurdle model (Leece 1995a). The estimation involves UK data using a pooled cross-section/time series sample. The study period spans pre- and post-financial deregulation. It is generally considered that disequilibrium credit rationing was significantly reduced, or disappeared, during the early 1980s (Meen 1990). The results reported here represent the only cross-section study of mortgage credit rationing for the United Kingdom covering the period of financial deregulation. The purpose of the exercise is to indicate changes in household behaviour during this time frame. The exercise also offers a basic example of the double hurdle methodology. The focus of the discussion is a truncated regression.

The truncated regression (see Table 6.1) is estimated on a sample of mortgage holders taken from the Family Expenditure Survey (1986). These estimates were made along with the estimation of a probit equation on mortgage and non-mortgage holders, implicitly a tenure choice decision. The choice to take out mortgage debt is the first hurdle, and the size of mortgage demanded is the second. The discussion focuses upon the second of these two hurdles. The research involved a number of sources of possible bias. The real mortgage balance, used as a dependent variable, was an estimate, thus introducing the possibility of measurement error.[4] Exact identification of who was, and who was not, rationed in the first hurdle (tenure choice) was also not possible. These difficulties all emerged from the limitations of UK household level data covering this time frame.

Despite data problems the estimated mortgage demand equation offers some insight into the effects of financial deregulation in the UK. A number of interactions were modelled to detect changes pre- and post-financial deregulation. For example, a dummy variable for pre-1980 observations was interacted with the nominal and the real gross mortgage

Table 6.1 Mortgage demand and rationing: truncated regression

Variable	Coefficient	t-value
Constant	262669.00	1.114
North	−2370.67	−1.217
Yorkshire	−2537.12	−1.640
Northwest	−1278.95	−0.900
East Midlands	−1423.83	−0.899
West Midlands	566.28	0.359
East Anglia	2502.97	1.119
London	9072.14	3.666
South East	9957.32	6.008
South West	2905.28	1.815
Pre-1980 mortgage (Yes = 1)	10927.00	0.036
Total household expenditure	8147.34	1.010
Age of head of household (HOH)	−750.70	−7.725
Gross HOH real income	79.93	3.481
HOH manual worker (Yes = 1)	−1158.40	−0.513
HOH married (Yes = 1)	1804.25	0.681
Pre-1980 mortage × gross HOH real income	−52.39	−2.645
HOH male (Yes = 1)	−2370.67	−1.217
Number of rooms in the property	3384.39	3.290
HOH manual worker × gross HOH real income	2.13	0.390
Child present age 5 and under 18 years	−1543.27	−1.668
Nominal gross mortgage interest rate at time of origination	2298.80	2.330
Pre-1980 mortgage × nominal gross mortgage interest rate at time of origination	−7205.30	−4.860
Real mortgage interest rate at time of origination	2153.26	2.185
Pre-1980 mortgage × real mortgage interest rate at time of origination	−1998.82	−2.106
Expected relative house price inflation	−646.83	−1.296
Loan-to-value ratio for first time buyers	−71154.40	−1.358
Pre-1980 mortgage × loan-to-value ratio for first time buyers	13655.90	0.196

Notes:
1. Total household expenditure is an instrument estimated from an expenditure equation.
2. The residual from the household expenditure equation is included as a test of exogeneity.

Source: Leece (1995a, Table 4, p. 58)

interest rate. The signs and coefficients on the interaction variables indicate that real interest rates had more sizeable effects post-financial deregulation. This might indicate a lessening of credit constraints, though the net of tax nominal mortgage interest rate had an unexpected positive sign. The income of the head of household was also statistically significant in the truncated regression, though this had not been the case in the probit. A key feature of the double hurdle model is the possibility that some different variables effect the discrete and the continuous choice.

Though real interest rate effects were stronger post-1980 in the UK the nominal mortgage interest rate was still a relevant specification in any post-1980 mortgage demand equation. Thus the overall conclusion of the study was that some households continued to be rationed post-financial deregulation. This was also the case for the discrete choice modelled by the probit equation. A log likelihood ratio test of the explanatory power of the double hurdle model compared to a Tobit estimated on this data offered a more powerful explanation of variation in mortgage demand. Thus the null hypothesis of perfect credit markets with no rationing was rejected. However, there was some easing of credit rationing post-1980, though the exact form of the rationing in either period was not identified.

The double hurdle model raised questions about the interdependence of discrete and continuous choices when analysing mortgage demand. Further analysis of these results can be found in Leece (1995a). The methodology facilitated a testing of the likelihood, if not the exact extent, of mortgage credit rationing. The empirical study also indicated the impact of deregulation on household behaviour in the UK mortgage market. However, mortgage markets have changed even more since the mid-1980s. Generally, financial deregulation has been accompanied by the increased securitisation of mortgage debt, particularly in the US. These factors should have contributed to the significant lessening, or removal, of anything other than equilibrium credit rationing based upon default risk. However, temporary or dynamic credit rationing might be evident if mortgage market adjustment is sluggish.

Mortgage market adjustment and dynamic credit rationing

The mortgage markets can be in temporary disequilibrium when interest rate adjustments are sluggish. The slow adjustment of interest rates on debt can also reflect the impact of credit rationing, though not necessarily (see Berger & Udell 1992). For example, lenders may enter an implicit risk sharing agreement with borrowers. Slow upward adjustments of the cost of debt can also create temporary excess demand. How quickly and in what manner mortgage interest rates adjust to exogenous shocks also reflects upon the integration of mortgage markets with other capital markets. Securitisation should increase the speed of interest rate adjustments, as changes are rapidly passed on to MBS investors. The existence of dynamic rationing has always been disputed. For example, Kent (1980) found no evidence of dynamic rationing in the United States, though a number of studies did suggest that it was evident (Huang 1969; Ostas & Zahn 1975).

Several pieces of research have attested the stickiness of mortgage interest rates. Allen *et al.* (1999) noted that mortgage rates generally do not adjust downwards as quickly as they adjust upwards. Historically the UK has experienced sluggishness in both directions as mutuals have smoothed changes in interest rates (Heffernan 2002). This is compatible with the theoretical predictions of Stiglitz & Weiss (1981), where adverse selection leads to interest rate stickiness. Allen *et al.* present an argument for the reluctance of lenders to lower mortgage interest rates, in the US. Low interest rates increase the duration of debt and increased duration increases price volatility. This increased volatility demands a risk premium which lenders collect by less than full adjustment to declining capital market rates.

A further cause of 'sticky' mortgage rates is the choice of interest rate index that the rates track. This is important in the US where adjustable rate debt requires lenders periodically to adjust the mortgage interest rate. Insofar as different mortgages use different indices, which in turn demonstrate different sensitivities to underlying rate changes, then there is an important source of cross-sectional variation in mortgage interest rate adjustment. Though UK rates track changes in the Bank of England base rate there can still be significant lags in interest rate adjustments. Miles (1994) noted that at times sluggish response in the variable rate of interest has made this debt similar to a fixed rate mortgage, a factor that influences the choice of mortgage instrument in the UK (Leece 2000a). This is not a problem for the increasing number of mortgages that are designed to track the base rate of interest.[5]

Stanton & Wallace (1999) examined the dynamics of the commonly used indices for ARM pricing in the US. This area of research is particularly applicable to the issue of mortgage valuation and pricing, to be treated more generally in Chapter 8. The relevance of the research here is the lag between the adjustment of the ARM coupon and the term structure of interest rates. For some ARM mortgages the lag makes them closer in characteristics to a fixed rate mortgage.[6] The study finds that the interest rate sensitivity of an ARM depends upon the terms of the contract (e.g. the presence of an interest rate cap), the dynamics of the pertinent interest rate index, and mortgage prepayment behaviour. So for new borrowers searching current contracts there may be significant lags before coupon rates adjust to interest rate levels, though this does not necessarily lead to dynamic credit rationing.

A number of US and UK studies find sluggish mortgage market adjustment to long-run equilibrium values. For the UK Drake & Holmes (1997) use three stage least squares to estimate an error correcting representation of mortgage demand for 1981–1992. They find that both mortgage supply and demand are slow in adjusting to their long-run equilibrium values.

Following Stiglitz & Weiss (1981) the research finds a backward bending supply curve for mortgage finance. The loan-to-value ratio for first time buyers had a larger impact upon mortgage demand than the mortgage interest rate, implying equilibrium rationing. For the US Zumpano *et al.* (1986) finds a partial adjustment model more applicable to mortgage market adjustment than instantaneous adjustment. Even using more recent data Buist & Yang (2000) found mortgage demand slow to adjust though this was not the case for the supply of funds.

There are a number of more recent developments that might have led to faster rates of interest rate and market adjustment in mortgage markets. One is the increased use of mortgage securitisation. The second is the growth in the sub-prime lending market. These are not entirely separate issues. For example, improved information on the observed default risk in the sub-prime market could encourage securitisation of sub-prime loans. This in turn would depend upon the efficient pricing of sub-prime debt to reflect its additional risk (Van Order, 2000). Sub-prime lending should add to market efficiency by providing loan finance to previously rationed households. Socioeconomic changes such as higher divorce rates, increased part-time work and self-employment have led to new classes of borrower with risk profiles that can be accommodated by sub-prime lending. Sub-prime lending should be an increasingly important focus for future mortgage market research.

The growth in the securitisation of mortgage debt should also have improved market efficiency and effected the speed of mortgage market adjustment. There is some evidence for the UK that interest rate changes have occurred more rapidly for lenders who have used securitisation (Pais 2002). Dynamic rationing should be less evident in this case. For the US, Gabriel (1987) found that changes in fixed rates had become more responsive to changes in the cost of finance. Roth (1988) argued that securitisation had increased both the volatility of interest rates and the speed of interest rate adjustment.

There is some debate in the US over the relative importance of securitisation or financial deregulation in integrating capital and mortgage markets. Goebal & Ma (1993) argue for the importance of financial deregulation while Devaney & Pickerill (1990) consider securitisation more influential. Heuson *et al.* (2001) suggest that the observed negative correlation between securitisation and the mortgage interest rate should be interpreted as securitisation responding to lower rates, rather than vice versa. Allen *et al.* (1999)[7] finds that financial deregulation has led to mortgage rates responding more quickly to changes in riskless rates of interest. Rudolph & Griffith (1997) use co-integration analysis to test for the integration of mortgage markets and capital markets from 1963–1993, unusually finding integration over the whole period, in addition to the integration of national and local mortgage markets. The general agreement is that mortgage markets are now more integrated with other capital markets. Dynamic rationing should certainly be less. A key question is whether mortgage credit rationing can still be found after financial deregulation, in a form compatible with equilibrium in the mortgage market?

Equilibrium rationing separating equilibrium and liquidity constraints

This section examines the evidence for equilibrium credit rationing (Stiglitz & Weiss 1981; Williamson 1986, 1987). Given that empirical research in this area is sparse, then both UK and US work are discussed together. The US is particularly interesting in that default risk is fully insured for the Federal Housing Association, but not for the alternative conventional lenders. This has led to a number of interesting studies. For example, Duca & Rosenthal (1991) use time series data to explore the FHA/conventional loan decision, and the persistence of equilibrium rationing. Ambrose *et al.*, (2002) analyse variations in default risk and the proportion of FHA/conventional borrowing by state to detect credit rationing. The latter study exploits the fact that the FHA is not allowed to vary its lending criterion on a geographical basis. UK research in this area is even more sparse but there is some tentative evidence of a separating equilibrium, where the choice of mortgage design might signal a group of borrowers that continued to be rationed after financial deregulation (Leece 2000b).

The extent to which non-price terms are used to offset default risk will depend upon the ability to vary interest rates according to each individual borrower's risk (Stiglitz & Weiss 1981; Riley 1987; Duca & Rosenthal 1994). This redlining (Stiglitz & Weiss, 1981), or rate sorting, will reduce the need to use non-price terms for credit rationing. In this case non-price terms will have little or no influence on observed household behaviour, for example the size of borrowing, tenure choice and life cycle consumption and saving. However, some studies have shown that non-price terms do impact upon household mortgage choices (Duca & Rosenthal 1991, 1994; Cox & Jappelli 1993; Perraudin & Sorensen 1992). Duca & Rosenthal (1994) analysed data on FRM rates (1981 to 1983) taken from the 1983 Survey of Consumer Finances and found no substantive evidence of red lining. The major explanation for this was the existence of fair lending laws constraining price discrimination.

A key issue is how far credit rationing attributable to variations in default risk is likely to persist after financial deregulation? Duca & Rosenthal (1991) conduct a time series analysis of the extent of credit rationing pre- and post-financial deregulation. They use the unique institutional feature of the US market that FHA loans are fully insured against default risk. When the likelihood of default risk increases overall in the national economy then any credit rationing apparent in the conventional loans sector will increase the take up of more costly FHA loans, but with some borrowers remaining credit rationed. The study found that from 1973 through 1987 originators of conventional mortgage loans used non-price terms of mortgage contracts to ration mortgage credit. The FHA partly offset this rationing effect. Linnemann et al. (1997) find some evidence of credit rationing after financial deregulation in the US, while Leece finds tentative evidence for this in the UK (Leece 2000b). This form of post-financial deregulation rationing is most likely to take the form of equilibrium credit rationing, though this still requires more explicit empirical verification.

Brueckner (2000) points to the payment of higher mortgage indemnity premiums on large loans as a form of price discrimination that might induce separating equilibrium. Such differential insurance payments are also characteristic of the UK mortgage market. Harrison et al. (2004) find evidence to support separating equilibrium based upon affordability criterion though credit rationing is not necessarily an outcome. The empirical aspect of the work is based upon a 'rich data set' which contains measures of the level of default costs of borrowers, and a variety of proxies for default risk. The data pertains to originations from December 1989 to June 1991 with a recording of default status up to mid-1997. The estimated regression model used a number of interaction terms (e.g. default costs[8] multiplied by self-employment) and suggested that less risky borrowers borrow more. Given this challenge to conventional wisdom then this is an area where further work would be welcome, say in different economies for different points of the business and housing cycles.

Sub-prime lending is another area that raises challenges for the detection of credit rationing. The interesting questions in relation to the sub-prime lending market concerns the efficient pricing of the credit risk, and how far the self-selection on sub-prime loans overcomes problems of asymmetric information? Analysis of this market has revealed that third party mortgage originations lead to significantly higher default rates (see

LaCour-Little & Chun 1999; Alexander *et al.* 2002). Thus information asymmetry may still be a significant problem in mortgage markets where loans involve third party originations, that is sales by mortgage brokers. Lack of information on the part of borrowers can also lead to 'churning', with brokers encouraging prepayment and the unnecessary origination of new mortgage contracts. Alexander *et al.* argued that agency risk was not initially priced during the industry growth stage in the US, but that it is correctly priced now.

Mortgage brokers in the UK have also been a source of controversy, with sub-prime lending attracting increased critical attention, but no substantive academic study as yet.[9] The question remains as to whether equilibrium mortgage credit rationing is evident in the sub-prime lending market, in the US or the UK? Ben-Shahar & Feldman (2003) noted the signalling effects of credit scoring and the possibility that within each credit scoring category there is a menu of mortgage contracts that screen borrowers. Thus asymmetric information and separating equilibrium with credit rationing might still persist, a theoretical issue that invites empirical research.

There is some evidence for the UK that the choice of mortgage instrument during the mid-1980s might have signalled which borrowers were liquidity constrained, and possibly continuing to be mortgage rationed (Leece 2000b). The repayment mortgage is a more flexible mortgage instrument than the endowment mortgage and might therefore have appealed to liquidity constrained borrowers wishing to vary their payment patterns via changes of maturity, etc. Leece estimated separate truncated regressions on samples identified by this mortgage type. The research made no pretence at being a direct test of the separating equilibrium outlined in Chapter 5, though it is indicative of the potential importance of self-selection and screening in the UK mortgage market.

Repayment (annuity) mortgage holders displayed behaviour consistent with liquidity constraints, that is they responded to changes in nominal interest rates, and showed no significant sensitivity to changes in expected house price inflation. Endowment mortgage holders were more responsive to user cost arguments. The estimation indicated that income, reflecting affordability constraints, was a significant explanatory variable for annuity mortgage holders only. The evidence tentatively suggested a group continuing to be credit rationed after financial deregulation. The results might also reflect credit rationing of non-housing finance but if borrowers cannot substitute cheaper mortgage debt then some mortgage credit rationing is at least inferred.[10]

There is much work yet to be done on determining the extent of equilibrium credit rationing in the major mortgage markets, where the development of sub-prime lending, mortgage instruments that allow flexible amortisation, and mortgage securitisation raise the question of its continuing importance. Equilibrium credit rationing is bound up with the explanations of default behaviour, to be discussed further in Chapters 9 and 10. Whether affordability issues drive default, or if default is explained by the option theoretic approach, is also discussed in those chapters. These issues reflect upon the behaviour of low risk borrowers, and whether they borrow more or less than they would under full information equilibrium. Empirical findings may vary by time and economy, and this area merits significantly wider and more in-depth investigation.

Mortgage credit rationing in other economies

The study of mortgage rationing and its removal has been of interest in countries other than the UK and the US. For example, Deutsch & Tomann (1995) noted the tight collateral rules obtaining in Austria and Germany. The application of a maximum 75% loan-to-value ratio minimises default risk but restricts access to owner occupation for low-income groups. A study of Australia by Bourassa (1995), estimated a tenure choice model incorporating a direct measure of rationing, income, wealth and the comparative cost of homeownership and renting. The methodology followed Linneman & Wachter (1989). Bourassa found that measures of rationing reduce the effect of income and relative cost variables suggested that these might have acted as proxies for mortgage market rationing in previous studies.

Moriizumi (2000) considered the case of public corporations in Japan. These corporations lend to individuals for house purchase at low interest rates, but apply credit limits. Thus a household wishing to exceed the credit limit must then borrow from the private banking system. The work again followed the procedure of Linneman & Wachter. Rationed and non-rationed samples are formed and parameter estimates derived from switching regression analysis. Households who do not top up their borrowing from private banks are assumed not to be rationed. Once again the results of the study emphasises that housing and mortgage demand equations that do not explicitly account for rationing criterion will produced biased coefficient estimates.

Summary and conclusions

The discussion in this chapter adopted the classification of types of mortgage credit rationing presented in Chapter 5. Time series studies and pooled cross-section/time series research had indicated that periods of disequilibrium rationing had existed in both the US and the UK. This was also true of other economies. Financial deregulation had generally ameliorated this form of rationing. However, mortgage credit rationing could persist because of lags in the dynamic adjustment of the mortgage market, or from equilibrium credit rationing. Mortgage securitisation and the growth in sub-prime lending should have improved mortgage market adjustment. However, if interest rates could not be varied according to the individual borrower characteristics then any evident credit rationing could represent an equilibrium based upon credit risk.

There is a dearth of empirical research into the contemporary presence and extent of equilibrium credit rationing in the mortgage market. For the US there was some evidence of equilibrium rationing reflecting variations in default risks under conditions of asymmetric information. The particularities of the US housing finance system allow the indirect detection of credit rationing through variations in FHA compared to conventional mortgage loans. Separating equilibrium was a more elusive phenomenon though there was some limited evidence from the UK that liquidity constrained individuals, who valued flexibility in payment scheduling, were attracted to standard annuity mortgages. Borrowers may self-select into a separating equilibrium on the basis of a wide range of contract characteristics, and theoretical and empirical research should incorporate this heterogeneity.

The discussion in this chapter highlighted some key points for the estimation of mortgage demand under liquidity constraints and credit rationing. A case was made for using a truncated regression and for including the nominal mortgage interest rate in addition to, or instead of, real interest rate arguments. However, we must recognise the segmented nature of the mortgage market, and the different types of household behaviour that we might observe. It might even be the case that high default costs combined with an emphasis upon affordability leads to a separating equilibrium where credit rationing is not apparent. These are issues that require further research. An analysis of household behaviour across different housing finance systems where default costs can be demonstrated to differ might also be fruitful. The study of why we observe heterogeneous mortgage contracts can also offer insight into mortgage choice behaviour and the possible bases of separating equilibria.

Guide to further reading

Information problems and the design of incentive compatible contracts, and the extent of equilibrium credit rationing are important areas of research. It is also possible that under changing economic circumstances economy-wide rationing might re-emerge as a significant policy concern and may currently be evident in some housing finance systems. The most innovative work of late has been the theoretical adaptations of asymmetric information models to the mortgage market (Brueckner 2000; Posey & Yavas 2001; Harrison *et al.* 2004). The most innovative empirical work has occurred in the area of choice of mortgage instrument where such instruments can generate self-selection of relevance to default probabilities (see Stanton & Wallace 1999).

The paper by Leece (2000b) highlights some significant aspects of self-selection and is worth a critical read, though the data applies to the immediate aftermath of financial deregulation in the 1980s. A more up-to-date paper by the same author (Leece 2000c) does explore the issue of mis-selling in the endowment mortgage market which represents an important information problem that might lead to specification problems for any mortgage demand equation. North American readers might enhance their appreciation of the UK mortgage market by reading those particular pieces. There is little econometric treatment of the sub-prime lending market as yet and this is clearly an area for further research.

Notes

1 Generally, if levels of these non-price terms are statistically significant in a mortgage demand equation then this is evidence of equilibrium rationing. This conclusion is reinforced if changes in the lagged values of non-price terms are not statistically significant, that is such terms have been used to clear the market (see Nellis & Thom 1983 and Holmes 1993) and so disequilibrium rationing is not evident.
2 Haurin (1991) follows a similar procedure and estimates the unconstrained demands for housing services using a sub-sample of households whose wealth is above a given level. The remainder of the sample is used to estimate constrained demand. The results indicate that the down payment constraint has a significant impact upon the probability of home ownership and on the amount of housing services consumed.
3 Households are indicated as highly, moderately or severely constrained according to how far their desired level of housing services exceeds their observed demand.

4 The estimate involved a backward calculation from current mortgage payments and using the history of interest rate changes over the life of the mortgage (see Leece 1995a).

5 The emergence of base rate tracking mortgages in the United Kingdom was very much a response to controversy over the apparent reluctance of building societies and banks to lower mortgage interest rates in the face of a declining base rate. Tracker mortgages are proving another reaction to increased competition in UK mortgage markets with new lenders appearing continuously in this market (see Interactive Investor, August, 2000; **www.iii.co.uk**).

6 See Stanton & Wallace (1999, p. 50).

7 The mortgage rate in this case is the average *prime* lending rate for conventional 30-year mortgage debt. The analysis therefore applies to new rates on long-term fixed rate mortgage finance (see Allen *et al.*, 1999, p. 213).

8 Default costs in this case were measured by the FICO score developed by Fair, Isaac & Co., a system endorsed by both Fannie Mae and Freddie Mac.

9 The principal agent problem can lead TPOs to indulge in passive or active gaming with the credit rating criterion. Passive gaming occurs when sellers were lax in their application of the rules. An example of active gaming would be where the agent colluded with an appraiser to overstate property values (see Devaney 2000). This type of principal agent problem under asymmetric information would lead to high defaults compared to direct lending.

10 One complication here is mis-selling. Lenders may have considered any increased risk of default as fully compensated by endowment commissions. The mis-selling may have represented a distortion of the option to default, rather than misrepresenting affordability. Thus mis-selling is quite consistent with the reported results, with currently liquidity constrained borrowers opting for the annuity mortgage. That is, some borrowers may not have been aware of potential default risk, this does not mean that they were currently liquidity constrained. There is a limited amount of research on this issue for the UK (see Leece 2000c).

7

The Household's Choice of Mortgage Design: Theory

Introduction

The issue of mortgage contract design has formed an important aspect of the discussion in previous chapters. The design of the mortgage instrument has implications for the tilting of real mortgage payments, the ability to match housing expenditures with life cycle plans; it could potentially bring about a separating equilibrium in the mortgage market, thus influencing the extent of mortgage rationing. Fundamental to understanding these issues is the question of how individuals and/or households choose from the menu of mortgage contracts available to them. In principle the rationale for the existence of different mortgage designs or the determinants of mortgage choice are complementary perspectives. For example, the existence of 'private information' might lead lenders to offer mortgage contracts inducing borrowers to reveal their propensity to prepay or to default, then the borrowers' expected response to various contract features inform our model of their choices.

Though securitisation of mortgages can impose some standardisation of loans approved for bundling, the mortgage market is characterised by contract heterogeneity. Mature mortgage markets can exhibit a bewildering array of choices. Chapter 1 noted how meeting borrowers' preferences was an important dimension of the efficiency of a housing finance system. So, why do so many types of mortgage instrument coexist in the marketplace? Do consumers treat these alternative choices as perfect substitutes? Is contract heterogeneity truly an example of separating equilibrium? On what basis do consumers actually make their choices? The attempt to answer these questions impinges upon the theoretical and econometric treatment of mortgage demand, with correspondingly important implications for the secondary mortgage market and for mortgage valuation. For example, a case will be made for the simultaneous determination of mortgage/housing demand with the choice of mortgage instrument. Dunn & Spatt (1988), also note that in equilibrium, contract design, expected prepayment rates and default probabilities are simultaneously determined, along with the price of the mortgage.[1]

This chapter provides a confluence, or collecting point, of ideas and themes explored in previous chapters. Four approaches to mortgage contract heterogeneity are discussed.

- The first is the idea that borrowers have different preferred payment schedules that are better represented by some mortgage designs than others. Thus we have clear links here with the discussion of contract designs and amortisation in Chapter 4.

- Second, there are approaches to the choice of mortgage instrument that rely upon the arguments that we find in the modelling of mortgage demand in Chapter 2, such as wealth and its variance.

- Third, some mortgage designs can act as signalling devices for lenders when information is hidden; so we refer back to the discussion of asymmetric information and separating equilibrium outlined in Chapter 5.

- Fourth, we look again at both the role and nature of interest rate expectations. For example, there is a stream of literature that concerns itself with how the total interest rate cost varies with the choice of mortgage instrument, and recommends mortgage choices on that basis.

It is also important to consider borrowers' attitudes to interest rate risk, that is variations in their degree of risk aversion. If costs are considered as a certainty equivalent, that is, at what fixed interest rate would a borrower be indifferent between the known rate and expected value of a variable or adjustable rate, then risk aversion becomes critical to the choice of contract. For example, the FRM–ARM differential can be viewed as an insurance against interest rate increases.

The chapter concludes by drawing together the predictions emanating from the various theoretical approaches that can then be used to inform econometric estimation.

Theoretical determinants of the choice of mortgage instrument and contract heterogeneity

Various dimensions of mortgage design can represent the heterogeneity of mortgage contracts. In the US there is a trade off between front loaded mortgage points and the coupon or interest rate on the debt. In the UK there is a bewildering variety of contracts offering different tradeoffs between interest rate terms, 'cash back' arrangements, flexible payment scheduling and a variety of combinations of arrangement fees or penalties for prepayment. In the USA there is the FRM/ARM choice, or a combination or hybrid mortgage, while in the UK the choice is between the FRM and the variable rate mortgage (VRM). Both the ARM and the VRM frequently have discounts ('teaser rates') and can be subject to caps or collars on interest rate adjustments. Thus there are a large number of features of contracts to consider in mortgage choice.

There are, of course, explanations of mortgage contract heterogeneity, over time, across different countries, in terms of funding requirements/regulations, as to why some mortgage instruments are absent, suddenly appear, or become more prevalent. For example, increased interest rate risk led the ARM to become more attractive to lenders in the US, and the FRM became more prevalent with the shift from retail funding to mortgage securitisation. The discussion in Chapter 1 noted how well borrowers preferences were met as a indicator of the efficiency of a housing finance system. So we need to understand on what basis borrowers choose between different mortgage instruments. This would also be a prequisite of any assessment of welfare losses arising from restrictions on the choice of contract, and assessing the full cost of mortgage provision. The discussion that follows expands upon the analysis of earlier chapters and presents the main explanations for observed mortgage contract heterogeneity, and household decision making.

Payment scheduling and mortgage contract heterogeneity

Chapter 4 considered the tilting of mortgage payments towards the early life of the mortgage. In particular the constant payment mortgage would not necessarily reflect the desired or optimum payment schedule for borrowers. This would certainly be true of households who expected their incomes to rise. Thus an optimal mortgage instrument would better align payment profiles with income expectations. The issue of optimum mortgage design also involves interest rate risk, and the sharing of risk between the borrower and the lender. An initially lower payment on a mortgage may better suit those with expectations of growing income, but they may have to bear more, or all, of the risk of adverse change in interest rates (Dokko & Edelstein 1991; Brueckner 1993). A fixed rate constant nominal payment mortgage would impose interest rate risk on the lender, but at the possible expense of a less desirable payment profile for the borrower. These issues offer one explanation for the heterogeneity of mortgage instruments and present a rationale for the ARM (Brueckner 1993).

Lenders are usually large financial institutions with the capacity to diversify, hedge against risk, obtain access to futures and options contracts and interest rate swaps. For these reasons lenders might be expected to be risk-neutral. This means that they will be interested in the size of the cash flows rather than the risk of these flows. Baesel & Biger (1980) suggest that the often limited diversification opportunities open to borrowers makes it more likely that they will be risk averse. This leads to the paradox noted by Brueckner (1993), that theory would indicate borrowers having a preference for the FRM, that is shifting interest rate risk onto lenders, yet we observe consumers choosing ARMs. In theory therefore, the ARM is a sub-optimal contract and ought not to be observed. Why then have ARMs been so prevalent in the US mortgage market (or VRMs in the UK)?

Dokko & Edelstein (1991) explored the idea of an optimal mortgage design and presented a single-period theoretical model. The model demonstrated that if both borrowers and lenders were risk averse, and if borrowers behaved according to the precepts of a von-Neumann & Morgernstern utility function, then it would not be optimal for the borrower to take out 100% interest rate protection (that is a fixed rate mortgage). Subsequent research has used two-period frameworks, which allow the simultaneous examination of optimum payment profiles and interest rate risk.

Arvan & Brueckner (1986) develop a two-period model of optimum mortgage design where there is no constraint on the payment profile. Their work assumed risk-neutral borrowers. The Arvan & Brueckner model demonstrated that when the borrower was more impatient than the lender, then the graduated payment mortgage was the optimum mortgage instrument. It is instructive to examine briefly the framework of this model.

$$V(y - i_0) + \lambda \int V[y - R(r_1)d_r]f(r_1)dr_1 \qquad (7.1)$$

$$i_0 - r_0 + \eta \int [R(r_1) - r_1]dr_1 \qquad (7.2)$$

The borrower's utility function is given by expression (7.1), with $V(\cdot)$ representing the general form of the utility function. The argument y is income which is constant between the two periods, λ is the discount rate and r_0 and r_1 are the prevailing interest rate (cost of lenders funds) in period 1 and period 2 respectiveley. The argument i_0 is the first period payment by the borrower. The borrower's utility is a function of the difference between income and the mortgage payment in the first period, and the discounted value of this difference in the second period. The complication is that the interest rate outcome in period two is stochastic, hence the integral which represents a probability density function. There also has to be some rule for determining the interest charged in the second period, and this is represented by $R(r_1)$. The stochastic outcome and the pricing rule determine the second period mortgage payment. Thus utility is derived from the borrower's residual income after recognising the uncertain nature of interest rate outcomes and the lender's pricing policy.

The constraint is the lender's profit function given by expression (7.2). If a lender is risk-neutral then he or she will only be concerned with the cash flow arising from the loan. Of course, cash flows in the second period will still be discounted, hence the lender's discount rate, η. Now the lender's income arises from the difference between the cost of funds and the mortgage payment (we are assuming an interest only mortgage). The payment received by the lender in the second period is a function of the random draw and the pricing rule or loan function applied. Assuming a perfectly competitive market for loans then the lender will operate under the zero profit constraint discussed in Chapter 5. The optimisation problem is to find the first period payment and a loan rate function which maximises the borrower's utility, subject to the zero profit constraint. The solution to this optimisation problem depends upon the borrower's impatience relative to the lender's.[2] In the case where the borrower is the more impatient then the optimum mortgage instrument is a graduated payment mortgage.

The problem is that the GPM is not always a prevalent mortgage instrument. The key to the analysis is the loan rate function. Brueckner (1993) argues that borrowers will seek their optimum payment profile by finding mortgage instruments whose loan functions best suit their optimum choice. It is assumed that this loan rate function is both linear, and held to consistantly between the two periods. The borrower chooses the best fitting combination of payment profile and interest rate risk.[3] For example, if the term structure of interest rates is upward sloping then the expectation is that the cost of funds will be higher in the second period. This will suit a borrower who is impatient and desires lower initial payments.

However, this payment profile is purchased at the risk of a high draw from the interest rate distribution in the second period. There will be some circumstances where the ARM provides a desireable combination of gradient on the payment profile, and acceptable interest rate risk. Hence the rationale for the existence and sometimes prevalence of the adjustable rate mortgage.

It is useful to look briefly at the loan rate function, as it is suggestive of some other important characteristics of the mortgage market. For example, some empirical work for the United Kingdom has suggested that lags in pricing adjustment can influence borrowers choices. Brueckner (1993) presents a nice example of a linear loan rate function, given in expression (7.3). The term $R(r)$ is the loan rate function where r is the cost of funds, α is a constant indicating a given mark-up and β is a parameter determining the impact of changes in the cost of funds. In the case of the ARM the parameter value is $\beta = 1$ while for the FRM $\beta = 0$.[4] While noting that this linear form is mathematically restrictive, Brueckner argues that it is probably a realistic representation of pricing.

Interestingly, the VRM in the UK has not always responded quickly to changes in the cost of funds ($\beta < 1$). The recent introduction of tracker mortgages means that there are now mortgage instruments where $\beta = 1$. Lags in interest rate adjustment are not insignificant and mean that variable rate debt can sometimes behave like fixed rate mortgages (see Miles 1992; Leece 2000a). The discussion of credit rationing in Chapter 5 noted how lags in interest rate adjustment reflect the structure of competition in the lending market (Heffernan, 1997). In the US adjustable rate mortgages are also known to have this element of fixity, through their varied speed of response with respect to the interest rate indices used to determine them (see Stanton & Wallace 1999). The possible empirical significance of interest rate adjustment lags for the choice of instrument is returned to in Chapter 8.

$$R(r) = \alpha + \beta r \qquad (7.3)$$

Table 7.1 presents the theoretical predictions which follow from Brueckner's analysis. The table expresses the decision in terms of the choice of an FRM compared to an ARM. A large variance in the cost of funds represents high interest rate risk and will encourage FRM take up. A normal yield curve will encourage the adoption of an ARM. In fact, a flattening yield curve will progressively discourage ARM take up as the benefits of a graduated payment profile fall. The theoretical predictions of other approaches to modelling the choice of mortgage instrument are also represented in Table 7.1 and are discussed in the appropriate sections below. (Note that some expected signs will differ from those in the published work which have the ARM as the dependent variable.) Though the models which focus upon interest rate risk and payment profiles do not incorporate prepayment or default risk, they offer some key theoretical insights that can be used to guide empirical specifications of choice of mortgage instrument equations.

Mortgage demand under uncertainty and mortgage contract heterogeneity

A number of models approach the choice of mortgage instrument using similar arguments to those encountered in the theoretical analysis of mortgage demand in Chapter 2. In particular, the modelling of mortgage demand under uncertainty where borrowers are risk averse. The household utility function presented in that chapter (expression 2.5) included wealth and its variance. Portfolio theory stresses the covariance of asset returns. If a household is focused upon portfolio wealth and its variance – where housing is a part of that portfolio – and where interest rates and inflation are stochastically determined, then mortgage choice needs to be examined in the context of the relevant covariances. For example, if income is negatively correlated with interest rates does this induce the choice of a fixed rate mortgage? In this case a rise in interest rates would correspond with a fall in income and create liquidity problems for the borrower. We proceed to examine the main models of choice of mortgage instrument that have considered such covariances, and highlight their theoretical predictions.

The Baesel and Biger and Statman Models

Baesel & Biger (1980) base their analysis of the choice of mortgage instrument on the existence of capital market imperfections. With fewer diversification possibilities than financial institutions, the choice of mortgage instrument by a consumer then depends upon the 'characteristics of other components of their income stream'.[5] Thus lenders may be indifferent to different mortgage designs, but borrowers are not. They demonstrate how it is possible for both an FRM and an indexed linked mortgage to coexist. Thus mortgage choices are treated as being along a continuum rather than discrete decisions. Statman (1982) extended this model and it is this extension that is considered here.

Table 7.1   Summary of theoretical expectations regarding the choice of mortgage instrument (fixed rate mortgage choice=1)

Payment profile and risk sharing models		
Variable	Expected sign	Comment
Interest rate variance	Positive	Increased interest rate risk
Term structure of interest rates	Negative	Flat term structure means smaller benefits from any graduated payment profile
Borrower's degree of risk aversion	Positive	–
Impatience of borrower	Negative	–
Income of borrower	Negative	Derived from Dokko & Edelstein (1991) who deal with a VPM rather than an ARM
Payment burden (mortgage to income ratio)	Positive	Derived from Dokko & Edelstein (1991)

Mortgage/housing demand related models		
Variable	Expected sign	Comment
Interest rate variance	Positive	Alm & Follain (1987)
Correlation between housing price and mortgage interest rate and other covariances	Negative	Alm & Follain (1987)
Demand for housing	Positive	Alm & Follain (1987)
Variance of inflation	Positive	Unambiguous in Alm & Follain (1987) and Szerb (1996)
Variance in the real interest rate (real shock)	Positive/negative	Of ambiguous sign in Smith (1987)

Signalling and self-selection models		
Variable	Expected sign	Comment
Income variance	Negative	Posey & Yavas (2001)
Term structure of interest rates	Positive	Posey & Yavas (2001)
Personal characteristics of borrower	Positive/negative	Posey & Yavas (2001)

Interest rate expectations		
Variable	Expected sign	Comment
Level of the mortgage interest rate	Positive/negative	Regressive interest rate expectations would produce a negative sign
FRM–ARM premium	Positive/negative	Effect depends upon whether this is a relative cost or a forecast of interest rate changes and volatility. In principle both of these variables should be separately modelled

Though indexation is not currently a 'hot' issue in mortgage design, we can view both indexation and the adjustable rate mortgage as means of allocating the effects of inflation between the borrower and the lender. Dokko & Edelstein note that 'even in a disinflationary or deflationary world, the standard periodic fully amortised mortgage with constant payments would likely be less than optimal....'.[6] In any case, a paper by Smith (1987) adapts the Basel & Biger model to accommodate the ARM choice and this model will also be briefly considered below.

It is worthwhile briefly exploring the mechanics of the Baesal & Biger/ Statman model as the reasoning is assessable, and it offers a sharp focus upon some important variables that might underpin mortgage choices. Subsequent research builds upon this model by adding new covariances (Statman 1982; Smith 1987) or by extending the modelling into a two-period framework (Alm & Follain 1987; Szerb 1996). The model is for a single-period and assumes that borrowers are interested in the value of their terminal wealth W. As with mortgage demand under uncertainty, expected utility increases with terminal wealth and is negatively related to the variance of wealth. The particular form of the utility function, given by expression (7.4), reflects a risk averse borrower, and θ is a measure of the borrower's degree of absolute risk aversion. Once again the notation is adapted to make it compatible with that used elsewhere in this book, the one modification being the asterisk which indicates real values.

$$U(W^*) = E(W^*) - \frac{1}{2}\theta(\sigma^2(W^*))$$
(7.4)

An expression for terminal wealth is given by (7.5). This wealth is the difference between income and mortgage payments during the period but also, following Statman (1982), includes the real value of property. The argument h is the proportion of the mortgage $M(M = 1)$ that is fixed rate debt. Thus the mortgage costs are a weighted average of the holdings of fixed rate or index linked debt. Note that the fixed rate of interest rises with inflation, where π^{-1} is one plus the rate of change in the consumer price index. Due to the inflation risk that lenders face with fixed rate debt the interest payment is always greater than that for the index linked mortgage. Income $\tilde{y}$ is assumed to be stochastic.

$$W^* = \tilde{y}\pi^{-1} - \left[hr_F\pi^{-1} + (M - h)r_1\right] + p_h H\pi^{-1}$$
(7.5)

Though it is possible to analyse the discrete choices of 100% fixed rate or index linked debt the key focus of the model is on intermediate choices. Because an FRM is always more expensive, the choice of a fixed rate instrument always has a negative impact upon wealth. However, the key point of interest is the impact of the choice of fixed rate debt on the portfolio variance, that is the risk attached to the wealth. Several factors influence the impact of FRM choice on portfolio variance. The key determinants here are the size and sign on key covariances; relative to the variance of inflation, and the size of the premium on the FRM. The two covariances are income with inflation $Cov(\hat{y}\pi^{-1}, \pi^{-1})$ and real house prices with inflation $Cov(p_h H\pi^{-1}, \pi^{-1})$. Remember that residual income (income after mortgage payments) and the real house price are the components of wealth in this case.

The optimal combination of the two types of borrowing is rather complex, and depends upon the assumptions we make about the behaviour of incomes and house prices. For example, we might assume that real wages are determined independently of inflation, and so the covariance between wages and inflation is zero. We might also assume that house price inflation is faster than the general rate of inflation and so the covariance between real house prices and inflation is positive. The assumptions we make about the labour and housing markets, and the size of the covariances, effects the predicted combinations of fixed rate and indexed debt. For example, a negative covariance between real income and inflation induces the choice of indexed debt to protect borrowers. Once again the main theoretical predictions from this model are summarised in Table 7.1.

It is interesting to note the amendment of the Baesel & Biger model by Smith (1987) who now accommodates the FRM/ARM choice. So as to gain a better understanding of the discrete choice between an FRM and an ARM the model examines the extreme mixes of mortgage instrument. The key difference between the indexed linked and the ARM choice is that with the ARM the real value of the mortgage interest rate can change. This now introduces two new covariances into the analysis, that is the covariance between the real interest rate and income, and the covariance between the real rate of interest and the net value of the property. The ARM will typically be priced with reference to some index or chosen interest rate. The behaviour of the ARM price now depends on the fundemental determinants of this reference rate.

In the Smith model the determinants of the reference rate are the real rate of interest and the price level. Wealth in this model is based upon real income and the price of property. If there is a positive correlation between the determinants of the price of the ARM and the components of wealth then choosing an ARM will reduce portfolio variance. For example, an increase in the real interest rate will correspond with a rise in the price of the property and income. This offsets the negative impact on wealth of having to pay the higher real rate. When the determinants of the ARM price and the components of wealth are negatively correlated then the effect of ARM choice is to increase portfolio variance. For example, a higher real borrowing rate will be accompanied by a fall in wealth. The model once again emphasises that it is the signs on the covariances between key variables that are critical to the effect of mortgage choice on wealth and its variance. Choice of mortgage instrument is based upon the ARM–FRM differential and the portfolio impact of this choice, where at times the FRM–ARM premium will be considered an appropriate level of insurance against adverse interest rate movements to pay. The theoretical expectations are added to the list of theoretical variables considered in Table 7.1.

The importance of the early models of mortgage instrument choice lies with the highlighted relationships, particularly the covariances. They can be criticised for focusing upon combinations of mortgage types rather than reflecting the possibly more typical discrete choices (Alm & Follain 1987). However, hybrid mortgages and the mixing of fixed and adjustable rate debt in the US and 'pick and mix' combinations in the UK suggest that this might be an increasingly relevant focus, though unwieldy perhaps in the setting of more complex models. There is the important implication for lenders that offering a variety of mortgage contracts could be optimal, though theoretically lenders are usually assumed to be indifferent to the mortgage instruments that they issue. Another criticism might be that the early models of Baesel & Biger and Statman are too simple, that is, they are single-period and do not incorporate an alternative asset to housing that completes the portfolio picture. These considerations have to some extent been rectified by Alm & Follain. However, the earlier simpler analysis is tractable in adddition to being informative.

Extending the portfolio perspective (Alm & Follain)

The above models have not considered the choice of mortgage instrument in the context of the demand for housing services and mortgage debt as modelled under conditions of uncertainty. This involves the trade off between housing and non-housing consumption and investment in an alternative asset to housing. Alm & Follain rectify this omission and adopt the mean variance approach to mortgage choice that was outlined in Chapter 2, equations 2.5 to 2.8. We have already seen how the choice of mortgage instrument can impact upon the variance of the borrower's portfolio. Plaut's model of optimal amortisation discussed in Chapter 4 also emphasised the impact of payment scheduling on wealth and its variance. The Alm & Follain model evaluates the discrete ARM/FRM choice instead of the continuous choice between the FRM and indexed debt. Though implicitly in a two-period model the borrower attempts to maximise wealth at the end of period 1.

$$E(U) = U(\Omega^*, \text{Var}(\Omega^*)) + U(C, H) \qquad (7.6)$$

The outline of the Baesel & Biger model was useful in highlighting the importance of the covariance between various key variables in mortgage choice. The work of Alm & Follain is also important in this regard. Extending the modelling to two periods allows consideration of interest rate variations. In a one period model no meaningful distinction can be made between a variable (adjustable) rate and a fixed rate mortgage. The adjustable rate mortgage can be seen as an alternative mechanism for allocating inflation. The more extensive modelling is not quite so mathematically transparent as the simpler models, but the first order conditions do conform to those likely to be found in a conventional mean-variance portfolio framework.[7] Alm & Follain draw their key insights using this approach from a numerical simulation, using a specific form of utility function.[8]

The general form of the utility function for this analysis is given by expression (7.6). The impact of key variables on the FRM/ARM choice can now be determined in one of two ways. Firstly, the consumers utility function can be maximised under the assumption that a particular mortgage (and thus interest rate path) is chosen. Performing this calculation for both types of mortgage leads mortgage choice to be determined by that mortgage instrument which yields the highest utility. Alternatively, a willingness to pay criterion can be used based upon the FRM–ARM differential that leaves the consumer indifferent between the FRM and ARM; this is then compared with the market differential. Alm & Follain conducted both of these exercises, deriving some important predictions for both potential time series and cross-section studies of mortgage instrument choice.

The results from Alm & Follain are presented as key variables in Table 7.1. The most important factors influencing mortgage instrument choice where the degree of correlation between house prices and the real mortgage interest rate, the variance of the mortgage interest rate, and the level of housing demand. The first two results confirm the findings of the simpler modelling approaches discussed above. Generally, the demand for an ARM was greater when the demand for housing was lower, when there was less uncertainty surrounding the mortgage interest rate, and when there was a high positive correlation between the house price and the mortgage interest rate. Positive covariances generally encouraged ARM take up, as this choice then minimised the impact upon portfolio variance.

The Alm & Follain results suggested interesting tests for time series/panel studies. They noted that cross-section work might focus upon the correlation between incomes and the mortgage rate, in the absence of detailed data perhaps using occupational categories. Income, income growth and wealth all had small effects in the model. It is interesting to note the smaller proportion of housing expected to be found in the ARM holder's portfolio. This suggested that the ARM does little to stimulate housing demand, and that any positive effect found by empirical study is likely to be the product of 'teaser rates'. The issue of the effect of choice of mortgage instrument on housing demand will be considered in Chapter 8 along with an analysis of 'teaser rates' or discounts on interest rates.

Szerb (1996) offers an extension to the choice of mortgage instrument literature. He argues that previous models only deal indirectly with uncertainty surrounding inflation and nominal shocks, whereas mortgage choices can be influenced by real shocks to the economy. The Szerb model is restrictive in that it does not consider the intertemporal trade off between housing and non-housing consumption, and it does not have an alternative asset to housing. We have seen how the latter and the variance of the rate of return can have a significant impact upon housing and mortgage demand and therefore at least indirectly on mortgage choice. Consequently we shall refer to the results of the more comprehensive Alm & Follain model as the basis of our theoretical expectations.

The work of Szerb does offer some important insights. Real shocks that impact upon the real interest rate can influence mortgage choices via the borrower's chosen exposure to such shocks. The work also makes the important point that the expected effects of independent variables, income in particular, will vary according to whether borrowers are constrained or unconstrained in their borrowing. This might be one reason why aggregate empirical studies may detect small or insignificant effects for income. The model also gives some insight into why wealth is often found to have a small impact upon mortgage instrument choice, or varies in sign. The impact of wealth operates through its substitutability with mortgage size when purchasing a property. However, it was not possible to say unambiguously whether the amount of FRM or ARM borrowing would reduce by a larger amount if wealth increased. The result depended upon the comparative variances of inflation and the real interest rate.

The Alm & Follain model does not, of course, incorporate all of the simultaneous choices that a borrower/house purchaser must make. Housing and mortgage demand are not part of a general equilibrium model. Neither does the modelling explicitly account for the trade off between borrowers' impatience and interest rate risk, that is optimum payment profiles (Brueckner 1993). In common with other models prepayment and default risk are not considered. We will see that the latter omission is partly rectified by the new models of mortgage instrument choice under asymmetric information. The models considered so far do give insight into some of the key variables that should inform the econometric specification of reduced form mortgage choice equations. It would be a monumental task to incorporate all of the various aspects of mortgage instrument choice into a single theoretical model. If the various dimensions of mortgage choice are to be captured then it is necessary to move between different world views on the efficiency and completeness of markets

Information asymmetry and mortgage contract heterogeneity

The theoretical discussion of rationing in Chapter 5, and its empirical treatment in Chapter 6, focused upon the importance of asymmetric information in the mortgage market. There is now a rich vein of largely theoretical literature arguing that mortgage contracts of different design exist as screening devices that signal important, and otherwise unobservable, characteristics of borrowers to lenders (Dunn & Spatt 1988; Brueckner 1992, Chari & Jagannathan 1989; Brueckner 1994b, c, 2000; LeRoy 1996; Yang 1992; Stanton & Wallace 1998; Posey & Yavas 2001; Harrison *et al.* 2004). The theories provide further explanation of why we might observe mortgage contracts of different design.

Theoretical work in the US has been mainly concerned with the trade off between mortgage points and the interest (coupon) payable on mortgage debt (Dunn & Spatt 1988; Yang 1992; Stanton & Wallace 1998). A few cases have explored the possibility of a separating equilibrium for the FRM/ARM mortgage choice (Brueckner 1992; Posey & Yavas 2001). The points/coupon trade off is important partly because if it leads to a separating equilibrium then the points attached to a mortgage can be used to predict the likelihood of prepayment. This is particularly useful to financial analysts who wish to value pools of mortgage-backed securities (Stanton & Wallace 1998).

Highly mobile borrowers may be keen to avoid paying high points if they are likely to be taking out a new mortgage contract soon. Thus the highly mobile borrower will opt for a high interest rate and low points combination, while the less mobile borrower will go for higher points and a lower interest rate. There is some empirical evidence for this relationship (see Brueckner 1994b; Hayre & Rajan 1995). Formal modelling of this potential separating equilibrium has been undertaken by Chari & Jagannathan (1989), Brueckner (1992), LeRoy (1996), Yang (1992) and Stanton & Wallace (1998). The balance of research is in favour of separating equilibrium (Chari & Jagannathan 1989; Brueckner 1994b, c, 2000; Stanton & Wallace 1998) or a semi-pooling equilibrium, that is with some separability (LeRoy 1996).

Mobility is important because the majority of mortgages in the US have 'due on sale' clauses, meaning that a mortgage must be paid off on the sale of the property, thus mobility determines the holding period of the mortgage and therefore impacts on the value of the mortgage debt.[9] The work of Stanton & Wallace (1998) significantly advances research in this area by introducing transaction costs into the analysis and incorporating prepayment through refinancing rather than just mobility. We shall meet this contribution again when we examine mortgage valuation in Chapter 10. For now the main focus of analysis is on the separating equilibrium that might characterise the choice between a fixed and an adjustable rate mortgage. This fits with the focus here on FRM/ARM choice and is compatible with our attempt to understand the variety of classes of mortgage instrument. It is also the case that mortgage market competition has generally reduced the significance of points (Bennett *et al.* 1998, 2001), though they are still a phenomenon worthy of further research attention.

The FRM/ARM mortgage choice and separating equilibrium

If it can be demonstrated that different mortgage instruments signal important characteristics of borrowers then the study of mortgage choice has important implications for several areas of mortgage market economics. Forecasting prepayment and default probabilities is one such area. Moreover, if the selection of different contracts yielded information to lenders on the expected holding period of mortgage debt then those contracts could be efficiently priced. The lender's profitability is a positive function of the holding period. Brueckner (1992) provides a model where self-selection and changing contract choices effect expected holding periods and the efficient pricing of ARMs and FRMs. The discussion which follows explores the possibility of a separating equilibrium in this market.

Posey & Yavas (2001) demonstrate the possibility that the FRM/ARM choice will lead to self-selection on the basis of potential default costs.

The Posey & Yavas (P & Y) model predicts that low risk borrowers will choose an FRM, while high risk borrowers will choose an ARM. Risks here are defined in terms of the probability of experiencing a fall in income. Borrowers are assumed to face significantly high default costs. The model focuses upon the ability of borrowers to meet mortgage payments out of income (that is 'affordability') as a trigger for default, rather than negative equity ('ruthless default'). A separating equilibrium can emerge from this model. The two-period model has stochastically determined income and interest rates in the second period. If the income of the borrower falls below the mortgage payment due in the second period, then default takes place.

The P & Y model presents an interesting decision problem for the borrower. A sufficiently large fall in income in the second period will lead to default in the FRM case, but with the choice of an ARM, default also depends upon the interest rate outcome. Thus all is not lost for the ARM borrower if interest rates, in addition to income, also fall. Of course, a cost here is the risk that an increase in income might be offset by an even greater increase in the interest rate. The choice between the FRM and ARM now depends on whether the borrower's risk of default is high or low. Remember that risk in this case refers to the risk of a fall in income. Borrowers with a high risk of default (income fall) are more likely to obtain the benefit from lower interest rates. Thus high risk borrowers will be predisposed towards the ARM choice. Conversely, borrowers with a low risk of default are more likely to choose the FRM. Borrowers who have high income variance are more inclined to select an ARM.

Given the potential relevance of separating equilibrium in the FRM/ARM (VRM) market for the US, the UK and possibly other mortgage markets, then it is worth noting the technical aspects of the Posey & Yavas model in a little more detail. Figure 7.1 is taken from Posey & Yavas and demonstrates the possibility of a separating equilibrium in the FRM/ARM choice. There are also conditions where a pooling equilibrium is the predicted outcome. The vertical axis is the interest rate charged on fixed rate debt (incorporating interest rate expectations and risk of default), the horizontal axis is the margin that lenders charge ARM holders to cover the risk of default. Thus borrower preferences and mortgage contract designs are both represented in Figure 7.1.

The indifference curves exhibited in Figure 7.1 are determined by choosing a margin, a, which at a given interest rate, i, leaves a borrower, with a given risk and cost of default indifferent between an FRM and an ARM. The indifference curve for the low risk borrower is depicted by $i(a;pl)$ and

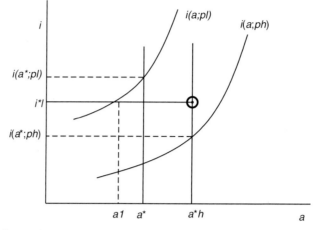

Figure 7.1   Separating equilibrium based upon the FRM/ARM choice.

Source: Posey, L. & A. Yavas (2001) Adjustable and fixed rate mortgages as a screening mechanism.

i(a;ph) is the indifference curve for the high risk borrower. It is possible to demonstrate that for a sufficiently high disutilty of default the indifference curve of the high risk borrower lies below that of the low risk borrower.[10] The choice of an FRM or ARM is indicated by the position of the contract, that is the combination of *i* and *a*. When the contract is above the borrower's indifference curve then an ARM is chosen. This is because above the curve for the FRM becomes increasingly more expensive. If the contract is below the indifference curve then an FRM is preferred. This is because below the indifference curve the FRM becomes relatively cheaper. Thus an interest rate/margin combination lying above the high risk indifference curve, but below that for a low risk borrower, indicates that the high risk borrower will adopt an ARM; conversely a low risk borrower will adopt an FRM.

A separating equilibrium is indicated in Figure 7.1 by the contract offering at *i*l* and *a*h*, that is, with this contract low risk individuals obtain an FRM at the rate *i*l*, and high risk individuals obtain an ARM with margin *a*h*. Moreover, this contract lies to the right of the zero profit constraint indicated by the vertical line at *a**. Thus this contract will be offered by lenders. The basis of the separation is the argument that those borrowers with a high risk of default will prefer an ARM contract because they are more likely to experience the benefits which arise when the mortgage interest rate falls.

The stability of the FRM–ARM separating equilibrium in the P & Y model can be seen by considering the contract depicted by *a1* and *i*l*. This contract represents the highest margin at which both types of borrower are indifferent between an FRM and an ARM. Given that a^* is a zero profit contract, and that $a1 < a^*$, then there is no common (pooling) contract that can generate positive profits. This separating equilibrium is only feasible if under full information the high risk borrowers would still prefer an ARM. In most signalling and screening models high risk borrowers achieve their full information equilibrium loan. Separating equilibrium can also be established with positive profits, and there are also unique conditions under which an FRM or an ARM pooling equilibrium can occur.[11] With sufficiently high levels and variations in default costs and default risks the FRM/ARM choice can act as a screening mechanism for lenders, and assist in the efficient pricing of contracts.

It is important to note the characteristics of the Posey & Yavas model that distinguish it from the separating equilibrium models of Rothschild & Stiglitz (1976), and the models considered in Chapter 5 of this book. Those models have contracts differentiated along a continuum of loan size (balance) interest rate combinations, or allow a mix of mortgage instruments. In the Posey & Yavas model borrowers have either an FRM or an ARM, and not a combination of both. This reduction in the degrees of freedom means that it is theoretically possible for both a pooling equilibrium to exist, and for a positive profit to be earned on at least one of the contracts under separating equilibrium

The Posey & Yavas model focuses upon the unobserved risk of default (through affordability problems) and the role of the FRM/ARM choice in acting as a screening device. Posey & Yavas assert that in the absence of default risk, or with zero default costs, the FRM is the dominant optimal risk sharing contract. Brueckner (1993), offers a similar argument that ARMs exist to better match preferred payment profiles, but it is default costs that lead to the absense of a graduated payment mortgage, giving the rationale for the ARM. Both models have the feature that that there is no unsecured borrowing available to overcome liquidity problems, obtain an optimal time distribution of consumption or mitigate default. Both models also have the common feature of unsettling the strong risk sharing rationale for the FRM, and generating contract heterogeneity.

The empirical predictions that follow from the Posey & Yavas model are summarised in Table 7.1. The model suggests that borrowers with variable incomes, and a correspondingly high risk of default are more likely to choose an ARM in a stochastic interest rate environment. Also, given the possibility that costs and risks of default are likely to vary according to personal characteristics (though how much so is open to question), then with asymmetric information borrowers' characteristics are more likely to be influential determinants of mortgage choices. The model also predicts that default rates will be higher for ARM holders a prediction with some empirical validity (see SA-Aadu 1988). These and other empirical predictions emanating from these models are discussed more fully in Chapter 8.

Interest rate expectations and mortgage contract heterogeneity

Several of the models discussed above have focused upon interest rate expectations. For example, the slope of the yield curve was an important determinant of ARM choice (Brueckner 1993). Also the models were based upon draws from probability density functions of interest rates, which if they are to explain borrowers' choices imply an interest rate expectations mechanism, or at least knowledge of the variance of the interest rate distribution. In this section we consider the question of interest rate expectations as a source of contract heterogeneity more explicitly. Interest rate arguments have been the more empirically successful of the predictors of mortgage choice.

A key variable in the empirical analysis of the choice of mortgage instrument is the impact of the FRM–ARM price differential. The determination of the optimum premium on the FRM is not explicitly considered in the models reviewed so far. For example, Alm & Follain assume that the margin is exogenously determined: choices are then based upon a comparison of the FRM–ARM differential which leaves a borrower indifferent between the two types of mortgage with the actual differential charged. Posey & Yavas conclude that their screening model is too complex to arrive at explicit solutions to the efficient pricing of the FRM and the ARM, leaving the rather intriguing question of how prices are determined when choices are discrete and information incomplete.

Insofar as mortgage instruments are not efficiently priced, so as to leave borrowers indifferent between them, then econometric analysis requires that the FRM–ARM margin be included as a measure of relative costs, with other variable(s) included as an indicator(s) of interest rate expectations. Of course, the FRM–ARM differential is itself an indicator of the expected change in interest rates and their volatility. However, relying solely upon this as a measure of interest rate expectations in empirical work may place too much of a burden on the one variable. There can be different expected outcomes of the impact of the term structure on the choice of mortgage instrument. Brueckner (1993) indicated that a positively sloping term structure encourages the choice of an ARM, while Posey & Yavas suggested the opposite. This difference follows from the focus of the two models, with one concerned with the impatience of the borrower, and the other the risk of default from variations in income. These contrasting perspectives suggest some ambiguity in the expected sign on term structure variables with much depending upon the underlying determinants of the risk of default.

Typically then the difference between the FRM–ARM rates have been used in empirical work as a measure of relative mortgage costs. Supply side determinants of this difference have tended to be neglected with the comparative mortgage costs being treated as exogenously determined (for an important exception see Jones *et al.* 1995).[12] Interest rate expectations are usually modelled by including some measure of the term structure of interest rates. However, there are a number of interesting theoretical perspectives on how borrowers might form their interest rate expectations. These perspectives offer insights into both the determinants of the choice of mortgage instrument (contract heterogeneity), and the endogeneity of this choice in mortgage and housing demand equations.

Brueckner & Follain (1989) adopt an interesting calculation for estimating the expected comparative mortgage costs of the ARM compared to choosing an FRM. While the FRM interest rate cost is clearly fixed until maturity or prepaid, whichever comes first, the expected ARM cost is a function of the term structure of interest rates. The difference between the FRM and the ARM rate now represents the expected increase in interest rates over time, and the degree of perceived volatility in rates. This suggests another role for the FRM–ARM premium in estimation, that is as an indicator of expected interest rate changes.

The calculation is represented by expression (7.7). The term R_a is expected interest rate costs, the arguments r_a and r_f are the current interest rates on adjustable and fixed rate debt respectively, B is a constant, ρ is a parameter which results in expected costs expressed as a positive function of the premium on fixed rate mortgage debt. Notice the presence of a borrower's mobility, *MOB*. More mobile borrowers who prepay their debt on moving have a smaller risk of facing a large interest rate rise.

$$R_a = Br_a(r_f - r_a + 1)^P \exp(\pi MOB) \tag{7.7}$$

A main argument of the Brueckner & Follain paper is that expected interest rate costs are endogenous to housing/mortgage demand. That is the actual costs depend upon the probability of choosing a particular mortgage instrument. This requires a synthetic measure of mortgage interest rates, to be discussed more fully in the consideration of empirical research. Though subsequent theoretical and empirical work would suggest a more sophisticated mortgage pricing mechanism; for example, pricing itself as endogenous to the FRM–ARM decision (Brueckner 1992), the model highlights the importance of the FRM premium as a potential indicator of mortgage interest rate expectations. The modelling also focuses upon the endogeneity of interest rate costs in mortgage and housing demand equations. The work of Bruekner & Follain does not present an explicit theory of instrument choice and so no theoretical predictions appear in Table 7.1. The model does suggest the possible simultaneous determination of mortgage/housing demand and the household's choice of mortgage instrument.

Modelling mortgage instrument choice should include some measure of interest rate expectations, whether this is the FRM–ARM differential, the term structure of interest rates, adaptive expectations, or whatever. There are a number of observations that suggest that modelling expectations is problematic. For example, consumers may have contrary interest rate expectations. Goodman (1992) notes that this is evident in the University of Michigan consumer survey. Contrary views are not inconsistent with unbiased forecasting of interest rate changes. On average, consumers may still forecast the direction of change correctly, if, occasionally, they get this wrong. However, the presence of contrary interest rate expectations is an interesting, if ad hoc, explanation of why some consumers may choose an ARM in preference to an FRM, or vice versa.

There has also been some largely empirical research that suggests that at a particularly high or low mortgage interest rate borrowers might expect the rate to regress back to the mean. This effect has been empirically detected by Jones *et al.* (1995) for the US and by Leece (2001a) for the UK. Though consumers' expectations based on this form of behaviour are not well developed theoretically[13] the possibility of regressive expectations offers an interesting perspective on why at some interest rate levels, and *ceteris paribus*, consumers may prefer an ARM to an FRM (or VRM in the UK). This perspective in particular suggests a concern with short-run interest rate movements, which may be of special relevance in imperfect capital markets (Leece 2001a). Another argument is that borrower behaviour might simply be myopic, perhaps unduly attracted to 'teaser rates' (Brueckner & Follain 1989), or concerned only with immediate comparative costs (Earley 2000). The interpretation of these possible effects will be fully discussed in Chapter 8.[14]

There is some interesting work on the comparative costs of the choice of different mortgage instruments over time (Milevsky 2001; Tucker 1991; Sprecher & Willman 1993; Templeton *et al*. 1996). Though largely normative it could be suggestive of the drivers of mortgage choices. The discussion in Chapter 4 outlined the cost minimisation hypothesis that might determine the choice of mortgage maturity. Households who were not constrained by affordability considerations might also look at the total costs of different mortgage instruments, over the expected life of the mortgage. Most of the studies involve simulating future interest rate scenarios using Monte Carlo techniques. Taking the characteristics of prevalent contracts then allows a forecast of the expected differential in payments between mortgage instruments. This differential is typically discounted, with a variety of assumptions regarding the opportunity cost of mortgage debt (see Tucker 1991), or a future value is calculated (Milevsky 2001). The findings generally note that under conditions where the yield curve is normal (or even flat) the ARM or the equivalent spot rate mortgage is the least costly choice in the long term.

The mortgage cost literature adopts a number of different approaches to the manner in which short-term interest rates are thought to be generated. Some studies assume reversion to a mean value (Milevsky 2001), while others assume a form of random walk (Templeton *et al*. 1996). It is clear that there are times when short-term money market rates are below long-run expectations. In the latter case there is always the possibility that on occasion the FRM will prove the cheaper option in terms of costs. Thus the cost minimisation literature suggests some optimum strategies for cost minimisers, one of which would be to lock into an FRM at historically low interest rates and expect regression to the mean.

However, there are some problems in using the approaches in the mortgage cost literature as the basis for hypothesis testing. There is the question of whether observed cost differences over time are optimal. For example, is the cost difference an acceptable and efficiently priced risk premium? Costs will also vary with expected holding period, which might also vary by mortgage instrument. However, cost minimisation in the short-term by liquidity constrained households, and in the long-term by consumers exploiting pricing inefficiencies may be valid ways of examining consumers actual mortgage choices. There may also be significant differences in the expected holding periods for mortgage instruments generating different expected costs, and differences in risk aversion that can also alter expected costs (Capone & Cunningham 1992).

In theory the borrower will compare the discounted costs of the ARM to that of the FRM. However, the ARM holder also has exposure to interest rate changes. Capone & Cunningham note that the borrower utilising an ARM will calculate the certainty equivalent of the discounted stream of mortgage cost over the expected holding period, and then compare this with the discounted cost of the FRM. This is an important perspective because the discount rate and the certainty equivalents will reflect risk aversion. The FRM–ARM differential is essentially an insurance premium to protect against adverse interest rates changes. In empirical work borrower characteristics may proxy both differences in risk aversion and differences in expected holding periods (Capone & Cunningham 1992).

Another potentially interesting perspective on mortgage instrument choice and mortgage market choices in general, that has not been fully explored, would be a psychological or behavioural approach. There are some aspects of mortgage market behaviour that do suggest that an understanding of consumer psychology might help. For example, mortgage prepayment cannot always be fully explained by a rational financial decision making model (see Deng *et al.* 2000) and it has been suggested that many borrowers are simply financially unsophisticated. Behavioural finance might prove a productive avenue of future research for understanding consumer choices in the mortgage market. For now myopic behaviour might be considered a 'catch all' category for as yet unexplained determinants of mortgage choices.

Summary and conclusions

Understanding more about the variety of mortgage contracts that households face is important in several respects. Contract choices can impact upon individual economic welfare and determine the risk and payment profiles that households face. In a world of asymmetric information, different types of mortgage instrument can signal the characteristics of borrowers to lenders including their propensity to default. Such information is important if lenders are to price mortgage contracts efficiently. Secondary mortgage market participants can also benefit from the information yielded by contract choices. Choice of mortgage instrument is a potentially important influence upon mortgage/housing demand. There is also the question of 'inappropriate choices' arising out of agency problems that can have significant effects on the borrower's economic welfare, a matter to be raised in Chapter 8.

This chapter has explored the theoretical basis of mortgage contract heterogeneity. Why should we observe anything other than the optimal risk sharing contract, the FRM? The answers to this question could be found in desired payment profiles, the portfolio impact of mortgage choices, information asymmetry and signalling, interest rate expectations and variations in risk aversion. Each of the perspectives discussed offered some theoretical predictions (summarised in Table 7.1) that might explain mortgage choices in practice. The modelling approaches explored the phenomenon from different perspectives and adopting different assumptions; a reflection of the complexity of this decision, particularly if capital markets operate imperfectly. There is still much theoretical work to be done in this important area of mortgage choice; for example, general equilibrium modelling or more sophisticated models of how borrowers deal with uncertainty. The chapter which follows will assess the empirical contributions to the mortgage choice literature, from both the US and the UK, for their compatibility with the various theoretical perspectives.

Guide to further reading

The research and formal modelling in the area of asymmetric information and self-selection in the mortgage market is comparatively recent. I would recommend that the student of this subject reads the paper by Dunn & Spatt (1988) which is not a mathematical exposition, but clearly sets out the interdependencies between contract designs, prepayment behaviour and self-selection by borrowers. The paper by Posey & Yavas (2001) is also useful for its succinct but enlightening review of the pertinent literature on signalling and screening. This is an area to watch for more theoretical and empirical treatment. The simultaneous determination of contract design, pricing and prepayment and default probabilities is a rich but extremely complex area ripe for further development.

Notes

1 Dunn and Spatt (1988, p. 47).
2 The solution to this optimisation problem is not straightforward. Brueckner notes that it is a problem in optimum control but a 'heuristic solution' can be achieved by creating a Lagrangian multiplier and differentiating with respect to the integrals with respect to R at each value of r_1, see Brueckner (1993, p. 336).
3 The analysis is conducted using a quadratic utility function (see Brueckner 1993, p. 341).

4 It is interesting to note that elsewhere Brueckner (1986) has noted that increases in the cost of funds may not always be passed on to borrowers, and provide a further form of risk sharing in mortgage pricing.

5 Baesel & Biger (1980, p. 458).

6 Dokko & Edelstein (1991, p. 59).

7 Alm & Follain (1987, p. 4).

8 Simulations are conducted using an iso utility function.

9 In the United Kingdom mobility driven prepayment is typical of the repayment mortgage, whereas the endowment provides a debt that is transferable between properties. Increasing competition in the mortgage market has led to an increased emphasis upon 'portability' so that this issue might be less relevant for the United Kingdom with most prepayment reflecting refinancing. However, the existence of prepayment penalties on many United Kingdom mortgages introduces impediments to financially driven prepayment.

10 See Posey & Yavas (2001, pp. 65–6 and Appendix, pp. 75–7).

11 It is important to note that the P & Y model deals with outcomes that are 'mutually exclusive but they are not all inclusive' (Posey & Yavas 2001, p. 71).

12 Some research has treated the premium on fixed rate debt as an exogenously given pure risk adjustment. This is rather incompatible with the other influences on FRM pricing such as mobility and endogenously determined pre-payment.

13 It would not be true to say that regression to the mean as a phenomenon was under-researched for financial markets in general, but is an apt comment for consumer decision making in this area.

14 Jones *et al.* note the difficulty of disentangling affordability effects in this case. A given level of mortgage payments is compatible with different combinations of house prices and interest rates. When house prices are high and interest rates low then the borrower is more at risk from interest rate increases, thus an ARM may be a less likely choice. This argument is compatible with the portfolio view of Alm & Follain (1987). See Jones *et al.* (1995, pp. 83–4).

8

The Household's Choice of Mortgage Design: Empirical Evidence

Introduction

This chapter presents the results of the empirical analysis of the household's choice of mortgage instrument, reporting work from both the UK and the US. This area is one of the most thoroughly researched dimensions of mortgage choices, though there is comparatively little work for the UK (see Leece 1995b, 2000a, 2001a). Once again the main focus is upon cross-section studies of household behaviour, without neglecting any important time series work on mortgage instrument choice. For example, models outlined in the previous chapter indicated the importance of interest rate expectations and the term structure of interest rates. The discussion in Chapter 1 noted the significance of the different features of housing finance systems, and how the choices available to borrowers represent an important dimension of efficiency. The research discussed in this chapter will highlight the importance of these choices, the impact of differences in housing finance systems and the general applicability of theories and empirical methodologies.

It is a prime purpose of this chapter to evaluate how well existing theoretical perspectives on the choice of mortgage instrument are substantiated by empirical studies. We will find that some recent theoretical developments in the modelling of asymmetric information and separating equilibrium in the mortgage market, discussed in Chapter 7, have to some extent left the empirical literature behind. Thus the discussion in this chapter is structured in a more general way. However, the theoretical modelling can offer interesting perspectives on the interpretation of empirical studies; more ad hoc empirical research has also yielded some very interesting results.

The main focus of the empirical research in the US has been on the ARM/ FRM choice (see Dhillon *et al.* 1987; Alm & Follain 1987; SA-Aadu 1987; Brueckner & Follain 1988; SA-Aadu & Sirmans 1995). In the UK work has focused upon the repayment/endowment choice (Leece 1995b, 2000b) and the FRM/Variable Rate Mortgage (VRM) choice (Leece 2000a, 2001a). These mortgage choices have important implications for consumer welfare and macroeconomic policy, in addition to impinging upon other mortgage and housing choices (Brueckner & Follain 1989). For example, in the UK the prevalence of variable rate mortgages has been argued to introduce elements of instability into the economy (Britton & Whitley 1997; Earley 2000; Maclennan *et al.* 1998) while some studies have explored the potentially stabilising impact of the ARM choice in the US (see Brueckner & Follain 1989; Goodman 1992).[1]

The chapter begins with a presentation of the main research findings on the choice of mortgage instrument in the US. This is followed by a discussion of the results of UK research and a section briefly comparing US and UK work. For example, UK households appear to adopt, or are constrained to adopt, a more short-term perspective in their mortgage choices. Two important issues are explored within each of the reviews of the empirical research. The first is the importance of the variety of mortgage contracts to be found in the mortgage market, which has implications for consumer decision making and econometric estimation. The second issue is the possibility that the choice of mortgage instrument is endogenous to mortgage/housing demand, a result which if true has important policy implications. For example, the choice of instrument might help overcome credit market constraints on desired house size and facilitate access to owner occupation. The chapter concludes with an overview of the general contribution of empirical research to understanding the choice between contracts.

Figure 8.1 shows the varying fortunes of the ARM as a proportion of the mortgage market in the US. Note the peaking in 1985 and 1988, and the troughs of 1986, 1993 and 1998. The marked fluctuations in the popularity of the ARM invite an explanation. We might also note that this is an aggregate picture, the ARM is adjustable over varying time periods; also there are a wide range of variations in mortgage designs including caps collars and initial discounts ('teaser rates'). Inevitably, there are times when it is necessary to aggregate mortgage types, or focus upon a particular feature. For now, there are several important questions to ask. Does the heterogeneity of mortgage contracts matter? Do the empirics suggest why such a variety might exist? What are the links between the choice of mortgage instrument and mortgage/housing demand?

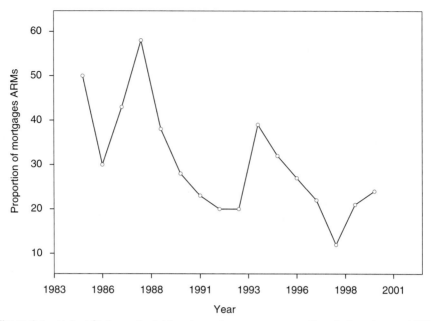

Figure 8.1   United States, adjustable rate mortgages as a proportion of all mortgages (1983 to 2001).

Source: Federal Housing Finance Board: Terms on Conventional Mortgages: Annual Summary.

Figure 8.2 shows the changing fortunes of the FRM in the UK, with a significant peaking in 1994. Once again this choice is an important one for the UK, and invites explanation, but is also aggregated, subsuming the endowment/repayment and other mortgage instrument choices. Again we can ask similar questions to those addressed to the FRM/ARM choice in the US. What then does the UK research show regarding the key determinants of the choice of mortgage instrument, and the relationship between this choice and the mortgage/housing market?

Choice of mortgage instrument in the United States

It is worthwhile recollecting some of the pertinent differences in the housing finance systems of the UK and the US, outlined and discussed in Chapter 1. Note that typically the FRM in the US has a longer period for which the interest rate is fixed than its counterpart in the UK. The UK FRM is typically fixed for 1 to 5 years while the US FRM rate is generally secured for 15 or 30 years. US mortgages are also more extensively packaged into securities, thus allowing some of the risk of variations in cash flows due to prepayment and default to be offset in the secondary mortgage

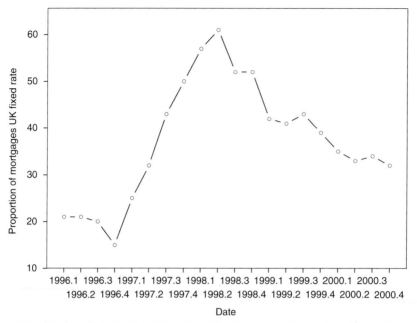

Figure 8.2   United Kingdom, fixed rate mortgages as a proportion of all mortgages (1996 to 2000).

Source: Council of Mortgage Lenders.

market. There is also less use of retail funds to underpin housing finance, whereas in the UK mainly savings in the retail finance sector finance the VRM. The importance of these differences will be apparent as we explore and compare the studies of mortgage instrument choice in the two countries, but also need to be kept in mind as we consider the results of empirical research in the US.

We begin the evaluation of US evidence with a review of the main empirical findings of the primarily cross-section research. The theoretical discussion in Chapter 7 noted the reasons why a variety of mortgage contracts might be observed. Empirical studies do not necessarily correspond directly with the theoretical models or restrictions discussed in Chapter 7. We saw how the choice of mortgage instrument was a multifaceted decision. However, the theoretical work can be referred to broadly when considering empirical results. This chapter also considers whether the observed heterogeneity of mortgage contracts leads to excessive search costs for consumers, together with a brief consideration of the problems that this heterogeneity might raise for researchers. Given such contract heterogeneity it is natural to ask if the choice of mortgage type has any impact upon mortgage and housing demand, an issue that has received attention in empirical work, mainly in the US.

The main findings of United States research

The most common empirical finding in US work is the statistical significance of the interest rate difference between the FRM and the ARM. Considering the ARM as the innovation, and the focus of interest, it is typically designated as the dependent variable (that is ARM choice = 1) in a probit or other discrete choice model. The discussion in Chapter 6 highlighted that the FRM–ARM differential can be interpreted in a number of ways. For example, it can be an indicator of expected changes in interest rates, including their volatility (that is more volatile rates would command a larger FRM–ARM differential). More simply the FRM–ARM differential can be viewed as the relative price of the two mortgage instruments. If the premium is treated as a relative cost of the two mortgage types then the expected sign is positive (ARM = 1); this is generally found to be the case (Phillips & Vanderhoff 1994; Brueckner & Follain 1988, 1989).[2] Cross-section studies typically have a time series component that allows the detection of interest rate effects, and/or there are regional variations in interest rates.

Another important, and statistically significant independent variable found in US specifications is the own price of the ARM, which is generally found to have a negative sign (Dhillon *et al.* 1987). This could again be a cost effect, with expensive ARMs discouraging take up. However, there is also the possibility that at high ARM rates consumers feel overexposed to further interest rate increases (Alm & Follain 1987). Alternatively, if high ARM rates reflect a level of interest rates significantly in excess of the historical mean rate, then some households might expect interest rates (and ARM rates) to fall. Thus there would be less incentive to adopt fixed rate debt at high ARM rates. This form of regressive interest rate expectations has found some credence in both US (Jones *et al.* 1995) and UK research (Leece 2000a, 2001a). Clearly, how households form their interest rate expectations is crucial in assessing the determinants of the choice of mortgage instrument.

Some independent variables in the econometric models have been less successful in explaining the choice of mortgage instrument. Two such are wealth and the personal characteristics of the borrower, e.g. age. The few studies that have used measures of wealth in the estimating equation tend to find that it has a negligible impact upon choice probabilities and/or the measure is not statistically significant (Dhillon *et al.* 1987; Phillips & Vanderhoff 1994). This small impact of wealth is consistent with the results of the theoretical simulations conducted by Brueckner & Follain (1989) reported in Chapter 7, and the work of Szerb (1996), also discussed in that chapter. Recall that wealth and mortgage debt may be substitutes and the impact of wealth on mortgage choice depends upon various key variances and covariances (e.g. inflation and real wages).

Generally the characteristics of borrowers do not have statistically significant effects upon the choice of mortgage instrument, exceptions are SA-Aadu & Shilling (1994), SA-Aadu & Sirmans (1995) and SA-Aadu & Megbolugbe (1995). Capone & Cunningham (1992) estimated a binomial logit model for mortgage instrument choice as a selectivity equation in a model of mortgage termination behaviour. Key borrower characteristics used were the age of the borrower, the mortgage payment-to-income ratio, and net worth per dependent. These measures were taken as indicators of the degree of risk aversion. For example, younger households with high levels of net worth were considered less risk averse. However, no borrower characteristics were statistically significant at the 5% level. If the choice of mortgage instrument signals default risk then the characteristics of borrowers should have an influence upon choice, unless, of course, these differences in risk are efficiently priced.

One reason why personal characteristics might appear not to influence the choice of mortgage instrument is the manner in which different types of mortgage are aggregated. Once we start to recognise the heterogeneity of mortgage instruments then there may be some hidden behaviour. This is also interesting because, as we shall see later, the heterogeneity of mortgage contracts might generate excessive search costs, and lead to more misclassified observations, that is a household being recorded as having the wrong type of mortgage (see Leece 2000a, 2001a). The problem of misclassification in particular, has important implications for the reliability of statistical results.

The significance of contract heterogeneity is highlighted in research by SA-Aadu & Sirmans (1995) who found that personal characteristics do influence the choice between ARMs with different adjustment periods. The work applied a multinomial logit model to data from a large saving and loan institution, giving a sample size of 345 mortgage loans over the period 1979 to 1984. ARM choices could be taken to reflect the consumer's chosen degree of risk exposure. This is a very important piece of work; borrowers reacted differently to contract prices and the impact of price differs across contracts due to the different lock-in periods. Thus there may be some self-selection by borrowers according to mortgage contract. For example, results show that younger, and presumably more mobile, borrowers prefer an ARM where the interest rate is fixed for a comparatively short period of time.

An early study by Brueckner & Follain (1988) pointed to the rather dramatic rise in the market share of the ARM (2/3 of market share in 1984) and its subsequent fall from favour (falling to nearly 20% by June 1986) (see Figure 8.1). The research used the Residential Finance Database compiled by the National Association of REALTORS, using a final sample of 475 observations for 1985. Variations in the FRM–ARM difference are captured in monthly and regional variations (40 different values in total). Their empirical model uses proxies[3] to capture several key theoretical variables, namely the borrower's risk aversion, his or her discount rate for future consumption and the strength of the demand for housing. Other important variables are the level of income and its expected growth path, and household mobility. As with other studies, the FRM–ARM price differential is included, noting that high FRM–ARM differentials make fixed rate debt less attractive, but also indicate expectations of increasing rates.

The results of the Brueckner & Follain study indicated that the level of the FRM rate and the FRM–ARM price differential were important contributors to ARM choice. The proxies for risk aversion (the presence of children in the household) and the tilt of the income stream (age of the borrower) did not have significant effects upon the choice of an ARM. Of course, these may have been poor measures of the theoretical variables. Income level and regional mobility did have statistically significant effects. Simulations comparing forecasts ARM market share with actual suggested that the rapid rise of the ARM could be attributed to the high interest rates in the US in the early 1980s which made borrowers more sensitive to the price differential on the FRM.

In summary, cross-section/time series studies using US data have found the FRM–ARM differential and the level of either the ARM or the FRM rate to be important determinants of the choice of mortgage instrument. In pure cross-section research, rather than pooled cross-section/time series, variations in the FRM premium will reflect relative cost differences rather than variations in interest rate expectations. There is also evidence that mobility and income are significant influences upon choice. More mobile households are less likely to pay the premium on fixed rate debt if they expect to remortgage soon. Borrowers appear to be influenced both by affordability and the different degrees of risk exposure evident in the choice of mortgage type, particularly among ARMs with different adjustment periods.

Time series studies, or some pooling of cross-section and time series data, provide the most favourable means of detecting the influence of changing interest rate expectations on the choice of mortgage instrument. Jones *et al.* (1995) estimated a time series model of ARM market share focusing upon interest rate variables. The research included supply side factors, e.g. the percentage of ARMs securitised. The general assumption in the studies of mortgage instrument choice is that the supply of mortgage finance, for any contract design, is infinitely elastic. A major research question was how far supply side factors impacted upon pricing, and thus the demand for ARMs?

The sample period covered 1986 to 1992 inclusive. This period included a number of peaks and troughs in the aggregate ARM market share (see Figure 8.1). The main empirical findings pointed to the importance of the term structure of interest rates, with steeper term structures encouraging the take up of ARMs (that is a positive sign); a result compatible with the theoretical predictions of Brueckner's model (1993). The current level of the mortgage interest rate had a negative impact upon the probability of choosing an ARM. The latter effect suggested that some consumers took the view that interest rates regress to the mean.[4] The research also indicated that securitisation, through its impact upon mortgage pricing had a significant impact upon ARM take up. The research highlighted the importance of interest rate expectations.

Mortgage contract heterogeneity in the United States

The theories of mortgage choice discussed in Chapter 7 offered some explanations for why we observe a variety of mortgage instruments available in the marketplace. Explanations included the presence of liquidity constrained borrowers, signalling and self-selection and heterogeneous interest rate expectations. Some of the empirical studies are also suggestive. For example, SA-Aadu & Sirmans indicate that borrowers take differing risk positions, and that a variety of ARM adjustment periods accommodate these choices. The choices facing consumers are also increased by the presence of 'teaser rates', or initial discounts on new business, and these discounts can vary between providers.

The noted complexity of the mortgage market raises two concerns. First, is there excess contract differentiation that merely raises consumers search costs, and poses particular difficulties for the packaging of mortgage-backed securities? Second, does the extent of contract heterogeneity lead to a significant degree of misclassification of the borrower's choice? Misclassification here could include consumers making inappropriate choices, borrowers misreporting their choice, researchers misrecording the observed mortgage, or inappropriately aggregating mortgage designs.

The issue of misclassification will be explored more fully in the discussion of the empirical evidence for the UK. We note the issue here as not being entirely unrelated to excessive heterogeneity.

The possibility that the heterogeneity of mortgage contracts is 'excessive' can be technically considered as a problem of 'independence of irrelevant alternatives' (SA-Aadu & Shilling 1994). This involves identifying which choices are close enough substitutes to be considered in the same set. A multinomial logit model of contract choices can be estimated and tests conducted to see if choices are close or near perfect substitutes. One test is to see how sensitive estimates are when one of the types of contract available are excluded. Stability of parameter estimates in the presence of this exclusion would suggest that the contracts form distinct choices. If parameter estimates are not stable when some of the choices are excluded then we are dealing with close substitutes (SA-Aadu & Shilling 1994).

SA-Aadu & Shilling use the Hausmann & McFadden specification test procedure to assess how far consumers consider adjustable rate mortgages as distinct entities. Different contract designs are identified by the size of the interest rate cap, and the length of the interest rate adjustment period. The estimation indicated that a large number of ARMs are considered to be close substitutes. This excess heterogeneity may impose additional search costs upon consumers, and inhibit the securitisation of ARM as opposed to the more typically securitised FRM. This is an area of work that suggests the importance of the competitive process among lenders and merits much further research. A further important research question relates to the impact of mortgage choice on mortgage and housing demand, an issue that has received attention by US researchers.

The simultaneous determination of mortgage demand and choice of mortgage instrument (US)

The research reported under this heading relates back to the demand for mortgage debt discussed in Chapter 2 and the possibility, raised in Chapter 7, that mortgage costs were endogenous to mortgage/housing demand equations. In Chapter 2 we noted the possibility that the choice of mortgage instrument and the size of the mortgage debt might be simultaneously determined. Theoretical work has suggested the possible importance of this simultaneous determination (Brueckner & Follain 1988; Brueckner 1994a).[5] Not allowing for such endogeneity in mortgage demand equations can lead to biased and inconsistent parameter estimates. There is a surprising neglect of this simultaneity in the literature.

Early work by Brueckner & Follain (1989) estimated a discrete choice model of the selection between an FRM and an ARM; the predicted probabilities were then used to weight the FRM and the ARM rates applying to the mortgage choices. This technique created synthetic measures of interest rate costs to be included in a housing demand equation, and controlled for the endogeneity of the choice of mortgage instrument. The expected ARM rate was based upon the FRM–ARM differential.[6] The research found a significant impact of ARM choice on the level of housing demand, and established the simultaneity of the choice of mortgage instrument and the demand for housing.

A piece of research that found little evidence of any significant impact of ARM choice on housing demand was that of Gabriel & Rosenthal (1993). The study based the choice of mortgage instrument on the lowest cost over a known period of residence. The focus was then on tenure choice conditional on choosing an ARM. Tenure choice was measured by the percentage of recent movers who chose to own their property. Estimates from a logit model of tenure choice were used to simulate the impact of ARM choice on this percentage. A semi-Markov model estimated the long-run steady state proportion of owner occupiers. The results showed that for the economic environment evident during the 1980s ARM choice had little effect on the net demand for owner occupied homes. This was mainly explained by the small impact of different choices of mortgage instrument on the relative cost of owning and renting. The tendency for more mobile borrowers to choose ARMs further weakened any effect.

The small impact on housing demand, found by Gabriel & Rosenthal, contrasts with the more significant effects detected by Brueckner & Follain (1989). There are several possible reasons for this. The studies adopted different perspectives, Brueckner & Follain examined the impact on mortgage demand rather than tenure choice. The impact of ARMs on tenure choice might also be significantly greater under conditions where the FRM–ARM interest rate gap is much larger. This gap is, of course, much greater in the presence of 'teaser rates' on ARMs, a factor not accounted for in the empirical analysis of Gabriel & Rosenthal. 'Teaser rates' have become increasingly important in both the US and UK mortgage markets improving affordability and lowering user costs.

Phillips & Vanderhoff (1992), explored the impact of initial discounts or 'teaser rates' on housing demand and extended the work of Brueckner & Follain (1989). Phillips & Vanderhoff argue that 'teaser rates' can have several potential effects on the demand for housing services. First, there may be a significant reduction in the user cost of owner occupation over the life of the mortgage, particularly so if the holding period is short. Second, the impact of interest rate risk is reduced for borrowers because the initial benchmark rate is lower. Finally, borrowers who might normally be constrained by any binding payment-to-income ratio can now possibly overcome this constraint. These arguments, to some extent, parallel the reasoning of Brueckner (1993) as to why we observe ARMs in the market, that is that they offer a preferred pattern of payments over time for some borrowers. 'Teaser rates' which are typically attached to ARMs may enhance this effect.[7]

Estimating a probit model for mortgage choice, Phillips & Vanderhoff confirm the importance of relative cost effects, that is the impact of the FRM–ARM differential, initial discounts and variations in up front fees or points. Also, borrower characteristics had no significant impact upon the choice of mortgage instrument. A conventionally specified housing demand equation including terms representative of user costs, along with synthetic interest rate measures, had all of the correct signs and statistically significant parameter estimates. The results confirmed the significant and positive impact of ARM choice upon housing demand for the period 1986–1988 in the US and highlighted the importance of high initial discounts on ARM mortgage contracts. So research into the discrete choice of mortgage instrument must account for the influence of 'teaser rates', whenever possible. The question of the impact of ARM choice on housing demand is not settled, and as Gabriel & Rosenthal (1993) contend, may require a general equilibrium approach.

The choice of mortgage instrument in the United Kingdom

Many of the questions explored in the US research are relevant to the UK mortgage market. In the UK the innovation was the fixed rate mortgage (fixed rate = 1) which became popular in the early 1990s (see Figure 8.2). Mirroring US research we can ask several pertinent questions. What is the impact of the FRM–VRM interest rate differential on the choice of a fixed rate mortgage? Do wealth and personal characteristics influence mortgage choice? Are the choice of mortgage instrument and mortgage/housing demand simultaneously determined? The UK also exhibits marked heterogeneity of mortgage products which has implications for consumer decision making and econometric analysis of the choice of mortgage instrument. Thus we can see how far the research findings evident in US work are applicable in the UK.

The main UK research findings

There is considerably less research into the choice of mortgage instrument
for the UK, compared to the US. This applies to both cross-section and
time series studies. This is surprising given the importance of the mortgage market for the UK economy but less surprising given a paucity of
data, at least compared to the US. UK research has focused upon the
endowment/repayment mortgage choice (Leece 1995b, 2000b) with more
recent work considering the FRM/VRM choice (Leece 2000a, 2001a), and
the possible simultaneous determination of mortgage/housing demand
with the choice of mortgage instrument (Leece 2001a).

The choice between a repayment mortgage and an endowment mortgage
is peculiar to the UK, but given that it is a possible savings/portfolio
decision, the results of empirical research may have wider implications
for understanding household behaviour. The repayment mortgage is an
annuity mortgage with a constant payment consisting of capital and
interest. The endowment mortgage is an interest only mortgage with
contractual savings in a diversified portfolio of assets, making a single
(balloon) payment on maturity. The endowment has the added advantage
that maintaining the principal until the debt is paid off maximises any tax
relief on the interest payments.

Given an interest only mortgage, then the savings vehicle used to eventually pay off the debt on maturity should reflect the opportunity cost of
equity in the property, that is if a repayment mortgage is adopted then the
return on this alternative asset is forgone. Thus the choice of an endowment mortgage is indicative of a portfolio decision (see Plaut 1986; Leece
1995b, 2000b). There is an opportunity here for testing the amortisation
models presented in Chapter 4 of this book where an interest only mortgage represented zero amortisation (see Plaut 1986).

Using a sample of mortgages taken from the 1986 Family Expenditure
Survey, Leece (1995b) estimated a probit model with correction for any
selectivity bias arising out of tenure choice. Econometric investigation of
the choice between a repayment and an endowment mortgage did not
indicate any significant portfolio influences upon the decision (Leece
1995b). The main influences on the choice of the endowment mortgage
were income and the nominal mortgage interest rate, suggesting the importance of affordability and cash flow. Thus endowments were popular
when they were comparatively cheaper. These arguments are compatible
with those models that emphasised borrower impatience and the 'tilt' that
were presented in Chapter 7 (e.g. Brueckner 1993).

The sale of endowments in the UK has been at the centre of some contro-versy, with suggestions that third party originations (mortgage brokers rewarded by commission on sales) have led to widespread 'mis-selling'. The 'mis-selling' relates to the contention that consumers were not made aware of the risk that endowment funds might not grow sufficiently to eventually pay off the mortgage debt. The appropriateness of using a risky investment vehicle for this purpose has also been questioned. A low interest rate environment and depressed stock market returns in recent years have led to widespread endowment shortfalls. The analysis of so called 'mis-selling' is a linguistic and analytical minefield and an issue that has not really been explored in the mortgage analysis literature (for an exception see Leece 2000c), though there is US research on agency prob-lems and third party originations that is relevant to this issue (see LaCour Little & Chun 1999; Alexander *et al.* 2002). Econometric analysis of the endowment/repayment choice has assumed that borrowers had expect-ations of a rate of return in excess of the net of tax mortgage rate, even if endowments were 'mis-sold' (Leece 1995b).

There is some UK research into the choice between a fixed and a variable rate mortgage (Leece 2000a, 2001a). The results suggested that UK borrow-ers took a short-period view, basing their choice upon expected move-ments in the variable mortgage interest rate. The age of the head of household was the only statistically significant personal characteristic, with older borrowers having a greater likelihood of choosing variable rate debt.[8] The use of a limited amount of wealth data produced no statistically significant effects on the choice of mortgage instrument, for either the level of wealth or a measure of liquidity (Leece 2001a). This was also true for a measure of the covariance between interest rates and income though the research did involve the use of a fairly short panel, just five years.

The distinctive aspect of the UK research is the lack of statistical sign-ificance on the FRM–VRM differential. Thus an econometric model generally specified along North American lines did not produce the expected statistical results. There was evidence of regressive interest rate expectations with consumers more reluctant to lock into fixed rate debt at high mortgage interest rates.[9] Borrowers were also more willing to adopt fixed rate mortgage debt the greater the discrepancy between the mortgage rate and the base rate of interest. The latter variable was a control for the stickiness of mortgage rates, which gives even variable rate debt some element of, albeit uncertain, fixity. Thus this analysis emphasised the importance of the loan rate function as discussed in Chapter 7.

Model 3 in Table 8.1 reports the results of estimating an econometric model of the choice of mortgage instrument using UK data. The sample of mortgage holders was drawn from the British Household Panel Survey, covering the years 1991–1994. The estimates confirm the lack of statistical significance of personal characteristics (e.g. age) and the negative sign on the absolute level of the mortgage interest rate, that is regressive expectations. However, such rules and heuristics may be contingent. For example, the post-1995 behaviour of UK borrowers appears different. This is illustrated in Figure 8.3 which plots the proportion of UK fixed rate debt against the FRM–VRM differential for 1996–2000.

The relationship in Figure 8.3 is quite distinct and suggests that households respond negatively to larger FRM–VRM differentials. However, the salient point is the fact that the FRM–VRM premium over a range of values is negative (covering 1997 (4) to 1999 (2)), reflecting the inverse yield curve obtaining at the time. It is perhaps not surprising that the rule based upon regression to the mean might be obscured, or no longer pertinent, when fixed rate mortgages are selling at a discount to variable rate debt. For example, even with a lower expectation of an interest rate rise a negative premium on the FRM would induce increased take up of that type of mortgage contract.

Table 8.1   Comparison of treatments of the misclassification problem (2).

	Model 1 Probit with correction for misclassification		Model 2 Probit incorporating misclassification		Model 3 Probit with jack-knife correction (excluding points with high relative influence)	
	Coefficient	S.E.	Coefficient	S.E	Coefficient	S.E
Constant	21.5024	8.3082	11.0669	2.5117	20.3578	3.8913
Age	−6.4592	2.3851	−3.5329	0.8201	−6.4583	1.1984
Variable rate	−1.5857	0.5783	−0.7641	0.1599	−1.3875	0.2564
Gap	−1.3990	0.5797	−0.6319	0.2679	−0.9332	0.3065
Lincome	0.1015	0.2685	−0.0151	0.1394	−0.0441	0.1668
Trend	−0.3385	0.1849	−0.1522	0.07152	−0.3256	0.1118
Corriv	−0.1849	0.3032	−0.7373	0.1689	−0.0899	0.2145
Had	0.4736	0.5068	0.2355	0.2619	0.2828	0.3062
Alpha	0.1285	0.0490	–		–	–
Log likelihood		−165.2252	−167.1500		−96.77313	

The table shows the coefficient estimates and standard errors for three different ways of dealing with classification problems in a dependent variable, including estimates that make no attempt to correct for this problem. The results shown as *Model 1* are derived from a maximum likelihood technique that estimates the degree of classification error and controls for this. *Model 2* is estimated on a sample that is not corrected for classification error. *Model 3* is estimated using a sample where possibly misclassified observations are excluded.

Source: Leece (2001a, p. 603)

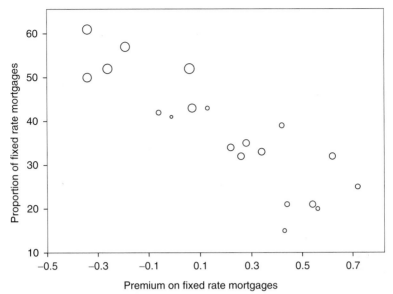

Figure 8.3 United Kingdom, the proportion of fixed rate mortgages and the fixed rate premium.

The higher interest rates, indicated by larger bubbles in Figure 8.3, correspond with high take up of FRMs. This is due to the negative or small average premium and the fact that the level of the VRM rate has a strong negative correlation with the size of the differential (−0.66). Thus high FRM take up corresponds with comparatively high rates of interest but negative premiums. This is all rather suggestive of borrowers' concern with the comparative costs of mortgage instruments.[10] There is no research into the nature of household decision making in this market when negative premiums obtain and the diagram is suggestive of potentially very interesting research into the contingency of rules and heuristics, and the manner in which interest rate expectations are generated among consumers.

The mortgage choices that have been considered in this section of the book have been particular to the UK, that is the repayment versus endowment, and the choice between generally short-term fixed rate debt and a variable rate mortgage.[11] However, they offer important insights into the nature of household decision making. Both types of mortgage choice appeared to be effected more by cash flow and short-term considerations rather than portfolio planning. UK households adopting a cash flow perspective have benefited from and been encouraged by intense competition, and periods of heavy discounting of mortgage debt. There has also been a proliferation of mortgage contracts from which to choose. One of the most interesting aspects of the UK research is the possibility of a misclassified dependent variable, an issue that relates to mortgage contract heterogeneity.

Mortgage contract heterogeneity in the United Kingdom

Growing competition in the mortgage market has been accompanied by a proliferation of mortgage contract designs. This can be a good thing, in that consumers can adopt different positions with regard to interest rate risk, and their desired payment profiles. Chapter 1 noted these choices as an important dimension of the efficiency of housing finance systems. However, we have seen that some empirical research suggests the possibility of excess of innovation in the mortgage market. Certainly the increased extent and complexity of mortgage choices available might lead to consumers misreporting their mortgage type. Mortgage choice research is based upon discrete choice modelling, and it is known that this type of statistical estimation is particularly prone to problems if the choices are misclassified (Hausmann & Scott Morton 1994; Leece 2000a, 2001a). This is far from being a trivial or over technical econometric problem. This type of error can lead the researcher to draw erroneous conclusions relating to the impact and statistical significance of key variables.[12]

Leece (2000a) and Leece (2001a) estimate a discrete choice model of FRM/VRM mortgage choice, which allows for classification error in the dependent variable. The research did not identify the extent of classification error due to misreporting by borrowers; most of the errors arose from an algorithm designed to deduce the mortgage type from other data, but it did demonstrate the likely significance of this problem for the estimation of mortgage choice equations. Classification error had a large impact on the estimated impact of key variables such as interest rates and personal characteristics such as age. The importance of this type of error can be gauged from the statistical results reported in Table 8.1.

Table 8.1 shows three sets of results. The first column is the biased sample which includes the misclassified observations. The second column reports results using a technique that includes the extent of classification error as a further endogenously determined variable – thus this controls for such error. The third column is a sample with what are thought to be misclassified observations removed, so that the problem should not be evident at all. Casual inspection of the results across models by variable indicates the extent to which the estimates and their precision and efficiency, as indicated by the size of standard errors, varies. There are, in fact, a number of reasons for using two techniques (*Model 2* and *Model 3*) which control for classification error in the dependent variable.

First, estimating *Model 2* involves the use of complex non-linear estimation techniques that are often unstable, so that finding an alternative means of controlling for this problem provides a useful check and might be preferred. Second, *Model 3* actually identifies and excludes potentially misclassified observations and this can be very useful if we wish to estimate simultaneous equation models, say, the potentially simultaneous determination of mortgage demand and choice of mortgage instrument. Third, *Model 3* allows some triangulation of the estimation results by providing another means of dealing with classification error. The observations thought to be misclassified are identified using a 'jack knife after bootstrap' which is a method that estimates the statistical model on a number of samples which excludes a given observation to detect its impact; it is thus able to pinpoint those observations exerting a high degree of leverage on any bias in the estimated coefficients.[13]

The research used data from the British Household Panel Survey (BHPS 1991–1994) consisting of 304 observations. The results in Table 8.1 reveal the potential variation in the standard errors of estimates when estimated equations suffer from classification error in the dependent variable. The standard errors in *Model 1*, which does not control for the problem, are generally larger than those for the same variables in *Model 2* and *Model 3*. For example, look at the standard errors on 'Age'. *Model 3* which excludes potentially misclassified variables altogether provides the most precise estimates. We might tentatively view *Model 3* as representing the 'true' picture, but be wary of any biases arising out of the exclusion of some observations, though no particular selectivity problems were detected in this study.

The research indicated that resampling techniques can provide acceptable estimates in the face of bias induced by classification error.[14] It was shown that the heterogeneity of mortgage contracts can create potentially important measurement problems for the investigator. Not only might a wide variety of mortgage instruments generate excessive search costs, but it might also increase the likelihood of measurement error in the form of misclassification. Dealing with such an error is not straightforward; for example, the researcher must have some confidence in the actual specification of the discrete choice model and be sure that there are no significant missing variables. More research is needed in this area of econometric analysis and this will be of great interest to the study of mortgage choices.

An interesting argument is that misclassification may actually reflect some underlying phenomenon in addition to misreporting. It might be the case that the increasing complexity of the mortgage market results in some consumers making 'inappropriate' choices. Misclassification is then endogenous to the process of mortgage market competition and innovation. Another example is 'mis-selling' (or agency problems) which might be a phenomenon that revealed itself through detectable classification error (see Leece 2000c). Thus classification error may not just be a measurement or recording problem, but be inappropriate sales or decisions endogenous to competitive mortgage market innovation and proliferating mortgage choices.[15] Again much more research into consumer choices and lender behaviour in this area would be welcome.

The simultaneous determination of mortgage demand and choice of mortgage type (UK)

The study of the simultaneous determination of the choice of mortgage instrument and the level of housing services, and implicitly mortgage demand, is far more advanced in the US. It is clearly a potentially important issue and relates to the impact of mortgage market innovation on housing demand and the demand for housing finance. The previous discussion noted how in principle mortgage costs are endogenously determined. However, the theoretical discussion in Chapter 7 also argued that correctly priced mortgage instruments ought to have no effect on mortgage/housing demand. This is clearly an important issue for macroeconomic policy in the UK where there is an argument that a movement towards long-term fixed rate debt would add to macroeconomic stability.

Interestingly, UK research has found no evidence for the simultaneous determination of mortgage size (or real housing expenditure) and choice of mortgage design. This result applies to both the endowment/repayment choice (Leece 1995b, 2000a), and the choice between the VRM and the FRM (Leece 2000a, 2001a). Of course, in a no arbitrage perfectly competitive economy there is no reason for the choice of mortgage instrument to have any impact upon housing/mortgage demand. However, the lack of simultaneity does not necessarily reflect optimum pricing in a risk-neutral no arbitrage economy. There are a number of reasons why this simultaneity may not be evident in the UK case.

The 'mis-selling' of certain mortgage contracts may have induced some separability in the two decisions (Leece 2000c)). That is housing and mortgage decisions may become decoupled where there are agency problems resulting from the reward to third party salespersons. Empirical evidence also points to borrowers making their decisions on the basis of the relative cost of the various types of mortgage and adopting a rather short-term perspective on costs and interest rate expectations (Leece 2000a, 2000b). For example, the choice between a VRM and an FRM has been characterised as a gamble against short-run interest rate movements, often informed by the current level of the nominal mortgage interest rate (Leece 2000b). In this case housing expenditures and instrument choice may not be so closely related, and simultaneity will not be apparent. Once again these results may be contingent upon circumstances obtaining in the early to mid-1990s, and invite further research.

A comparison of United States and United Kingdom research

Fixed rate mortgages in the UK still remain largely short to medium term in the period for which the interest rate is fixed. In the US 15-year and 30-year fixed rate deals predominate. The widespread use of variable rate debt is also a key and important characteristic of the UK economy. Though the UK and US mortgage markets differ in important ways it is still possible to draw some general conclusions regarding research into the choice of mortgage instrument. For example, research in both economies has suggested the importance of the level of mortgage interest rates for informing interest rate expectations.

The negative sign found for the impact of the FRM–ARM differential on ARM choice in US studies has suggested the importance of comparative costs. The equivalent FRM–VRM differential in the UK was not found to be significant, at least for the early to mid-1990s. However, a cursory view of recent UK mortgage choices does suggest a strong negative relationship between the FRM–ARM premium and FRM take up. The increased use of discounts ('teaser rates') and a period of negative FRM premiums may account for much of this relationship. 'Teaser rates' or discounts have been demonstrated as important in US research and merit more attention from UK mortgage market researchers.

The question of the simultaneity of mortgage/housing demand and the choice of mortgage instrument is another important area where there are interesting contrasts between the two economies. The need to correct for the endogeneity of mortgage choice and interest rate costs in US housing demand equations is reasonably well established.[16] This was not the case for the UK. This may reflect the existence of agency problems in third party sales of mortgages ('mis-selling'), or it may be a result of the short-term nature of UK contract designs and borrowers behaviour. In either case the choice of mortgage instrument may become decoupled from the demand for housing services and mortgage size.

The other key issue identified in this chapter is the heterogeneity of mortgage contracts. This raised the interesting question of whether or not such heterogeneity generated excessive search costs for borrowers. Findings from the US suggested that there was an excess of mortgage designs, though more research into this is needed, particularly for other economies and at other times. Of more general concern were the potential estimation problems that faced the investigator when mortgage choices might be subject to the risk of misclassification. Such misclassification could also reflect agency problems. It would be interesting to test misclassification models on US data.

An overview of empirical work on the choice of mortgage instrument

The introduction to this chapter noted the importance of understanding how individuals, or households, actually choose from the menu of mortgage contracts available to them. Chapter 7 introduced some theoretical explanations for mortgage contract heterogeneity. These ranged from the desire to achieve a preferred payment profile to establishing a separating equilibrium in the mortgage market. In many ways theory has raced ahead of empirical application in this area. However, empirical research has revealed a number of important influences upon mortgage choices. This is particularly true of interest rate variables such as the FRM–ARM premium, and the term structure of interest rates. The discussion in Chapter 7 noted how different perspectives on affordability, or portfolio considerations could generate different models. For example, the importance of various covariances in the latter case.

Affordability is a key aspect of mortgage choice in both US and UK research. Brueckner (1993) predicted that at low interest rates FRM take up would be higher, a result that is generally confirmed. Borrowers will be more willing to lock in at low interest rates, though the possibility that borrowers may adopt regressive interest rate expectations should also be considered (Jones *et al.* 1995; Leece 2000a, 2001a). Interestingly, the Brueckner model also indicated a high take up of FRMs when the term structure was flat, that is when borrowers may be less worried about the gradient of their anticipated payment profile. The latter prediction was contradicted by two studies (Brueckner & Follain 1988 and Dhillon *et al.* 1987), albeit weakly, but more recent research by Phillips & Vanderhoff (1992) has suggested that the result may hold. Cursory evidence from the UK (see Figure 8.1 and discussion) also indicates the importance of affordability. It may be advisable to estimate disaggregated equations, or model interactions, to capture variations in behaviour between households.

The choice of mortgage instrument is invariably complex and some models have yet to be explicitly tested. For example, the theoretical simulations of Alm & Follain (1987) stress the covariance of house prices, incomes, inflation and mortgage interest rates. Data problems have probably been the main contributor to the lack of empirical testing of these relationships. Similarly more recent theoretical work on the role of different mortgage instruments as signals has not yet received full econometric treatment. However, there is some evidence that default and prepayment behaviour do vary by mortgage instrument (e.g. Ambrose & LaCour Little 2001). There is scope for considerably more empirical research in the area of signalling and screening via mortgage instrument choice.

For the UK Leece (2000b) has suggested that the endowment/repayment choice could reflect a sorting into liquidity and not-liquidity constrained borrowers, indicating a broader range of characteristics that might be signalled through mortgage choice. The issue of self-selection that arises out of separating equilibrium has important implications, not only for a better understanding of household behaviour, but also in forecasting the variability of cash flows to the securitised mortgage market, and thus the valuation of mortgage-backed securities. There are also implications for consumer welfare, for example the possibility of mortgage rationing for some borrowers, or even the inducement to borrow more than necessary under a full information credit market equilibrium. Though there is some empirical investigation of these matters (Harrison *et al.* 2004) more investigations are needed.

The analysis of lender behaviour also requires more extensive treatment. The work of Jones *et al.* (1995) is particularly important in incorporating the supply side of the mortgage market into the analysis of mortgage instrument choice. The authors argue that during periods when the term structure of interest rates is steep, that is interest rate increases are anticipated, US lenders encourage the take up of adjustable rather than fixed rate mortgages. The importance of supply side behaviour was also suggested in the discussion of complications arising out of the wide variety of contracts available. Agency problems and 'mis-selling' should also be part of any research agenda into mortgage choices. In a world where markets are not complete and there are significant information problems consumer welfare may be materially effected by the choice of mortgage instruments available, and the influences exerted upon the choice.

Summary and conclusions

The emphasis both in Chapter 7, and in this chapter, has been upon the basis of mortgage contract heterogeneity. In some world views correctly priced mortgage contracts should leave borrowers indifferent between them, and most models assume that this is the case for lenders. Thus if borrowers are observed to be making systematic choices then understanding the basis upon which they do this is important, and reflects upon the rationale for the existence of a variety of contract designs. The existence of systematic determinants of choice between different types of mortgage instrument also raises the possibility that this choice and mortgage/housing demand are simultaneously determined, though there is no evidence of this as yet for the UK.

The differences in the housing finance systems of the US and the UK was evident in both the different menus of mortgage contracts available, and the different findings of empirical research into the choice of mortgage instrument. Generally US research had found for the importance of the premium on fixed rate debt and long-term interest rate expectations evident in the term structure of interest rates. The UK research had highlighted the short-term perspective of decision making, and the focus on movements in short-term interest rates. This was partly the result of the contract choices available, such as short-term rather than long-term fixed rate debt, also through the treatment of prepayment risk through redemption penalties. There remains much more interesting research to be done on the short-versus long-run perspective in borrowers' choices and how this varies between housing finance systems.

One common factor between the US and UK was the wide range of mortgage instruments available. Contract heterogeneity also suggested two areas that merited much further research. First, the actual degree of substitutability between mortgage types and the link with search costs. Second, the consequences of increased consumer choice for potential problems in measurement and econometric estimation of choice models, together with the problems of asymmetric information and agency problems that estimates of misclassification might also be detecting. The heterogeneity of mortgage contract design has other implications. For example, loan performance, that is default and prepayment behaviour, might differ by mortgage type. However, before assessing the role of contract design further, there is a need to examine the basis of mortgage valuation and its links to prepayment and default.

Guide to further reading

For a clear discussion of some of the technical issues involved in the simultaneity of mortgage demand and the choice of mortgage instrument the student can do no better than read the seminal piece by Brueckner & Follain (1988). For a further exposition of the issues involved in detecting and correcting for classification error in a discrete dependent variable then see Hausmann & Scott Morton (1994), and for an application to mortgage choices including correction using 'jack-knife after bootstrap' see Leece (2001a). Research into the choice of mortgage instrument has been sparse in recent years, further research in this important area is eagerly awaited.

Notes

1 For example, it has been argued that the ARM increases aggregate housing demand and reduces the interest rate elasticity of housing demand (Goodman 1992, p. 1).
2 If the premium is viewed simply as a relative cost then interest rate expectations are typically modelled using a variable reflecting the term structure of interest rates, with variations in expectations assumed to be captured by the error term.
3 For example, the presence of children in a household is used as an indicator of risk aversion, and the discount rate; age is used as a measure of expected increases in income.
4 This result, of course, contradicts the usual cross sectional finding where estimation relies upon variations in mortgage costs across states with expectations assumed constant across individuals.
5 Also, see Green & Shilling (1997).
6 See the discussion in Chapter 7.
7 Interestingly, Brueckner & Follain (1988) find that the expansion of ARMs in the early 1980s had little to do with aggressive pricing and low 'teaser rates' but rather emerged from affordability and liquidity issues associated with the general level of interest rates (Brueckner & Follain 1987, p. 100).
8 This result may be specific to the time period studied as later developments such as heavy discounting of variable rate debt encouraged younger households to take up this form of mortgage contract.
9 Of course, this explanation is not incompatible with a simple affordability argument where at low rates the advantage of adopting cheaper ARMs (VRM) is less. However, given the inherent variability of the VRM, some short-run expectations mechanism is likely to be important for cash constrained borrowers. In a sense this is also emphasised by the importance of the degree of apparent stickiness of the VRM rate.

10 The difference between the FRM–VRM in this case also reflects discounts or 'teaser rates' which will be relevant when the premium is positive thus dampening demand for the FRM.

11 It is worth noting that the Canadian mortgage market exhibits similar contractual features to that in the United Kingdom (see Breslaw *et al.* 1996).

12 Equation (8.1) gives a standard probit log likelihood function. Equation (8.2) gives the same equation amended to incorporate estimates of the degree of classification error.

$$\ln L = \sum_{y=0_i} \ln\left[1 - \Phi(\beta'x_i)\right] + \sum_{y_i=1} \ln \Phi(\beta'x_i) \tag{8.1}$$

$$\ln L = \sum_{y=0_i} \ln\left[(1 - \alpha) + (2\alpha - 1)^* \Phi(\beta'x_i)\right] + \sum_{y_i=1} \ln\left[\alpha + (1 - 2\alpha)^* \Phi(\beta'x_i)\right] \tag{8.2}$$

For equations (8.1) and (8.2) β are the parameters to be estimated and x is the vector of independent variables. The usual standard normal probability distribution function Φ applies. The probit given in equation (8.1) is modified to allow for the endogenous determination of the extent of classification error (see Hausmann & Scott Morton 1994; Leece 2000a, 2001a). This involves estimation of the amended log likelihood given in equation (8.2); where α is the probability that an observation is misclassified. The particular correction given in expression (8.2) assumes that classification error is equally balanced between observations coded 1 or 0; other modifications are possible.

13 For a discussion of this technique see Efron & Tibshirani (1993).

14 It is important to note that classification error of this type is not determined by any missing variable and is more than the usual random error. With classification error in the dependent variable choices which would otherwise have a high probability of being coded correctly are incorrectly coded, as opposed to differences in classification through random error.

15 This perspective suggests that there is indeed an underlying or 'deep model' that constitutes the appropriate choice framework and that problems arising out of information asymmetry reveal themselves in subsequent biases. Leece (2000b) has demonstrated that information asymmetry between lender and borrower can be so high that agency problems lead to pathological mis-selling where the 'deep model' is not retrievable.

16 An exception, at least implicitly, is the findings of Goodman (1992) who in a time series study, notes that the introduction of the ARM had little effect on aggregate mortgage demand.

9

The Risky Mortgage Contract and Embedded Options: Mortgage Valuation and Household Behaviour

Introduction

This chapter explores the option theoretic approach to decision making and considers how a mortgage can be valued using the option valuation models developed in financial economics. Mortgages are particularly complex financial instruments to value and to price. The analysis requires several critical assumptions regarding the nature of the economic environment. There are no arbitrage opportunities, both borrowers and lenders are risk-neutral and there is no asymmetric information. Adopting an option theoretic approach to mortgage valuation can give important insights into the prepayment and default decisions of wealth-maximising households, it provides an important rationale for the study of these behaviours, that is the valuation of mortgage-backed securities. Lenders may benefit from knowing the prepayment (interest rate) risk of their portfolios of debt and mortgage-backed securities (Follain *et al.* 1992). Adopting this approach also offers some key insights into the basis of mortgage design.

The chapter begins with an overview of the approach to mortgage valuation and introduces the idea of the risky mortgage. Modelling stochastic behaviour is fundamental to valuing assets based upon contingent claims. Having demonstrated the general approach to valuing mortgage debt, and presented the stochastic differential equation that determines its value, the chapter considers the conditions (that is, boundary conditions) that fix the critical values of key variables. For example, the mortgage interest rate and the house price at which default and prepayment become optimal. To render this complex material accessible there is an emphasis upon diagrammatic treatment. However, there are several key equations and mathematical expressions that make it helpful to broadly understand.

An overview of the option theoretic approach to mortgage valuation

The valuation of a mortgage contract can be seen as the value of three different forms of security. The actual contract terms, and the discounted cash flows to the lender (using the current market rate of interest) can be represented as a non-callable bond. However, the borrower has both the option to prepay or to default on the mortgage. The option to default is a put option involving the possibility of selling the property back to the lender to repay the outstanding debt. The option to prepay is a call option involving the possibility of buying back the outstanding mortgage balance by prepaying the debt early. Consequently, the value of a mortgage is a composite of the non-callable bond, the call and the put option. An example of a mortgage option having value is a fixed rate mortgage which looks expensive at current interest rates. This makes prepayment look desirable, but if this was done then the option to default and the chance of refinancing under even more favourable terms would be lost.

The modelling presented in this chapter is based upon the idea that the household maximises its wealth by minimising the value of its mortgage debt. So what is meant by the value of a mortgage? Take the example of a household with a fixed rate contract. The cash flows on this contract can be discounted at the current market rate of interest. Assume that the current mortgage rate is lower than the contract rate. Discounting the mortgage payments at the current mortgage rate, over its expected life, will increase the present value of the cash flows. A wealth maximising mortgage holder will be tempted to quit this contract and adopt an alternative lower value mortgage. Remember that prepayment might not take place depending upon the values of the embedded call and put options. The value of these options reduces the value of the mortgage to the borrower. That is, they are benefits that reduce the liability.

$$NV(r, k) = A(r, k) - BOOK \qquad (9.1)$$

If the fixed rate on the mortgage is equal to the current market rate of interest then the discounted present value of future cash flows on that contract will equal the amount borrowed, or book value. Thus mortgage valuation also offers an implicit pricing formulae for a mortgage, that is setting a price where the value of the debt equals the current loan balance.

This equality requires that the term structure of interest rates is flat, that is there is no expectation of increases in interest rates and no premium for this in the price. Given this, then equation (9.1) represents the net value of a mortgage $NV(r, k)$. This is defined for a current market rate of interest r, and the time to maturity k. The net value is the difference between the cash flows due on the current contract discounted at the market rate of interest $A(r, k)$ and the book value ($BOOK$). The wealth maximising household will wish to minimise this difference. The net value in equation (9.1) can be alternatively described as the extent to which the option to prepay is 'in the money', or the intrinsic value of the debt. However, we also need to consider the value of the options to prepay or default, together with transaction costs arising from mortgage termination.

Kau *et al.* (1992) present a nice general form for the effects of prepayment and default on gross mortgage value. Expression (9.2) represents the value of a mortgage in terms of the noted present value of the contractual payments on the mortgage $A(r, k)$ discounted at the current spot rate of interest r, less a joint possibility of default or prepayment $J(r, H, k)$. Equation (9.3) shows the joint probability to consist of the put option to default $D(r, H, k)$ and the call option to prepay $C(r, H, k)$. The arguments in parenthesis are the variables that determine the value of the non-callable bond and the options. These are the interest rate r, the time to maturity k, and an additional factor influencing the value of both the call and the put option, the house price H. Note that time is represented in a variety of ways in the literature, being the age of the mortgage, current point of time, time to maturity and time of maturity. For purposes of consistency the discussion in this chapter generally uses the time to maturity, k, to represent time, the other indicators being implicit in this measure.

The value of the mortgage given by $V(r, H, k)$ in expression (9.2) can be described as the value of the risky mortgage, or a callable (and with Federal guarantees default free) bond. Clearly the value of the risky mortgage is a function of the stochastic behaviour of interest rates and house prices, that is, it is the stochastic behaviour of these variables that effects size of pay offs to the options. Having examined the components of the value of the risky mortgage, the discussion of prepayment and default, later in this chapter, will return to the kind of comparison made in expression (9.1). The contractual terms of the mortgage contract determine the boundary conditions for any option valuation model.

There are two important things to note regarding the general expression for the mortgage value given in expression (9.2). First, prepayment and default decisions are determined endogenously by the variables r, k and H.

This means that prepayment and default are treated as functions of these financial variables. However, some prepayment and default can arise out of exogenous effects, for example, moving house when the mortgage is not assumable will generate a prepayment. Equally, adverse life events such as unemployment may induce default. For the moment such factors are ignored and the focus is upon the financial calculations implied by the option theoretic approach.

$$V(r, H, k) = A(r, k) - J(r, H, k) \tag{9.2}$$

$$J(r, H, k) = D(r, H, k) + C(r, H, k) \tag{9.3}$$

The second point to note is that the prepayment and default decisions are interdependent. For example, exercising the default option precludes exercising the prepayment option. This is the reason for including house price behaviour in the prepayment function, that is at very low house prices default will dominate. In empirical work this interdependence has been recognised by the estimation of so called competing risk models, a topic to be considered in Chapter 10. The links between the prepayment and default decision are discussed below.

Of course, the valuation of mortgage-backed securities depends upon the valuation of the underlying risky asset (the mortgage). The value of this pass through security is modelled in the same way as the underlying mortgage. However, the cash flows to the pass through security holder are different. Pay outs on the MBS must reflect the fact that mortgage terminations lead to a return of the outstanding balance. It is worth noting that from the MBS security holders' perspective default and prepayment has the same effect, that is they are both terminations of cash flows. The main point is that the valuation of the MBS depends upon the prepayment and default behaviour of the underlying mortgage holders (Schwartz & Torous 1992). There are a number of alternative contingent claims models for valuing residential mortgages and pass through securities. These mainly differ in the number of variables used. Chatterjee *et al.* (1998) find models with the two variables, short rate of interest and building value, to be the most efficient. The discussion which follows uses these two state variables.

The stochastic economic environment

The pure financial decisions to default or prepay are examined in the context of a particular economic environment. The economy is assumed to be perfectly competitive and frictionless. There are no capital market imperfections of the kind considered in previous chapters. This perfectly competitive economy is one where it is not possible for traders in financial assets to arbitrage by taking profits on risky securities. Under these circumstances risk adjustments can be made to the price of risky assets such that their rate of return equals the risk-free rate of interest. In the absence of arbitrage all traders can adopt long or short positions in securities to obtain the risk-free rate of return. These risk adjustments are important because we can now value a security (mortgage) by discounting its expected cash flows at the risk-free rate of interest, equivalent to assuming that both borrowers and lenders are risk-neutral.

The general discussion of the option theoretic approach to valuing the risky mortgage noted the role of r and H in determining value. These are the state variables and it is the stochastic behaviour of interest rates and house prices that underpins the option-like characteristics of the risky mortgage. For example, interest rate volatility will determine the value of the option to prepay. It is assumed that the value of the contingent security (the mortgage) has no effect on the fundamental determinants of asset prices (e.g. house price). This analytical framework also means that the personal characteristics and preferences of individuals have no impact upon the value of the risky mortgage.

How then can we represent the stochastic behaviour of the state variables, which underpin mortgage valuation? Equation (9.4) represents the expected behaviour of interest rates. Interest rate changes, dr, are expected to occur at a rate $\mu_r(r, H, t)$ where r is the spot rate of interest, H is the level of house prices and t is a point of time t. The argument $\sigma_t(r, H, t)$ is the instantaneously adjusted standard deviation. The term dz_r is a Wiener process, which ensures that interest rate changes proceed in a random independently distributed unbiased manner, that is they follow Brownian motion. Equation (9.5) shows the same process for the stochastic determination of house prices, dH. The disturbance terms of interest rate and house price changes dz_r, dz_H may also be correlated through $\rho(r, H, t)$.

$$dr = \mu_r(r, H, t)dt + \sigma_r(r, H, t)dz_r \qquad (9.4)$$

$$dH = \mu_H(r, H, t)dt + \sigma_H(r, H, t)dz_H \qquad (9.5)$$

In a perfectly competitive no arbitrage economy continuously traded assets have an expected rate of return that equals the risk-free rate of interest. This is not a problem when we treat property as a continuously traded asset. Finding a risk adjustment for interest rates is a problem because a positive term structure with interest rates expected to rise can lead to a risk premium added to the current rate. In this case the no arbitrage modelling becomes extremely complex. One solution is to assume that the spot rate of interest contains all of the information implicit in the term structure. This is known as the Local Expectations Hypothesis (LEH).[1] This is the assumption adopted here.

The analysis has now established how the state variables behave stochastically through time, and noted that in a perfectly competitive no arbitrage economy risk-neutrality can be assumed. The general framework for evaluating the value of a mortgage can now be considered. That is, the expected value of the risky mortgage can be determined. This in turn will offer important insights into the default and prepayment decisions of households and the relationship between them.

Valuing a mortgage: the general framework

How then does the stochastic behaviour of the interest rate and house prices generate the value of a mortgage in an option's valuation framework? Equation (9.6) represents a general Black–Scholes valuation equation for a derivative asset, in this case the previously defined risky mortgage. The expression presents the present value of a mortgage $V(r, H, t)$ at time t, with an expected terminal value of $\overline{V}(r, H, T)$, discounted continuously at the risk-free rate of interest,

$$\left(e^{-\int_k^T \tilde{r}(t)dt}\right),$$

from the terminal date T. The expected value is a function of the final values of the two state variables H and r emerging from the stochastic processes given by equations (9.4) and (9.5). The term $\hat{E}$ is the expectations operator, the 'hat' indicating that the expected cash flows have been appropriately adjusted for the price of risk.

$$V(r, H, t) = \hat{E}[e^{-\int_t^T \tilde{r}(t)dt}\overline{V}(r, H, T)] \tag{9.6}$$

Equation (9.6) offers a way of understanding the nature of mortgage valuation in a perfectly competitive no arbitrage economy. However, the approach implies a method of solution, that is looking forward in time to the terminal value (see Kau & Keenan 1995; Schwartz & Torous 1989a, 1989b,

1991).[2] What would be useful is a means of backward rather than forward calculation. Forward calculation usually involves a projection of interest rate and house price paths using say a Monte Carlo simulation. This exercise involves a fundamental contradiction. The future value of a mortgage depends upon the termination date, which depends in turn on the decision to prepay or default. However, the decision to prepay or default depends upon the value of the mortgage. Though not without its own difficulties, backward calculation from a given terminal value does overcome this logical problem. The backward calculation begins with the known terminal value at which the mortgage matures, and works back incrementally to give a value of the mortgage at the initial interest rate and house price.

It should be noted here that there is a significant difference between the option to prepay and the option to default. The option to prepay can be exercised at any time. This makes the prepayment option equivalent to the so called American option for which there is no specific expiry date. In contrast it is not sensible to exercise the option to default having just made a mortgage payment. Therefore the default option is reviewed at the end of each payment period when the payment is actually due. In this sense there is not a single default option but a series of European-type options, that is options that have specific dates when they expire. Solving for the value-of the default option, say by using numerical analysis, then the value of the default option both before and after the last payment must be identified.

A method of evaluating equation (9.6) that involves backward calculation is represented by the second order differential equation given by (9.7) where equation (9.6) is a solution to this equation. This is the so called fundamental equation and it is based upon the no arbitrage solution that any security whose value depends upon contingent claims will have an expected return equal to the risk-free rate of return plus a risk adjustment. The value of any mortgage will still equal the risk adjusted present value of its expected net cash flows, as indicated in (9.6). The variables in equation (9.7) are as previously defined.[3] This equation can be solved using numerical methods. Some researchers have preferred to use the discrete time binomial pricing method. For a lucid application of this approach see Follain *et al.* (1992) and Kau & Keenan (1995) for a comparison of solutions involving assumptions of discrete or continuous time.[4]

$$\frac{1}{2}\sigma_r^2 \frac{\partial^2 V}{\partial r^2} + \rho\sigma_r\sigma_H \frac{\partial^2 V}{\partial r\partial H} + \frac{1}{2}\sigma_H^2 \frac{\partial^2 V}{\partial H^2} + \mu_r \frac{\partial V}{\partial r} + (r-s)H \frac{\partial V}{\partial t} + \frac{\partial V}{\partial t} - rV = 0$$

$$(9.7)$$

The discussion, which follows, will utilise the fundamental equation given by expression (9.7), though the explanation will also involve representing this equation graphically. The boundary conditions, which determine optimum prepayment and default, arise from the terms of the mortgage contract (e.g. the coupon rate). These termination decisions will be explored on the assumption that borrowers are wealth maximisers. The analysis will also proceed on the assumption that the mortgage is a fixed rate instrument. The implications of an adjustable or variable rate mortgage for mortgage valuation are discussed later in the chapter. The emphasis throughout is on the implications of the option theoretic framework for the analysis and prediction of household behaviour in the mortgage market.

The prepayment behaviour of the wealth maximising borrower

The option theoretic approach to mortgage valuation offers an explanation of prepayment behaviour. This behaviour results from breaching a boundary condition for the value of a risky mortgage involving those values of H and r which induce prepayment. This boundary is known as a free boundary because the borrower can prepay the debt at any time during the life of the current mortgage contract, and will do so depending upon the combination of r and H. This is the main reason why we work backwards to estimate the current mortgage value. The decision to prepay depends upon the future value of the mortgage so that working backwards allows the conditions when prepayment is likely to take place to be determined. This also has the important implication that the decision to prepay a mortgage depends not only upon whether it is currently 'in the money' but also upon the anticipated future values of H and r, and thus the value of the option to prepay.

The analysis in this, and the following section, proceeds on the assumption that prepayment and default are separate decisions. This is particularly useful when presenting diagrammatic explanations of either prepayment or default behaviour. We also retain the focus upon prepayment which takes place for financial reasons only. In other words, the prepayment decision is endogenously determined within the option based model. Such financial prepayment is compatible with the assumption that the borrower aims to maximise his or her wealth and will prepay when such behaviour is consistent with this objective. Other motives for both prepayment and default will be discussed in Chapter 10.

A call option on a mortgage can be said to be 'in the money' when the value of mortgage exceeds the outstanding balance on the debt (book value), as indicated in expression (9.1). The balance can also be considered the price that the borrower pays to exercise the option to prepay. There are two complications to this view of when a mortgage should be prepaid. It may not always maximise expected wealth to exercise the call option when it is 'in the money'. First, once the option is exercised then it cannot be used again, that is the option has value. Interest rates may fall further in the next period increasing the value of the current debt even further. Second, transaction costs may arise when prepaying the mortgage. Both of these features are readily incorporated into the analysis.

Expression (9.8) follows the logic of Follain *et al.* (1992)[5] and indicates the inequality, which would trigger prepayment. This includes the value of the option to prepay $C(r, k)$, that is we now use the arguments of the risky mortgage, and also include transaction costs TC. The outstanding mortgage balance is denoted by OB (or alternatively book value, $BOOK$). The borrower prepays when the gain on refinancing exceeds the transaction costs of prepayment plus the value of the call option treated as if it is a publicly traded security.

$$A(r, T) - OB \succ C(r, T) + TC \tag{9.8}$$

Green & LaCour Little (1999) make the interesting point that the loss of the value of the call option on prepayment is to some extent offset by the option acquired with the new mortgage. Assuming that these two options cancel out can be a useful device for empirical work where the focus can then be on the pure refinancing strategy subject to transaction costs.[6] Yang & Maris (1996) also offer an interesting perspective by examining the effect of uncertainty regarding the holding period of the mortgage, that is the T in expression (9.8) is considered stochastic. The results of Yang & Maris suggest that the model with certainty underestimates the interest rate differential required to financially justify prepayment. These considerations will be important when we address the issue of why some households do not prepay their mortgage debt when the financial conditions suggest that it is optimal to do so. The question will be whether premature, delayed or non-occurring prepayments represent sub-optimal behaviour.

A diagrammatic treatment of the wealth maximising prepayment decision

Further insight into the decision rule on when to prepay can be gleaned from a diagrammatic treatment of the issue. Figure 9.1 follows Quigley & Van Order (1990) and illustrates the optimal prepayment rule. The dotted line shows the inverse relationship between the value of the non-callable

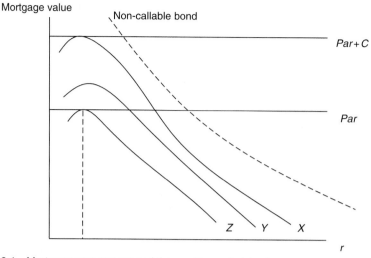

Mortgage value

Non-callable bond

Par+C

Par

Z   Y   X

r

Figure 9.1   Mortgage prepayment and the wealth maximising borrower.

bond component of the mortgage and the current interest rate. This would correspond to the value $A(r, T)$ in expression (9.8). The line labelled *Par* is the par or book value of the mortgage. The mortgage is assumed to be of a given age to maturity. The curves Z, X and Y represent the relationship between the value of a callable mortgage, that is the risky mortgage, and the interest rate. The three curves represent different solutions to equation (9.7) (using just the one state variable r in this case). Adopting the local expectations hypothesis we can interpret changes in the interest rate as changes in the term structure.

There are an infinite number of valuation curves, satisfying equation (9.7). These possibilities reflect the number of ways that the coupon rate and risk adjusted capital gains can be combined to produce the risk-free rate of return. The conditions of the mortgage contract (e.g. the coupon rate) and the face value fix the valuation curve and provide an interior solution where the par or book value provides the boundary. The optimal interest rate r^*, at which prepayment takes place is the point of tangency between the curve representing the value of the callable (risky) mortgage and the par value of the debt. Note that this equality implies that the market has already priced the value of the call option on the mortgage, that is it is presumed to be efficient from the borrower's point of view, no observable surplus accrues to the borrower at this point (Quigley & Van Order 1990).

The curve Z is relevant to the borrower who faces zero transaction costs. The curve X demonstrates the effect of transaction costs. From the borrower's perspective the par value of the debt they face is increased by transactions costs (C). The critical point now is the point of tangency between Y and $(Par + C)$. Introducing transactions costs do not markedly shift the interest rate at which prepayment occurs (r^*) and both points are examples of what is termed 'ruthless prepayment'. Quigley & Van Order note that the existence of transactions costs 'drive a wedge' between what the borrower pays and the lender receives. The curve Y takes the lender perspective whereby the lender only ever receives the par value of a loan at r^* whereas the mortgage is worth more than par to the borrower.

Transaction costs will feature in the empirical analysis of prepayment behaviour. Bennett *et al.* (2000) used the idea of the vega threshold in their theoretical work on prepayment. The vega is a measure of the relationship between the option value and changes in interest rate volatility. The theory suggests that volatility has its greatest impact when an option is 'near the money' rather than 'in the money'. Transaction costs, which may in turn be related to individual and household characteristics shift the value of the vega and increase the optimum refinancing threshold.

The preceding discussion has provided the basis of the option theoretic approach to mortgage prepayment in perfectly competitive markets. Mortgage prepayment can be described as 'ruthless' and is determined endogenously by purely financial considerations. The contractual terms and the outstanding mortgage balance establish the boundary conditions which along with the valuation of the risky mortgage determine the optimum r at which prepayment will take place. However, prepayment is not automatic when a mortgage is 'in the money' because the option to prepay has value. This option will be correctly priced in a perfectly competitive and efficient capital market. The modelling of prepayment behaviour assumed no default. Default behaviour, however, is not trivial and the mortgage valuation literature has paid increasing theoretical and empirical attention to this phenomenon.

The default behaviour of the wealth maximising borrower

The discussion of prepayment behaviour suggested that this could occur for purely financial reasons and be viewed as the 'ruthless' exercise of an option to prepay. Default can occur for many reasons, such as unemployment, and factors impinging upon affordability, or the reduced ability to service a mortgage such as a fall in income. Taking an option theoretic perspective, the exercise of the option to default can also be described as 'ruthless' if it is motivated purely by the maximisation of the borrower's wealth. A default option can be said to be 'in the money' when the value of the property is less than the value of the mortgage debt. However, the option to default also has value and a mortgage, which is 'in the money' in this sense may not necessarily result in default.

The analysis is simplified initially by assuming away the option to prepay. In this case the sole state variable is the house price and the path of this variable and the instantaneous variance of the house price determine the value of the put option to default. However, it will be shown that prepayment behaviour is also important in establishing the boundary conditions for the exercise of the default option. The interest rate is still important but we assume that it is non stochastic. Equation (9.9) expresses the default decision in terms of the inequality necessary for default to take place. Expression (9.9) reminds us that the value of the mortgage is reduced by the value of the option to default $(D(H, k))$ and that this alters the likelihood of default when the default option is 'in the money' (that is when the value of the non-callable bond exceeds the value of the house). Transactions costs, TC, must also be covered before default is triggered.

$$A(r, k) \succ H + D(H, k) + TC \tag{9.9}$$

A diagrammatic treatment of the wealth maximising default decision

Quigley & Van Order (1995) present a diagrammatic treatment of default behaviour when the interest rate is assumed to be non-stochastic. This is demonstrated in Figure 9.2. The horizontal line M is the value of the

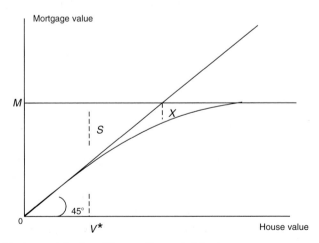

Figure 9.2   Mortgage default and the wealth maximising borrower.

Source: Quigley, J.H. & R. Van Order (1995) Explicit tests of contingent claims models of mortgage default, *Journal of Real Estate Finance and Economics* 11: 99–117.

riskless mortgage, that is a non-callable bond. The 45° line represents points where the balance of a mortgage equals the value of the house. Thus points where M is above this 45° line mean that the riskless mortgage is greater than the value of the house. However, default will not necessarily take place because the option to default itself has value. To determine the conditions for optimal default we must examine the value of the risky mortgage. This is represented by a PDE curve, which in this case is the lowest curve that satisfies the PDE given by equation (9.7) (with a known interest rate). The curve shows the relationship between the state variable (house value) and the value of the mortgage. Note that for a given book value of debt then different house prices represent different loan-to-value ratios, a key variable in the empirical analysis of default.

The distance X denotes the value of the option to default. This distance becomes zero at the point of tangency between the PDF and the 45° line and default takes place. Optimal default occurs therefore at V^* where the value of the mortgage is minimised. Also at this point the house is of sufficient value to cover the remaining mortgage balance after deducting the expected loss to the lender from default (S). The distance S is the amount by which the option must be 'in the money' at default. The PDE asymptotes towards the value of the riskless mortgage, that is the option to default approaches zero value as the value of the property increases. The extent to which the option is 'in the money' (X), is the amount that a competitive mortgage insurer would charge to cover the risk of mortgage default.

The model assumes that there are no transaction costs and no adverse effects on credit ratings arising from default, so called reputation costs, though these are easily incorporated into the analysis (see expression (9.10)). However, the approach clearly demonstrates the case of 'ruthless' default by the wealth maximising household. Default occurs when the value of the risky mortgage is less than the value of the house. There are similarities here with 'ruthless' exercise of the prepayment option where the option value must be entered into the equation. However, as earlier discussion suggested, the separate treatment of prepayment and default behaviour can be a little misleading. Closer analysis reveals some important interactions between these two phenomena.

The links between prepayment and default behaviour

Research using numerical simulation focuses upon the effects of changes in the state variables, and their volatilities, upon the value of the risky mortgage debt (Kau & Keenan 1995; Pereira *et al.* 2002). This involves analysis of the different components of the risky mortgage, that is the embedded options and the value of the cash flows on the debt. Default and prepayment are seen as a joint probability of mortgage termination. A related consideration, and the main focus of empirical work, is the likely rates of default and prepayment. Numerical analysis offers insights into interactions between prepayment and default value, and thus mortgage termination behaviour (Schwartz & Torous 1992).

It is necessary to examine the relationship between each of the components of mortgage value, including the value of the non-callable bond (discounted payments). These in turn determine the overall value of the risky debt which is a key element in the option to prepay or default (see Figure 9.1 and Figure 9.2). Thus the interactions can be quite complex and ultimately have a bearing upon the fair pricing of a mortgage and the valuation of insurance; default insurance in the US (Kau *et al.* 1993) and mortgage indemnity guarantees in the UK (Pereira *et al.* 2002, 2003).

It is useful to think in terms of different regions, delineated by combinations of the interest rate and house price, were the values of one or the other of the options to terminate dominates. Correspondingly, the likelihood of observing prepayment or default behaviour will vary in interest rate/house price space (Deng *et al.* 2000). For example, numerical analysis reveals that at low interest rates and high house prices the value of the prepayment option is high (Pereira *et al.* 2002). This is because when house prices are high the value of the default option is low and default is less likely.

Schwartz & Torous (1992) show that at low interest rates it is possible to have a mortgage value which exceeds the value of the property, which suggests default, and a house value which is greater than the mortgage balance which would argue against default. So the household would not be facing negative equity but the interest rate charge on alternative debt would be so low that it raises the value of the current mortgage above the value of the property. In theory both the value of the mortgage and the balance must be lower than the value of the property (see Figure 9.2) before default occurs. When the constraints are inconsistent in this way prepayment will dominate. Schwartz & Torous also note that at low house prices default is likely to dominate prepayment, reducing the likelihood of prepayment to zero.

Changes in the economic environment are represented by changes in interest rate and house price volatility. Increased interest rate volatility, *ceteris paribus*, raises the value of the option to prepay. Increased house price volatility, *ceteris paribus*, raises the value of the option to default. Thus the effects on the value of the risky mortgage depend upon the impact of the respective volatilities on the value of the components of the joint option to terminate. The volatility of interest rates also effects the value of the cash flows attached to the debt. Higher volatility of interest rates should increase the value of the cash flows to the mortgage. This effect occurs because the relationship between the net present value of the fixed cash flows and the discount rate is convex, so that lower discount rate outcomes have a comparatively high positive impact on NPV. However, greater interest rate volatility reduces the value of the risky mortgage via the option values, reducing the likelihood of default and prepayment.[7]

Increased house price volatility has no impact upon the value of cash flows attributable to the mortgage. However, higher house price volatility increases the value of the option to default at the expense of the option to prepay. With greater volatility of house prices it is more likely that a change in the house price would reach the default region (Pereira *et al.* 2002). Consequently, the value of the risky mortgage will fall with increases in house price volatility. This in turn makes prepayment less likely. These effects and the other possibilities discussed above demonstrate the complexity and competing nature of the interactions between default and prepayment behaviour. However, the analysis so far has been in terms of a fixed rate mortgage, a key question is how far option theoretic arguments apply to mortgage designs other than the FRM?

The valuation of alternative mortgage instruments and household behaviour

The analysis so far has focused on the case of a conventional (for the US) fixed rate mortgage. Given the importance of the adjustable rate mortgage in the US then the question naturally arises as to the implications of more frequent interest rate adjustments for the valuation of an ARM mortgage contract. This is also true of the variable rate mortgage (VRM) in the UK. In addition, the fixed rate mortgage in the UK has some distinctive features (Pereira *et al.* 2002); for example, the payment of redemption penalties on refinancing. Examining variations in termination behaviour by mortgage instrument further highlights the interaction between prepayment and default option values.

Many aspects of the valuation procedure remain the same. We still need to identify the underlying stochastic processes, which will determine the likely economic environment when the contract is terminated. The value of any contingent claim will still be determined by the second order partial differential equation given in expression (9.7) above. The interesting features for the ARM are the presence of caps, collars and 'teaser rates'. In the case of equality between the cap and the collar we effectively have the FRM which can be described as a 'degenerate'[8] ARM contract (Kau *et al.* 1993). The presence of caps and collars and/or 'teaser rates' mean that the option to prepay has value for the ARM borrower.

There is one critical problem with using the PDE for a contingent contract to value an adjustable rate mortgage. This is the problem of path dependency. Recall that backward solutions for the PDE are usually preferred. In the case of the ARM with a cap and a collar the coupon rate charged at the beginning of each new period will depend on past experience, that is it depends upon whether the cap or the floor were breached by the then current mortgage rate. Kau *et al.* adopt the ingenious solution of using a further (auxiliary) stochastically varying state variable, the past coupon rate. This device effectively controls for the whole range of possible past values of the coupon.[9]

A precise analysis of the financial behaviour of the ARM holder requires an evaluation of the comparative statics of the option theoretic/mortgage valuation model. Once again this usually involves numerical simulation. Collin-Dufresne & Harding (1999) do offer a closed form solution for valuing mortgages, though there are a number of severe restrictions including the use of just one state variable.[10] Kau *et al.* use numerical simulation to demonstrate the comparative statics of an ARM valuation model. The analysis reveals some fascinating interaction between the value of the options to prepay and default, in addition to presenting some specific theoretical predictions.

Kau *et al.*'s analysis confirms the usual expectations of default models, that is that the value of default is higher the greater the loan-to-value ratio, the lower the house price and the greater house price volatility. The value of the default option for an ARM is similar to that of an FRM. However, one of the most interesting findings is the large impact of 'teaser rates'. These significantly increase the prepayment rate. Rapid prepayment then reduces the expected life of mortgage loans, which insulates decisions from the effect of interest rate volatility. Prepayment is further encouraged by the reversion to a higher rate of interest when the 'teaser rate' finishes, that is on the reset date. The higher rate is, of course, compensation to lenders for the high prepayments that initial discounts induce. These are theoretical predictions that can be subject to empirical testing (see Ambrose & LaCour Little 2001).

The discussion in the previous section noted how increased interest rate volatility reduced the value of the mortgage through an increase in the value of the option to prepay. One reason for this is that the par value of the mortgage provides an upper bound on the value of the prepayment option. This produced the concave portion of the mortgage value graph at low interest rates (see Figure 9.1). Thus increased volatility in this region is more likely to place the option to prepay 'in the money'. This result also applies to interest rate caps on ARMs and the value function becomes concave around the point where the cap binds. Thus the major effects of interest rate caps are to introduce some of the changes in value and termination behaviour associated with fixed rate debt.

Chinloy (1995) and Periera *et al.* (2002, 2003) have undertaken theoretical modelling of mortgage valuation that incorporates mortgage contracts more typical of the UK. Chinloy examines the endowment mortgage, focusing upon the fact that the rate of interest is variable rather than fixed. This means that the UK borrower faces potential liquidity and affordability problems. Given that prepayment risk is not evident the analysis considers default risk that arises from both wealth maximising and liquidity constrained behaviour. Empirically, for the early 1990s, both the loan-to-value ratio and borrowers' real income were found to determine default. Prepayment risk was not considered relevant to an analysis of UK mortgage termination behaviour at that time.

Periara *et al.* (2002) examines the United Kingdom fixed rate mortgage where both the option to prepay and default have value. The numerical simulation incorporates the particular characteristics of UK fixed rate contracts, that is front loaded arrangement fees (equivalent to US points) and redemption penalties on prepayment. The paper applies a different form of backward calculation than that typical of US work, which is an explicit finance difference method. The model values the various components of the UK fixed rate repayment contract including third party insurance, and the lender's liability consequent to mortgage default. A main difference between UK and US contracts is the nature of default insurance. In the UK only part of the debt is insured against default and charged to the borrower with the residual risk laid off to insurers. Periara *et al.* also value this feature of UK contracts.

The option theoretic approach can be applied in the valuation of a range of different mortgage instruments. The numerical simulations discussed in this chapter can also be used to value and price the different components of a mortgage contract. For example, caps and collars, redemption penalties, mortgage insurance. Thus, while previous chapters have noted the importance of risk sharing and signalling for mortgage design, it is also true that the valuation of the different components of mortgage contracts offers a basis for design and an explanation for the variety of current contracts available.

There are several perspectives on how default and prepayment behaviour might vary by mortgage instrument. The mortgage termination literature has been concerned with the impact of household mobility on FRM/ARM mortgage terminations (see Vanderhoff 1996). Recent work on separating equilibrium based upon the FRM/ARM choice indicates that default probabilities arising from affordability problems can be signalled by the choice of mortgage instrument (Posey & Yavas 2001). In this case default probabilities are predicted to be higher for the ARM. It is also possible that households prepay a debt by switching between mortgage instruments, perhaps reflecting changes in their interest rate expectations (McConnell & Singh 1994). These perspectives differ from the pure option theoretical approach and invite recourse to empirical analysis, a matter for Chapter 10.

Summary and conclusions

The discussion in this chapter has outlined how a mortgage can be valued using an option theoretic framework. The building blocks of a mortgage where a non-callable bond plus a call option to prepay and a put option to default. Mortgage valuation was examined in the context of a stochastic economic environment where mortgage debt was a contingent claim. This led to the idea of the risky mortgage. The economic environment was also assumed to be a perfectly competitive economy with no arbitrage opportunities. These assumptions facilitated the analysis of the optimal prepayment and default decisions. Prepayment was a negative function of the current mortgage interest rate. Default was a positive function of the loan-to-value ratio, that is a negative function of housing equity.

An important consideration was the interaction between the prepayment and default options. It was possible that either default or prepayment could dominate depending upon the particular configuration of the house price and interest rates. This argued for viewing prepayment and default as competing risks, an issue of great significance for empirical estimation. Numerical simulations were able to capture these interactions and discriminate between prepayment and default behaviour for different mortgage instruments. The ARM with caps and collars became more like the FRM, while 'teaser rates' gave prepayment value to ARM and VRM contracts. The option theoretic framework could usefully inform decisions on the incorporation and valuation of these different features of mortgage design.

The prepayment and default decisions were based on the notion of 'ruthless' financial behaviour. That is the decisions were endogenously determined and explained by the option theoretical approach. The existence of capital market and other imperfections could reinstate the importance of personal characteristics and transaction costs might vary by individual. Affordability may also need to be viewed as a possible explanation of observed default and prepayment behaviour. The discussion now turns to the empirical evidence to determine how well the option theoretic approach explains the observed prepayment and default decisions of households.

Guide to further reading

Readers who are not familiar with the theory of options would do well to consult an introductory textbook on finance that discusses option theory. There are many such books, but the author would recommend the introduction to mathematical finance by Ross (1999). This book also presents a lucid account of the nature and significance of the no arbitrage assumptions.

The clearest and most comprehensive exposition of the option theoretic approach to mortgage valuation is the review paper by Kau & Keenan (1995). This work is a 'must read' for any serious student of mortgage market analysis. The paper examines both the underlying option theory, and the choices among numerical methods used to calculate the value of a mortgage. Further exposition of the diagrams used to depict optimal prepayment and default discussed in this text can be found in the respective papers by Quigley & Van Order (1990) and Schwartz & Torous (1992). Many of the empirical papers to be reviewed in Chapter 10 begin with an outline of the basic mortgage valuation model. Thus the student of mortgage market economics will find the option theoretic approach to prepayment and default behaviour an extremely well rehearsed argument. Anyone wishing to further ponder the relevance of US mortgage valuation research for the UK can profitably read Periera *et al.* (2002, 2003).

Notes

1 Assuming that interest rates tend to adjust to a mean value (Cox *et al.* 1985) also overcomes the term structure problem by absorbing risk premiums into other parameters.

2 A solution to this forward looking equation would involve the use of a Monte Carlo simulation to estimate the range of possible interest rate and house price paths and their impact upon mortgage value subsequently taking the estimated mean values to calculate the discounted present value of the debt.

3 Note also that the assumption of risk neutrality means that equation (9.4) does not contain either the expected rate of house price inflation or a risk premium for holding housing as an asset.

4 McConnell & Singh (1994) use a dynamic programming approach to backward solution that offers an alternative technique.

5 The notation used in previous equations is retained, but note the absence of the house price from the pure prepayment option.

6 See LaCour Little (1999, p. 47).

7 The net effect is a negative relationship between the value of the mortgage and interest rate volatility termed negative convexity. Convexity is often expressed in terms of Jensen's inequality. In the case of fixed interest rate securities such as a mortgage, negative convexity reverses Jensen's inequality.

8 Kau *et al.* (1993, p. 596).

9 The typical United Kingdom mortgage contract is a variable rate mortgage (VRM). Skinner (1999) has addressed this issue. Skinner notes that the main complication in valuing the VRM is once again path dependence. When the variable mortgage interest rate changes so to does the proportion of a payment that represents a capital repayment. In essence, the amount owed at a point of time depends upon the past sequence of changes in the variable mortgage interest rate. Skinner (1999) uses a Markov process to value the straight variable rate mortgage by backward calculation.

10 This model is nevertheless quite successful in predicting the market prices of mortgage-backed securities. It is primarily designed to assist portfolio management and hedging.

10

Prepayment and Default Behaviour: Empirical Evidence

Introduction

This chapter presents and discusses the empirical evidence relating to both prepayment and default behaviour. There are several reasons for discussing these behaviours in the same chapter. First, from the lender's or mortgage security holder's perspective both prepayment and default are reductions in cash flow and can be jointly described as mortgage terminations. Second, the theoretical and the empirical literature has increasingly recognised the importance of accounting for the interactions between prepayment and default that were discussed in the previous chapter. This is often expressed in terms of 'competing risks', and estimation incorporating this can be cited as the latest wave in an evolving and increasingly sophisticated research programme in mortgage termination behaviour.

Expected mortgage terminations, and their estimated impact upon cash flows, are clearly central to the valuation and efficient pricing of mortgages and pass through securities. Also, financial institutions need to manage the degree of risk exposure on their mortgage books. However, there are other reasons why terminations are generally important. The mortgage market is often cited as a channel through which the influences of monetary policy are transmitted to the wider economy. For example, in the UK the widespread use of variable rate mortgage debt has meant that UK households have often been subjected to severe liquidity squeezes when mortgage interest rates have risen (Chinloy 1995; Earley 2000). Phillips et al. (1996) note that a premium on mortgage rates reflecting prepayment risk raises the cost of capital with potentially adverse effects on the housing industry.

Mortgage prepayment can be a means of stimulating economic activity when borrowers refinance as interest rates fall. Conversely, mortgage default can have dampening effects when it reflects widespread negative equity, as it did in the UK during the early 1990s. Thus the study of mortgage termination behaviour is of wider economic significance. Credit rationing and the available menu of mortgage instruments will effect the efficacy of these transmission mechanisms, for example refinancing to increase indebtedness is less likely for the credit constrained (Peristiani *et al.* 1997). Behaviour may also vary according to the choice of mortgage instrument, a theoretical possibility explored in Chapter 9. The different loan performance of the ARM might explain its slower rate of adoption by the securitised mortgage market (Ambrose & LaCour Little 2001) and may have implications for the valuation of ARM backed securities (Calhoun & Deng 2002).

The chapter begins with an overview of some of the main features of empirical studies of prepayment and default. Topics include the nature of the data samples used in these studies and the problem of finding empirical counterparts to theoretically important variables. There is also a discussion of the main econometric techniques used in empirical work, including various approaches to estimating models of competing risk. The discussion of empirical results looks at studies of default and prepayment alone and more recent work on competing risks. Subsequent discussion considers how termination behaviour appears to vary according to the type of mortgage instrument.

The study of mortgage termination behaviour

There are two perspectives on mortgage termination research. One is to consider the 'ruthless' and endogenously determined exercise of the embedded call and put options (see, for example, Green & Shoven 1986; Schwartz & Torous 1989a, 1989b, 1992, 1993). A second perspective has recognised that exogenous factors may influence termination decisions. In the case of prepayment this is known as estimating an empirical prepayment function, while for default concern has been with 'trigger events'. These approaches are not always mutually exclusive with some studies adopting joint tests of the option theoretic and more ad hoc empirical approach (see Archer & Ling 1993).

One important modification of the 'ruthless' exercise of the call and put options arises in the case of transaction costs. In the case of mortgage default negative equity would be a necessary but not sufficient condition. Default with transaction costs might require a trigger event such as unemployment or divorce to justify exercising the put option. Examples of transaction costs of default would be the reputation and psychic costs recognised by Brueckner (1994c), including not wishing to be seen as a defaulter. Mortgage prepayment has also been modelled with transaction costs; examples here are the administration and legal fees due on taking out a new mortgage. Bennet *et al.* (2000) expressed the net benefit from refinancing in terms of variables which include a measure of the borrower's credit worthiness. For both the put and the call option, therefore, exercise may not be entirely 'ruthless', though still financially motivated.

Empirical work has increasingly recognised the need to isolate the motives behind default and prepayment. For example, households may refinance to obtain a cheaper mortgage, repay as a consequence of moving, increase their gearing or change their mortgage instrument. Even potential and actual defaulters may choose between default and mobility (see Pavlov 2001). Green and LaCour Little (1999) address the problem of varied motives by focusing upon a sample of borrowers where it is known that they refinanced for the cheaper coupon. Distinguishing between prepayment and default has been seen as an increasingly important thing to do. Other work (Vandell & Thibodeau 1985; Zorn & Lea 1989) has recognised the simultaneous choice between default, normal payment, partial prepayment and full prepayment, that is a range of continuous choices.

Household mobility can be a major cause of mortgage termination, independent of the exercise of the call and put options in the mortgage contract (see Green & Shoven 1986).[1] However, any assumed independence of household mobility and option theoretic arguments is dubious, given that expected length of stay in a residence determines the time horizon over which the value of the prepayment and default options will be evaluated. Also, low interest rates might trigger mobility while high rates can result in a lock in where the household on cheaper fixed rate finance does not move (see Quigley 1987). Archer *et al.* (1997) note the lack of any integrated theory of mortgage terminations.[2] More recent work by writers such as Pavlov (2001) has tried to bridge this gap. However, mortgage termination behaviour is generally viewed as a partial equilibrium problem.

Another salient feature of recent mortgage termination research is the recognition that estimates may contain a significant amount of unobserved heterogeneity. That is households may differ in their propensity to default or prepay in a variety of unobserved ways. This unobserved heterogeneity could be personal idiosyncratic factors such as attitudes to risk, or differing degrees of financial sophistication. Unobserved heterogeneity has been typically controlled for in the context of competing risk models of mortgage termination (see Deng *et al.* 2000). Some heterogeneity is observable and typically involves differences in contractual terms that vary according to the date that the mortgage is originated, for example the size of caps and collars on the ARM, along with adjustment periods. Comparing the influence on mortgage termination of contractual terms and borrower characteristics contributes to testing the option theoretic approach. Behaviour should not differ significantly according to the features of contracts *per se* but only in response to the value of the implied options.

Approaches to the econometric modelling of mortgage termination behaviour

In this section we examine the approaches adopted to the econometric modelling of mortgage termination behaviour. This includes a discussion of the sampling and data issues involved in any estimation. As with most other research endeavours data is not always complete and theoretical variables are represented by proxy measures which require careful interpretation. The discussion also encompasses the broad outline of the econometric methods used to evaluate mortgage termination. Particular attention is paid to the use of competing risk models.

Data and measurement issues

One important issue is the level of aggregation at which mortgage termination is analysed. For example, a number of studies have been concerned with the performance of mortgage pools (Peters *et al.* 1984; Richard & Roll 1989; Schwartz & Torous, 1989b, 1992; Foster & Van Order 1990; Mattey & Wallace 2001). Pool data studies tend to focus upon the endogenous modelling of termination behaviour, that is testing the pure option theoretic approach. There has been recognition of the fact that the proportion of mortgage terminations for pools can vary significantly, even for pools with similar interest rates on the underlying mortgages. This has led to the estimate of some empirical prepayment functions on pooled data that recognises significant sources of heterogeneity. For example, Mattey & Wallace (2001) control for regional variations in house prices. Low or weak house prices increase defaults and also inhibit prepayment due to lack of household mobility (Archer *et al.* 1996; Mayer & Genesove 1997). Chapter 9 also noted that prepayment probabilities are lower when house prices are low.

Prepayments from mortgage pools typically increase during the first four to five years, and then decline thereafter, a process known as burnout (Peristiani *et al.* 1997). Most empirical studies capture the burnout effect by including a measure of mortgage age in the estimation. Clearly as some homeowners quit the pool then it is possible that particular types of mortgage holder begin to dominate. The remaining borrowers may be credit constrained (Peristiani *et al.* 1997), or there may be significant variations in transactions costs across borrowers so that those with low costs refinance first (Stanton 1995). The latter effect is important because exogenous influences upon refinancing may not influence the distribution of transactions costs within the pool. However, endogenous refinancing for financial reasons will shift the characteristics of the pool so that subsequent refinancing is less likely (Stanton 1995). Thus there is a behavioural explanation for burnout.

Pool level data is an important source of information and a focus for players in the securitised mortgage market; the packaging of mortgage market securities originates from such pools. Practitioners have focused upon developing effective prepayment forecasting models that do not make excessive data demands (see Sanyal 1994; and Huang & Xia 1996) However, it has been increasingly recognised that more can be learned from loan level data. This is particularly so when combining cross-section and time varying observations. Such analysis facilitates testing for the influence of borrower, loan and property characteristics. The nature of the data means that loan level studies are often concerned with exogenously determined mortgage termination. This can be an important approach when assessing the role of credit rationing and variations in transaction costs. However, both mortgage pools and loan level data present measurement problems for the researcher.

Measurement issues in specifying mortgage termination models

One difficulty in testing option theoretic models is that the theoretical variables cannot always be measured directly. For example, the net value of the option to default or prepay which can inhibit mortgage termination, even when the option is 'in the money'. In the case of default, the value of the put option will depend upon the stochastic behaviour of particular house prices. Measuring the extent to which an option is 'in the money' (its intrinsic value) can also be problematic. Given that the precise valuation of options is difficult, research generally adopts a probabilistic approach, arguing that the embedded options are more likely to be exercised the further they are 'in the money'.

Several measures of the intrinsic value of the call option have been used in the prepayment literature. For example, the spread between, or ratio of, the coupon rate and the prevailing mortgage interest rate (LaCour Little 1999; Peristiani *et al.* 1997; Pavlov 2001). Richard & Roll (1989) measure intrinsic value by a present value annuity ratio, or the ratio of the present value of remaining payments on the mortgage at the coupon rate and the new interest rate (see Archer *et al.* 1997; Deng *et al.* 1996, 2000; Bennett *et al.* 1998, 2001).[3] However, for new mortgages they suggest that the ratio of the coupon and the market interest rate is a good proxy for the ratio of balances.[4]

Measures of the intrinsic value of the call option are imperfect, they do not account for transaction costs and there is no correction for the expected holding period of the mortgage. Peristiani *et al.* (1997) make a number of corrections for variations in holding period, none of which has a marked effect on their empirical findings. There is also a measurement issue for loan level analysis in assigning the value of the expected refinancing rate for those who do not refinance. For example, the points coupon trade off can produce interest rate variations. The literature has adopted a number of approaches to attributing the forgone rate for non-refinancers. For example, Bennett *et al.* (1998) use the average Freddie Mac commitment rate on a 30-year, fixed rate mortgage for the month that a loan was closed.

Some prepayment studies have distinguished between the intrinsic value of the option, which reflects the non-callable bond component of the mortgage (see expression (9.1)), and the value of the embedded option (Giliberto & Thibodeau 1989; Caplin *et al.* 1997a,b; Bennett *et al.* 1998, 2000, 2001). The net value of the call option will be effected by interest rate volatility. Giliberto & Thibodeau used the annual variance in the monthly FHLBB contract rate to measure the net value of the call option to prepay. Caplin *et al.* (1997a, b) used a GARCH measure of conditional variance. Bennett *et al.* (2000) measure interest rate volatility with the implied volatility from options on 10-year US Treasury-note futures contracts. The extent to which the call option has to be 'in the money' to trigger prepayment is of interest in itself. The impact of volatility on the value of an option is greatest when it is 'near the money'. The sensitivity of the option value to changes in volatility is known as the vega. Bennett *et al.* estimated this vega using it to infer the prepayment thresholds on a sample of mortgages.

To measure the extent to which the put option is 'in the money' requires an indication of the homeowner's equity in their property. This in turn requires a measure of the loan-to-value ratio. Moreover, this loan-to-value ratio is ideally measured subsequent to the origination of the mortgage, that is *exposte*. This *exposte* measure is not as readily available as data at the point of origination and is often estimated (see Foster & Van Order 1985; Quigley & Van Order 1990; Cunningham & Capone 1990; Capone & Cunningham 1992). This is also the case with other variables, such as income, and clearly these estimates add the potential for measurement error. Some studies have been fortunate enough to have data that does not require that these values be estimated (Archer *et al.* 1997).

The loan-to-value ratio is in fact a rather complex variable to interpret. Measured at origination it is more likely to reflect credit market constraints. Measured at this point of time it may also reflect information asymmetry between borrower and lender, say regarding property-specific house price volatility (see Deng *et al.* 2000). The loan-to-value ratio may also proxy personal characteristics such as attitudes to risk. There is the possibility that the loan-to-value ratio should be treated as simultaneously determined with the default decision (see Brueckner 1994b, 1994c). So the point of time to which the measured loan-to-value ratio relates is important. There is also a need to be precise regarding when a household defaults. This is often taken as mortgages subject to foreclosure, but a property might be sold during this period and thus avoid default (Phillips *et al.* 1996). Ambrose & Buttimer (2000) recognise this issue and follow Kau *et al.* (1992) by defining default as the lender's act of taking title to the property. Non-payment is termed 'delinquency'.

As with all econometric studies, default and prepayment research may also be subject to omitted variable bias. Mattey & Wallace (2001) note the effect on estimates based on mortgage pools of neglecting varying rates of house price inflation. A form of omitted variable bias is selectivity bias. For example, in the case of default studies lenders favour lending to borrowers who do not have an above average risk of default, thus any sample of borrowers is a particularly favourable selection. Ross (2000) has tentatively shown the merit of controlling for selection bias arising out of the approval process, and demonstrated how different databases, one for approval and one for defaulters and non-defaulters, can be used to correct for this bias. This requires an assumption that the underlying approval process is the same for both samples and that variables can be found that influence approval but not default (that is the approval equation can be identified). This is a potentially important source of selection bias.

More research into the multiple sources of selection bias in default and prepayment studies can be expected as more and better data becomes available. Pavlov (2001) clearly demonstrates the bias inherent in any estimation of a prepayment model that does not allow for the competing risk of default (moving). Deng *et al.* (2000) indicates the importance of unobserved heterogeneity for mortgage termination estimation. Competing risk and unobserved heterogeneity among borrowers are issues dealt with in the most recent application of econometric analysis. Thus, there are a range of omitted variable problems to be allowed some of which are related to the choice of estimation technique.

Econometric estimation

Several estimation techniques have been used in the mortgage prepayment and default literature, with the choice of approach depending upon the key research question(s), the nature of the data set and the current state of the art. The discussion in this section does assume some broad familiarity with methods of statistical estimation, though intuitive explanations are presented where possible. The main focus of the exposition is on the modelling of prepayment and default as competing risk.[5]

A large number of studies have used variations on the Cox proportional hazards model (Green & Shoven 1986; Follain & Ondrich 1997; Deng *et al.* 2000; Pavlov 2001). Others have utilised either a single logit or probit equation (Archer *et al.* 1997; Green & LaCour Little 1999), or have estimated a multinomial logit model with separate equations for a number of choices (Zorn 1989; Cunningham & Capone 1990; Clapp *et al.* 2001). The Cox proportional hazards model and the multinomial logit specification have both been used to model prepayment and default behaviour as competing risks (Deng *et al.* 1996, 2000; Clapp *et al.* 2001; Ambrose & Buttimer 2000; Calhoun & Deng 2002). Models of competing risk represent the most significant recent development in the estimation of mortgage termination equations. The approach was first adopted by economists to study the variety of mutually exclusive ways that individuals could exit unemployment (Narendranathan & Stewart 1993; Mealli & Pudney 1996; McCall 1996). This has proved to be an appropriate choice for modelling the competing nature of prepayment and default (Deng *et al.* 1996, 2000; Ambrose & Capone 2000).

The competing risk models recognise that durations can terminate (observations exit) for several competing reasons. The essence of the modelling approach is that each risk factor (that is reason for exit) has its own hazard (risk) function. Of course, when one event leads to termination it precludes termination due to the other risk factor, consequently observations are censored. For mortgage terminations prepayment risk is censored when default occurs, while for default the censoring occurs when prepayment is the reason for mortgage termination. This is equivalent to treating each hazard as if it has a latent duration that is not always observed. Thus the competing risk approach aggregates the separate hazard functions and corrects for the censoring effects. Applying this approach has demonstrated the inefficiency of parameter estimates in prepayment (default) models when default (prepayment) is not controlled for (see Pavlov 2001).

The general form of the competing risk model can be illustrated by reference to the appropriate log likelihood function. Equation (10.1) follows Deng *et al.* (2000) and illustrates the log likelihood to be maximised. Here we see the log likelihood as a sum of competing risks for individual i, beginning with the risk of prepayment (p), followed by the risk of default (d), and the risk due to censored observations such as mortgages which continue beyond the observation period (c). These choices are reflected in the subscripts in equation (10.1). Each argument (p, d, c) is an indicator variable taking the value of 1 when the appropriate exit or act of censoring occurs. The terms $F_j(K_i)$ are the unconditional probabilities of termination due to a particular cause j. The essence of this approach is the partitioning and summation of the different hazard (risk) rates.

$$\log L = \sum_i^N \delta_{pi} \log(F_p(K_i)) + \delta_{di} \log(F_d(K_i)) + \delta_{ui} \log(F_u(K_i)) + \delta_{ci} \log(F_c(K_i))$$

(10.1)

Estimation can be based upon the usual partial likelihood approach. Excluding alternative means of terminating a mortgage when looking at prepayment or default will result in inconsistent coefficient estimates (Pavlov 2001). Equally important, the chosen independent variables might have different effects on the individual hazards, or it might be that different variables should be included in the specifications. There are, in fact, a number of different algorithms and forms of the competing risk model. Deng *et al.* (2000) estimated a form which allowed for both the simultaneous determination of the two hazard rates and the presence of unobserved heterogeneity and time varying variables.[6] The results of the various estimations are discussed below.

An alternative econometric approach to modelling competing risks is to estimate the various exit routes using a series of logit models in the form of a multinomial logit (Clapp *et al.* 2001; Calhoun & Deng 2002). That is to model a selection of discrete choices. The proportional hazards model does have the advantage that the probabilities of the various forms of mortgage termination are restricted to sum to unity, and so any one termination is at the expense of the other. This appealing restriction is not true of the multinomial logit model. However, the multinomial logit does overcome some of the restrictive assumptions of other survival models. For example, survival models assume that the hazard functions for the competing risks are independent. There is also the assumption that the covariates have a constant proportionate effect on a hazard rate. However, the multinomial logit model does assume that the choices (competing risks) are independent (see Clapp *et al.* 2001). So each estimation technique has its own set of restrictions to note when evaluating competing risk.

The theoretical and econometric modelling of mortgage termination behaviour is undoubtedly complex. In principle one might argue that prepayment and default should be considered in the context of a system of equations which at the very least would include specifications for household mobility and the demand for mortgage finance. Elmer & Seelig (1999) note the need to link 'individual financial characteristics such as borrowing, savings, and insolvency, to house prices, home equity, and other option related variables'.[7] One might also recall the modelling of Buist & Yang (2000) and their incorporation of the labour market into the theoretical and empirical analysis. Inevitably studies of mortgage termination have been beset by data limitations, but the econometric modelling has developed significantly in its explicit recognition of the links between the various types of mortgage termination, and the existence of unobserved heterogeneity among borrowers.

Default specific studies

Though the emphasis so far has been on econometric estimation involving the competing risks of prepayment and default, a number of studies focusing upon one or the other of these behaviours have added important insights. Such research also provides a benchmark against which to judge the knowledge gained, and improvements in estimation following from adopting competing risk models. This and the following section also serve to remind us of the specific predictions of the pure option theory of default and prepayment. For example, the option theoretic approach to default makes predictions regarding the role of the borrower's equity and the timing of default. It would be a mistake however, to believe that default-focused studies entirely ignored prepayment, or vice versa, and indeed a number of papers examined default in the context of the multiple choices facing borrowers (see Vandell & Thibodeau 1985; Zorn & Lea 1989; Cunningham & Capone 1990).

Quercia & Stegman (1992) provide a comprehensive and clear review of the mortgage default literature pre-1992.[8] The authors identify three phases ('generations') in the development of research in this area. The first generation of studies adopts the lender point of view by examining loan and borrower characteristics at origination and attempting to predict the likelihood of default (Jung 1962; Page 1964; Von Furstenberg & Green 1969; Herzog & Earley 1970; Sandor & Sosin 1975; Von Furstenburg & Green 1974). A characteristic of this phase is its weak theoretical underpinnings.[9]

Second generation studies adopt the borrower point of view and consider default in the context of models of rational utility maximising behaviour (Jackson & Kasserman 1980; Campbell & Dietrich 1983; Foster & Van Order 1984; Epperson *et al.* 1985; Vandell & Thibodeau 1985; Zorn & Lea 1989; Cunningham & Capone 1990). The formal modelling recognises that borrowers make simultaneous choices between meeting scheduled payments, payment delinquency, prepayment or default. During the mid-1980s this research began to recognise the option theoretic basis of default behaviour. It is also at this time that the debate over the importance of transaction cost, borrower characteristics and trigger events begins to emerge.

The key research question was, and in many ways still is, how 'ruthlessly' the put option to default on the mortgage contract is exercised? Quercia & Stegman's (1992) summary of the findings suggested the importance of borrower characteristics with more ambiguous results for the effect of trigger events.[10] Estimation techniques involved multiple regression, logit, probit and the use of multinomial logit techniques. Though the latter can be adapted to estimate competing risk it was not done in these cases. The multinomial logit models did reflect the multiple choices available to utility maximising borrowers. Thus prepayment was not ignored in the modelling.

The use of the Cox proportional hazard model (survival models) distinguishes the third generation of default studies identified by Quercia & Stegman (Green & Shoven 1986; Quigley 1987; Van Order 1990; Quigley & Van Order 1991, 1992). Though not in all cases, there was a move towards studying mortgage pools and increased theoretical and empirical concern with mortgage pricing. Thus Quercia & Stegman (1992) identify third generation studies has having an institutional focus (e.g. studying a

Freddie Mac mortgage pool). The key research questions still centred on how 'ruthlessly', or otherwise, the option to default was exercised. Progress in third generation studies was mainly through methodological innovation. On this basis it may be reasonable to conclude that the competing risk approach to mortgage termination represents the fourth generation of research.

An interesting example of a third generation study is the work of Lekkas *et al.* (1993). The empirical estimation attempts to test the predictions of the model represented by Figure 9.2 on p. 192. The focus of this research is how far the put option needs to be 'in the money' before it is exercised. The intrinsic value of the put option is also known as loan loss severity. This research finds that the frictionless model of default does not offer a good explanation of loss severity. The research finds little evidence of wealth maximising behaviour and the results are more consistent with a model where borrowers 'get into trouble'. Quigley & Van Order (1995) estimate a proportional hazard model and obtain similar results, that is there is some confirmation of the 'ruthless' default model but with some inconsistencies, an issue that continues to be addressed by competing risk, fourth generation research.

Prepayment specific studies

A number of empirical studies have focused upon prepayment behaviour alone (Green & LaCour Little 1999; Abrahams 1997; Quigley & Van Order 1990; Bennet *et al.* 1998, 2000, 2001). This does not mean that default is ignored entirely. For example, Green & LaCour Little and Abrahams, assume that default patterns are modelled in the base hazard of a Cox Proportional Hazards model. Other studies offer some control by including a measure of equity, or the loan-to-value ratio, at origination (Quigley & Van Order 1990; Bennet *et al.* 1998). The importance of default may depend upon the sampling period and the associated economic environment. There are occasions when default is dominated by prepayment, and so presents a less critical selectivity or specification problem.

Of course, prepayment only studies fall far short of modelling the competing risk of prepayment and default. However, a review of this work is helpful in highlighting key issues in the analysis of prepayment behaviour. In particular, some research has been useful in pointing to the impact of structural changes in the mortgage market (Bennet *et al.* 1998, 2001). Prepayment specific studies have also stressed the importance of institutional factors and credit market constraints in explaining prepayment rates. There has been an increasing tendency to use loan level data to include personal characteristics including those factors likely to induce an household to move and thus prepay (Quigley 1987; Archer *et al.* 1996; Archer *et al.* 1997; LaCour Little 1999; Green & LaCour Little 1999).

One problem with early studies is that they seldom distinguish between the various motives for prepayment. In the case of the analysis of mortgage pools this extends to combining prepayment and default motivated terminations (Peters *et al.* 1984; Richard & Roll 1989; Schwartz & Torous 1989a, b, 1992; Foster & Van Order 1990). Brady *et al.* (2000) uses data generated by the University of Michigan Consumer Survey to analyse refinancing motives. They note that 21% of prepayments allowed a switch from an ARM to an FRM and 35% were to liquefy their equity in the property. This indicates the different purposes served by refinancing, some of which may be jointly determined. Caplin *et al.* (1997a,b) combined refinancing and mobility induced terminations in their data, finding that interest rate volatility, which effects the value of the call option, had no impact upon prepayment behaviour. Studies by Giliberto & Thibodeau (1989) and Bennett *et al.* (2000) did not confound these separate motives and detected a statistically significant negative impact of volatility on termination.

LaCour Little (1999) controlled for the various motives for refinancing by using a sample of borrowers who remained with a single lender, and only changed their mortgage rate and term with that lender.[11] Therefore the sample was standardised by restricting the observed prepayments to refinancing only. A probit was estimated with refinancing expressed as a function of the ratio of the current mortgage rate to the coupon rate, personal characteristics, and the transaction costs of refinancing. The research found that borrower and loan characteristics only have a significant effect when the option to prepay is at or 'near the money', a result consistent with the vega estimates of Bennett *et al.* (2000). Transaction costs, which differ across individuals create a new threshold before prepayment takes place (Bennett *et al.* 2000). In another study (Green & LaCour Little 1999) found that falling house prices,[12] and hidden transactions costs are not sufficient explanations for non-prepayment.

Transaction costs can include the difficulty of refinancing if a household is liquidity/credit constrained (Archer *et al.* 1996; Peristiani *et al.* 1997; Bennet *et al.* 1998, 2000, 2001). Transaction costs can also change as a consequence of structural changes in mortgage markets (Bennet *et al.* 1998, 2001; Sanyal 1994). An interesting feature of the US market is prepayment cycles. For example, there is an apparent acceleration of prepayment rates during the 1990s, compared to the 1980s. A number of important structural changes could account for this phenomenon. These include the spread of securitisation, mortgage lending by a wider range of financial institutions, faster processing of mortgage applications and the increased integration of mortgage markets with other capital markets. Such changes may also be responsible for high levels of mortgage refinancing observed in the UK.

Bennet *et al.* (1998, 2001) estimated a proportional hazard model on 12,835 observations, covering the periods 1984–1990 and 1991–1994. Shifts in the survival curves were interpreted as evidence of a positive impact of structural change on refinancing behaviour. The research confirmed the importance of credit ratings and homeowner equity for mortgage prepayment. The importance of liquidity constraints has been indicated by other work. Peristiani *et al.* (1997) estimated a logit model and found evidence of credit market constraints. The results highlighted the importance of the homeowner's credit history. Changes in the level of home equity and in the lending environment were also significant.[13] Refinancing was less responsive to interest rate falls during the 1990s. This phenomenon might be explained by poor credit histories arising from bankruptcies in the late 1980s.

There is a case for examining liquidity and credit constrained households separately. Archer *et al.* (1996) used American Housing Survey data to estimate a logistic regression. The estimation included a dummy variable to indicate those borrowers who were 'in the money' and not subject to income and collateral constraints (dummy = 1). The results showed that non-constrained borrowers were more likely to refinance. The research also indicated that demographic characteristics allocated households between the constrained and unconstrained groups. Bennet *et al.* (1998, 2001) found that credit constrained borrowers were less sensitive to changes in the intrinsic value of the option to prepay.

Prepayment focused studies have demonstrated the importance of identifying the motives for refinancing. They have also suggested the significance of structural change in explaining prepayment cycles. Liquidity and credit market constraints can discourage prepayment and prepayment certainly seems to have become increasingly important post-financial deregulation. The importance of refinancing motives, structural change and credit histories has been established. The negative impact of interest rate volatility upon the likelihood of prepayment suggests the importance of rational calculation (Giliberto & Thibodeau 1989; Bennett *et al.* 2000). However, if we wish to have efficient and consistent estimates of prepayment behaviour then the competing risks of prepayment and default must be recognised, and incorporated into our methodology.

Default and prepayment behaviour as competing risks

It has been increasingly recognised that default and prepayment behaviour are best viewed as competing risks, where exercising one option precludes the exercise of the other (Deng *et al.* 1996; Pavlov 2001, Deng *et al.* 2000; Clapp *et al.* 2001; Ambrose & LaCour Little 2001; Colhoun & Deng 2002). This work has been based on either the competing risk proportional hazard models, or the multinomial logit model. The research generally finds that the option theoretic approach is important and can explain household behaviour, but that trigger events and personal circumstances also have explanatory value, and that there is a significant measure of unexplained heterogeneity. Speculations on the nature of the unobservable factors have ranged from different attitudes to risk to variations in financial competence/sophistication (Deng *et al.* 2000). However, the use of a competing risk methodology has also resulted in a number of important improvements to estimation and new economic insights.

The use of a competing risk methodology has made significant improvements in the ability to predict mortgage terminations (Deng *et al.* 2000; Clapp *et al.* 2001). The approach also removes various biases in estimation and makes for more efficient and consistent parameter estimates (Pavlov 2001). Modelling unobserved heterogeneity has had a particularly important impact, and has actually enhanced the explanatory power of the variables reflecting the embedded call and put options in mortgage debt (Deng *et al.* 2000); though not all studies have corrected for this. New results have emerged from correctly identifying the competing risks. In particular, recognising household mobility and adjustments in housing demand, as a competing risk has led to different estimates of the influence of key variables on mortgage termination (Pavlov 2001; Ambrose & Buttimer 2000).

Household mobility is something that might be better explained by borrower characteristics and changes in economic circumstances than changes in the value of the mortgage. Generally, this is what the research finds. Pavlov (2001) notes that the value of the mortgage has no significant effect on the mobility decision, though the estimated model contains no borrower characteristics. Clapp *et al.* (2001) notes the smaller effect of income on prepayment if mobility induced refinancing is not separately identified. Clapp *et al.* find that financial factors are important for prepayment, but not for the moving or the default decision. Other socio-economic factors such as rates of divorce or unemployment have been found to be significant 'trigger events' and indicate the importance of liquidity constraints on both prepayment and default (Deng *et al.* 1996, 2000).[14]

Some research has indicated that it is useful to stratify the sample under study, for example by wealth or income. Deng *et al.* (1996) found that in terms of their propensity to default low income households were more sensitive to falling equity values, The 'ruthless' default model appeared most applicable to the very wealthiest households. Deng *et al.* (2000) note two clusters (high risk and low risk) of unobserved heterogeneity. This might represent the division between sophisticated and unsophisticated borrowers, though again the absence of several key variables (e.g. credit history) must leave the interpretation of this finding open to debate. A further interesting basis for segmentation is households who default for a second time. This group have had their mortgages re-instated only to possibly default again. Ambrose & Buttimer (2000) find that the economic factors that predict first defaults do not have the same influence on second defaults, for example interest rates had opposite effects.

Given the above, a key question is how far the competing risk approach confirms the option theoretic view of prepayment and default decisions? All of the competing risk studies reinforce the importance of the option theoretic perspective. Deng *et al.* (2000) find that controlling for unobserved heterogeneity actually improves the explanatory power of financial variables representing the call and put options. Competing risk studies highlight the differential influence of financial factors upon the prepayment, default and the moving decision. Some studies find that financial factors influence prepayment but have little effect on default (Clapp *et al.* 2001; Ambrose & Buttimer 2001). Deng *et al.* note that unobserved heterogeneity is more important for prepayment than default. There is a general view in the literature that there are aspects of termination behaviour that still require explanation.

Discussion in previous chapters has focused upon signalling and screening in the mortgage market, for example the role of points in screening for more mobile borrowers more likely to prepay. Interestingly, a number of studies have included mortgage points as an explanatory variable. Empirical tests confirm the expected relationship between points and mobility and prepayment, that is lower points correspond with a higher probability of prepayment (Pavlov 2001; Clapp *et al.* 2001). Mortgage term might also act as a signalling device with longer terms being favoured by less mobile borrowers (Clapp *et al.* 2001). The loan-to-value ratio at origination is a variable that can also reflect upon information asymmetry. Deng *et al.* (2000) noted that if borrowers know more about the price characteristics of their property (e.g. volatility) then the mortgage may represent an underpriced option to be exploited by higher gearing.

The competing risk studies have adopted a variety of econometric techniques. The most sophisticated is perhaps the modelling which involves the simultaneous determination of default and prepayment probabilities while controlling for unobserved heterogeneity, that is the so called HHSM model applied by Deng *et al.* (2000) and Ambrose & LaCour Little (2001). Clapp *et al.* (2001) apply a multinomial logit model but find little difference in the estimates compared to a standard Cox Proportional Hazards model. The importance of unobserved heterogeneity has been quite clearly demonstrated by these studies. However, there is a need to use richer databases that would allow for otherwise omitted variables (e.g. credit histories), incorporate post-origination data on incomes and housing equity and cover periods when defaults are more significant. There is much further research to be done in this important area of mortgage market economics.

Mortgage termination behaviour and alternative mortgage instruments

Previous chapters noted that economic behaviour might differ according to the type of mortgage instrument. This involves aspects of both signalling and selectivity. For example, it was suggested that households choosing an ARM might be more mobile and more inclined to default. Prepayment behaviour was generally considered for samples of fixed rate mortgage holders. However, the presence of interest rate floors and caps and the use of 'teaser rates' has meant that adjustable rate mortgages also have option theoretic features. Empirical research into mortgage default and prepayment has increasingly recognised the importance of the choice of mortgage instrument (Cunningham & Capone 1990; Capone & Cunningham 1992; Phillips *et al.* 1996; Vanderhoff 1996; Green & Shilling 1997; Ambrose & LaCour Little 2001; Calhoun & Deng 2002).

The essence of the ARM is that interest rate risk is passed on to the borrower. However, the default risk that lenders then face may have a significant impact upon their cash flows. This risk of default might arise out of the characteristics of the borrower (e.g. credit worthiness), or from the specific features of the mortgage instrument (e.g. periodic caps and their adjustment frequencies). Determining the relative contribution of these factors is important for the lender's cash and risk management, and for MBS valuation. Prepayment is also an issue insofar as the cap and adjustment terms establish boundary conditions that create a call option on the adjustable rate mortgage debt. There is evidence that the rates of prepayment on ARM mortgages in the US during the 1990s, have significantly exceeded the rates for FRM borrowers (Ambrose & LaCour Little 2001).

The methods and development of research in this area reflects mortgage termination work in general. For example, there is research covering aggregate ARM termination from mortgage pools (Huang & Xia 1996; Sanyal 1994). There are also studies using loan level data focusing upon prepayment (Lea & Zorn 1986; Zorn & Lea 1989; Cunningham & Capone 1990; Phillips *et al.* 1996; Vanderhoff 1996; Green & Shilling 1997); or default (SA-Aadu 1988; Cunningham & Capone 1990). Recent work has adopted the competing risk perspective (Ambrose & LaCour Little 2001; Calhoun & Deng 2002). Of course, a relevant issue not always considered is the extent to which the choice of mortgage instrument creates a selectivity issue for studies focusing upon a single mortgage type.

A concern of early studies using ARM data was the relative importance of the characteristics of the borrower and the features of the ARM contract (SA-Aadu 1988; Cunningham & Capone 1990). The research also used data from a single lender. The results of studies differ with SA-Aadu finding variables reflecting the borrower's credit worthiness generally statistically significant, and Cunningham & Capone finding only the net worth of the borrower to be significant. Cunningham & Capone conclude that differences in default rates between FRM and ARM contracts 'result from the contractual provisions of ARMs...and not from borrower clientele effects'.[15] The Cunningham & Capone study did use a multinomial logit model to account for prepayment, and utilised current data on house prices. A finding emphasising the importance of the features of the contract generally supports the option theoretic approach to mortgage default,[16] and variables indicating the extent to which the option was 'in the money' (e.g. equity net of moving costs) were also found to be statistically significant.

The option theoretic approach can be tested by analysing a household's response to interactions between key state variables and contract features (boundary conditions). The analysis can be extended by determining if households respond in the same manner to contract characteristics, regardless of whether they hold an FRM or an ARM. Calhoun & Deng (2002) separately estimated a multinomial logit, competing risk, model on ARM and FRM contracts. Though the research found similar responses to option theoretic variables for both ARM and FRM holders, there was some evidence that borrowers might self-select between these two forms of contract. This could reflect unobserved heterogeneity, or some other selectivity mechanism such as potential household mobility. A further indicator of selectivity was the lesser sensitivity of ARM holders to interest rate terms, possibly indicating a shorter expected holding period.

The theoretical work of Kau *et al.* (1993) discussed in Chapter 9 pointed to the strong impact of 'teaser rates' on prepayment behaviour, mortgage value and mortgage pricing. Any study of household behaviour of ARM holders must account for 'teaser rates'. However, some research has found that 'teaser rates' do not have a significant effect on, or discourage, prepayment (Green & Shilling 1997; Phillips *et al.* 1996; Vanderhoff 1996). More recent work by Ambrose & LaCour Little (2001) employing the competing risk framework of Deng *et al.* (2000), found a positive relationship between the size of discount and the likelihood of prepayment. Also ARM holders were found to be more likely to prepay than borrowers holding an FRM. Ambrose & LaCour Little (2001) provide empirical confirmation of the theoretical predictions and numerical simulations of Kau *et al.*

Though the more sophisticated recent research has detected the expected effects of 'teaser rates' on prepayment behaviour it is useful to consider why the results of studies might differ. Most studies of ARM prepayment behaviour have utilised sometimes limited data from individual lenders covering short time periods, thus inhibiting generalisation. The chosen period of the business or interest rate cycle could also significantly influence results (Phillips *et al.* 1996). Ambrose & LaCour Little (2001) note that Vanderhoff (1996) finds a lower risk of prepayment for ARMs during a period of recession when prepayment might have been inhibited, perhaps by default, again emphasising the importance of a competing risk perspective. The question of significant clientele/signalling effects in mortgage instrument choice and subsequent termination behaviour remains a crucial one for research.

Given the significant differences between the UK and US mortgage markets discussed in Chapter 1, and in other chapters, then there are also important variations in the features of mortgage contracts across housing finance systems. Unfortunately, there are few UK studies of mortgage termination behaviour available. Theoretical work on the valuation of UK mortgage instruments has been presented by Pereira *et al.* (2002, 2003). There is also empirical research on time to default Lambrecht *et al.* (1997), and default risk (Chinloy 1995). There is currently only one study of UK prepayment behaviour (Institute of Actuaries 2002). However, UK research does offer examples of both the application and the limitations of the option theoretic approach to the analysis of mortgage termination.

Lambrecht *et al.* note that in the UK 'ruthless' default is less likely because the liability for the outstanding mortgage balance remains with the borrower.[17] Using a duration analysis on a sample of defaulters, from 1987–1991, the researchers found that ability to pay variables exceeded equity variables in importance.[18] Chinloy also found in favour of the importance of liquidity constraints for default in the UK mortgage market, reflecting the liquidity squeezes that can arise with a variable (bullet) rate of interest. The Institute of Actuaries examined UK fixed rate contracts finding the age of the debt, house price inflation, interest rate differentials and prepayment charges effect the likelihood of prepayment. Especially given the theoretical lead of Pereira *et al.* there is much more scope for research into mortgage termination behaviour in the UK mortgage market.

Mortgage termination studies that have considered mortgage instruments other than the US standard FRM have also found for the importance of the option theoretic approach. The competing risk methodology has proved effective in analysing ARM loan performance. However, there has been some evidence of clientele, or selection effects. Research needs to account for potentially important selectivity biases arising from the choice of mortgage instrument. This has implications for mortgage security valuation and the balance sheet management of lenders. 'Teaser rates' on the ARM, or the VRM in the UK, appear to have a significant impact upon prepayment behaviour. There is no econometric study as yet of prepayment that reflects consumer search and switching between providers, a matter related to the heavy discounting of mortgage debt driven by mortgage market competition.

Another issue for further attention is the known lags in the adjustment of ARM rates to changes in indices. Simulations show that these different reactions can have significant effects on the sensitivity of mortgage price to interest rate variables (Boudoukh *et al.* 1997; Stanton & Wallace 1999). This may also be an imperative for UK research, where mortgage interest rates have demonstrated a variable lag with respect to base rate changes (Miles 1994; Leece 2000a).

Summary and conclusions

This chapter of the book has examined the empirical evidence for the 'ruthless' default and option-based prepayment models outlined and discussed in Chapter 9. The option theoretic approach certainly offers important insights into household behaviour in the mortgage market. There was empirical verification of the relevance and importance of rational financial calculation, and the wealth maximising behaviour involved in option theory. However, the analysis of loan level data to estimate empirical default and prepayment functions did suggest that borrower characteristics, affordability, liquidity and credit market constraints also have important effects on termination.

The study of mortgage termination behaviour exhibited increasing econometric sophistication. This sophistication represented a different way of viewing prepayment and default. Competing risk models recognised the importance of the interaction between the prepayment and default options. Generally, this work reinforced the importance and empirical validity of the option theoretic perspective. However, despite this sophistication and a sense that more and more of borrower behaviour was being explained, there was still some evidence that a proportion of the population in US studies apparently behaves in a sub-optimal fashion. More detailed loan level data may shed further light on this issue.

The empirical research also highlighted significant differences in the performance of different mortgage instruments, expressed in terms of prepayment and/or default behaviour. This was important from the point of view of mortgage securitisation, where the FRM had been more readily securitised than the ARM. Previous chapters had noted the signalling and screening characteristics of different mortgage designs. Though there was as yet little direct empirical evidence of the information role of contract design, differences in default and prepayment rates were indicative. Future research might further consider household mobility and the complexity and selectivity apparent in mortgage instrument choice. Flexible amortisation might also impact upon observed termination behaviour, as flexible mortgage instruments become more widely adopted. New data and increasingly the sophisticated competing risk methodology could generate yet more interesting and reliable results.

Guide to further reading

This is one of the most extensive areas of mortgage market research and the fastest moving. Thus this chapter has tried to cover the basic issues and give the researcher/student sufficient leverage to handle the burgeoning literature in this area. A must read for the student of default is the review of studies by Quercia & Stegman (1992). The chapter has noted the increasing tendency to focus upon default and prepayment as competing risks. Therefore recent papers such as those by Pavlov (2001) are recommended for further elucidation of this technique, discussions of its advantages in estimation and further review of the literature.

Notes

1 Green & Shoven note 'The point is that the effective maturity of the mortgage asset is endogenous to the evolution of interest rates and perhaps, other economic variables' (p. 42).
2 Archer *et al.* (1997, p. 160) note 'The approach in this study is fundamentally empirical. As noted, the state of theory on household mobility is highly incomplete, making the construction of an integrated theory of mortgage terminations problematic.'
3 Deng *et al.* (2000) present a clear exposition of the actual calculation of this measure in Appendix A on page 304 of their paper.
4 Another variation is the market value of the primary mortgage debt – the book value of the mortgage debt (see Archer *et al.* 1996, p. 249).
5 For a short and very clear exposition of some of the alternative techniques used in the literature see Calhoun & Deng (2002, pp. 11–12).
6 At the time of writing, and according to Clapp *et al.* (2001, p. 420, fn. 19) the software required to estimate this particular model is not commercially available.
7 Elmer and Seelig (1999, p. 2).
8 This includes some research in working paper form that subsequently emerges in published form post-1992.
9 The post-1969 research extends from using the characteristics of the loan. (e.g. loan-to-value, interest rate) to include a selection of borrower and property characteristics (see Quercia & Stegman 1992, p. 345).
10 See Quercia & Stegman (1992, p. 361).
11 This, as the author admits, introduces its own biases in terms of representing the general population (LaCour Little 1999).
12 The authors estimate that only about 25% of borrowers in the sample would have been constrained by falling house prices (LaCour Little, 1999, p. 246).
13 In this study changes in the lending environment are proxied by the average level of points and fees.
14 Particularly interesting in the Pavlov (2001) study is the finding that borrowers in low income areas exploit refinancing opportunities less than those in areas of higher income. Coupled with the insignificant impact of mortgage value on mobility then low income households are more likely to be refinancing under less favourable conditions, implying comparatively higher housing costs for such borrowers. Why low income groups should refinance less is not clear as Pavlov does not have credit history data available, but this or other aspects of transactions costs including levels of financial sophistication may underlie this phenomenon.
15 Cunningham & Capone (1990, p. 1699).

16 Variations in the contract features of the FRM can also be important. Phillips *et al.* (1996) estimated a multinomial logit model with default, prepayment and continuation as outcomes and found that termination probabilities vary by the term of the FRM, as well as between the ARM and FRM. For example, FRM 15-year prepayments are more responsive to falls in the interest rate than prepayments on the 30-year FRM.

17 There have been claims that repossessed houses have been sold off quickly at lower than expected prices and leaving such households in higher than expected debt. Thus there is an interesting agency problem for default studies in the United Kingdom.

18 This research was also unusual in finding a positive association between loan-to-value ratio and time to default. This may have been due to data measurement problems (second loans on homes could not be identified), and omitted variable bias (see Lambrecht *et al.* 1997, p. 487).

11

Conclusion: The 'Field' of Mortgage Market Economics

Introduction

I like to think that researching into the mortgage market can be viewed as something akin to research into black holes in physics. Cash constrained households with large mortgage debt will appreciate the analogy, but mortgage choices merit a similar place of importance in the study of economic performance and microeconomic behaviour in general. Early chapters of this book pointed to the size and importance of the mortgage market in many countries, its increasingly global nature and its critical impact on households, lenders, secondary mortgage market investors and national economic performance. At the very least the mortgage market can be viewed as a fruitful and insightful area for research, or even case study material for the application of key microeconomic concepts.

The US, Canada and the UK, with their large sophisticated mortgage markets, have been the main focuses of research into mortgage market economics. In the US the size of the securitised mortgage market has been a prime motivator for theoretical modelling, and empirical work. In the UK the prevalence of variable rate debt, the importance of the mortgage market as a monetary transmission mechanism, and the more extreme swings in house prices and borrowing have motivated much research. Research of the kind focused upon in this book has appeared in Australia, Japan, the Far East, India and Eastern Europe. The already extensive work on housing finance systems can benefit from the type of studies of mortgage choices presented here.

North American and European work can inform research in other economies. Institutional and policy features are clearly important. For example, mortgage markets in France or in Eastern Europe are very different from those in the UK or the US. Chapter 1 noted how different housing finance systems effected the menu of mortgage contracts available to the borrower. However, there are important theories, econometric techniques and empirically based perspectives on household behaviour that should inform any serious, rigorous research agenda. For example, option theoretic approaches are ahistorical but can aid the valuation of the components of very different forms of mortgage contract. The effects of credit rationing on the truncation of observed choices would be relevant to empirical methodologies applied elsewhere. Also, mortgage contracts of different design can be evaluated in terms of risk and optimum payment profiles. The evolution of other housing finance systems may produce the heterogeneity of mortgage contracts observed in the US and UK, and discussed throughout this book, highlighting information, signalling and agency problems, which are well treated by theory.

This final chapter is used to bring together the various dimensions of mortgage market economics discussed in this book, and highlight important and possible areas for future research. This is done in two ways. First, we look back at a previous review of the state of the art presented in a seminal paper by Follain, published in 1990. In that paper he surveyed the key research issues in mortgage choice, and took stock of progress up to 1989. Given the focus of this book on household decision making then the Follain paper is particularly apt. We will find some of his concerns enduring, while others are being addressed in new ways. Second, we revisit the main themes of this book. Finally, we reflect upon the changing nature of the mortgage market and issues in mortgage market economics, and consider some issues that the book has not had the time and space to cover.

The state of the art of mortgage market economics: retrospect and prospect

In his 1989 Presidential Address delivered to the American Real Estate and Urban Economics Association, James R. Follain noted that 'Mortgage choice is also the topic of this address because it is a challenging problem ripe for additional study'.[1] He defined mortgage choices to include the demand for debt (loan-to-value ratio), choice of mortgage instrument, and refinancing and default decisions.

In his review of the state of the art of research into mortgage choices there are several areas where Follain notes the paucity of literature. The choice of loan-to-value ratio, or mortgage demand, was seen as much understudied, with the mortgage demand observed to be a mere multiple of housing demand. This issue was explored in Chapters 2 and 3 of this book. There has been an increase in research that does not treat the link between housing and mortgage demand quite so mechanistically, and has extended analysis to consumption and portfolio decisions. However, it still remains true that more theoretical and empirical research is welcome in this area. The emergence of flexible amortisation scheduling in some economies raises new questions regarding the demand for housing debt. Flexible mortgage designs may overcome capital market imperfections and facilitate life cycle planning, presenting new challenges to financial intermediaries packaging mortgages into securities.

Follain also noted the importance of the points/coupon choice and considered little written on this topic. There is now a quite extensive literature in this area some of which was cited in Chapters 6 and 7. There have been significant theoretical developments in understanding how mortgage instruments can act as screening and signalling devices, though there is little econometric work. However, the theory is beginning to inform econometric specifications in prepayment and default studies. The researcher is faced with the complexity of the interdependence of mortgage choices. In theory mortgage termination, mortgage demand and choice of mortgage instrument are all simultaneously determined. Fully modelling this simultaneity remains a significant challenge.

Research into decisions to prepay or default had already received considerable attention by researchers by 1990, and Follain noted this. The different stages in the development of work concerning mortgage termination were outlined in Chapter 9. Both theoretical and empirical work on mortgage termination continues to expand; to the extent that such research almost demands a separate book. Recent studies have noted the competing nature of default and prepayment decisions and have contributed significantly to our understanding of household prepayment and default behaviour. Examining mortgage termination in the context of household mobility has led to a richer view of household decision making, and more efficient and consistent econometric estimation. Yet, more interesting work can be expected in this area.

Some of the greatest challenges in the field of mortgage market economics are in the development of appropriate theoretical models. Follain notes the division in 1989 between models based upon certainty and uncertainty models that facilitate the application of theoretical and empirical perspectives adopted from financial economics. This distinction was made much of in the discussion of mortgage demand in Chapters 2 and 3. The basic model with certainty has been used to explain loan-to-value ratios Other than option theoretic approaches uncertainty models have not yet received a lot of theoretical or empirical attention in the study of mortgage demand. More work on the portfolio setting of mortgage debt would be welcome, particularly critical approaches to the relevance of the propositions of Modigliani & Miller for a household's mortgage choices and financial decision making.

One of the greatest difficulties in modelling mortgage demand under uncertainty is combining this with liquidity constraints and capital market imperfections. Though some theoretical work, such as that by Plaut (1986) on amortisation, has included credit and cash constraints there is still more work needed in this area. The work of Stein (1995) and Ortalo-Magne & Rady (1999, 2002), covering down payment constraints and housing cycles could be extended to incorporate uncertainty in asset markets including the property market. Follain made an interesting appeal to link the results of empirical studies of liquidity constraints in housing and mortgage markets to broader debates in macroeconomics; this on the grounds that mortgage markets are where liquidity constraints are most likely to be found. To this perspective we can add the further likelihood of significant information and agency problems. These links were stressed throughout Chapters 4 to 6 of this book, as well as emerging again as considerations in the studies of prepayment and default behaviour evaluated in Chapters 9 and 10.

The option theoretic perspectives discussed in Chapters 9 and 10 are based upon uncertainty, but there are other important issues involved here too. Follain noted that empirical studies of prepayment did not allow for variations in the expected holding period of the mortgage. Insofar as a complete understanding of mortgage terminations requires a theory of household mobility, in which termination is embedded, then this has not yet been fully achieved. However, there have been significant attempts to incorporate mobility into termination decisions (see Pavlov 2001). Follain pointed out that there is no comprehensive model that covers all mortgage choices made by households. It remains true that the certainty models best explain the choice of loan-to-value ratio and liquidity constraints, while uncertainty models give important insights into refinancing and default decisions. Research in both of these areas and encompassing different worldviews continues to expand. This book has adopted both of these perspectives and pursued a number of key themes around which to organise the main issues.

Revisiting the themes of the book

Several major themes have been pursued in this book. One of these is the importance of household behaviour in the mortgage market and the validity of using a variety of perspectives to better understand it. The perfectly competitive no arbitrage economy, assumed in the option theoretic work, provided invaluable insights into behaviours based upon rational financial calculation. Increasingly sophisticated econometric modelling had established the empirical validity of this approach. Such work also facilitated the valuation of mortgage debt, and the efficient pricing of contracts. Effective mortgage valuation was an important issue for the management of financial intermediaries' balance sheets and risk positions, and ultimately the development of efficient mortgage markets. However, perspectives based upon affordability, liquidity constraints and incomplete markets are also valid and fruitful areas for research.

Despite the empirical success of the option theoretic approach it was the case that research into mortgage choices had identified a significant degree of sub-optimal decision making. Thus a second major perspective, discussed throughout this book, is the benefit of segmenting samples and recognising variations in microeconomic behaviour. For example, grouping samples by the extent to which credit constraints were binding, or by groups evidencing different degrees of unobserved heterogeneity. Liquidity constrained groups were evident in the study of mortgage demand, and the possibility of varying degrees of financial sophistication was apparent in the study of mortgage termination behaviour. Sometimes groups may have self-selected by choice of mortgage instrument giving the noted signalling role to different mortgage designs.

A key theme was mortgage contract design, and explanations for the heterogeneity of mortgage contracts that we observe. Of course, in a perfectly competitive economy with complete markets some mortgage choices, including mortgage demand and the choice of mortgage instrument, would be a matter of indifference to borrowers. When borrowers are risk averse and lenders risk-neutral then mortgage contracts involve important elements of risk sharing. Capital market imperfections and fundamental imperfections in mortgage design that involve the tilting of real payments towards the early life of the debt suggest the importance of payment profiles and the trade off with risk. Flexible amortisation scheduling raises new issues for risk sharing and contract design. Heterogeneity of contract design is apparent in the more sophisticated housing finance systems, it is important to continue to research the information and incentive problems attending or solved by such variety.

Throughout the book comparisons have been made between the research conducted in the US and the UK. The focus on these two economies reflects the sophistication of the their respective housing finance systems and the substantial body of work emanating from academics and private and government agencies in the two countries. The comparison also high-lighted the way in which some theoretical perspectives and econometric methodologies can be adopted for study in different forms of housing finance system, but also emphasised the importance of differences. For example, the different ways in which prepayment risk is priced with redemption penalties, rather than points in the UK, possibly contributes to a short-term perspective on decision making. A current concern in the UK is how to achieve the dominance of the long-term fixed rate mortgage instrument, which raises interesting questions regarding the future evolution and development of mortgage markets, and the nature of mortgage market economics.

Mortgage markets and mortgage market economics – where to?

One way of presenting the issues involved in mortgage market economics is to consider certain phenomena as puzzles. The benchmark for such puzzles is typically the outcomes of a perfectly competitive economy with complete markets. For example, why do countries have such different systems of housing finance, together with their domination by different mortgage contracts: Germany with its bond-funded long-term fixed rate debt, and variable rate mortgages in the UK? History, the evolution of institutional features and public policy all have a role in the emergence and development of such diverse markets. Chapter 1 noted some reasons why we might observe very different mortgage instruments in different economies, for example the long-term fixed rate contract prevalent in the US. This then raises the question of how we might expect mortgage markets to develop and what research issues might emerge or persist?

Lea (2000) considers the global trends in housing finance systems. Some of these trends have been noted earlier in the book, such as increased integration of the global economy. The adoption of a common currency by the European Union in 1999 is an example of this integration. The prevalence of variable rate debt in the UK is an example of where the dominance of a particular form of mortgage contract results in a barrier to integration. Securitisation encouraged the flow of housing finance across national boundaries. Lea notes the vulnerability of national housing finance systems to economic and financial crises occurring in other parts of the world. For example, the South East Asian real estate crises. The processes of integration and globalisation are far from complete and there remains a significant variety of market structures and contract designs.

The future evolution of actual housing finance systems is likely to be complex and difficult to predict. For example, flexible mortgages have optimal properties but have spread unevenly on an international scale. They are prevalent in Australia but they have not become widespread in the US. The mortgage market is ever shifting and complex. Van Order (2000) points to the dangers of forecasting its future shape. He notes that it would have been difficult from the viewpoint of the 1970s to predict the rise of the US secondary market in the 1980s, and then to forecast the competitive reaction of savings and loans institutions in the 1990s. However, it may not be unreasonable to forecast that competition, technological advance and improved information will render markets more complete.

One spreading feature in mortgage markets is the unbundling of origination, servicing, investment and risk management of mortgage debt via securitisation. The trend towards unbundling mortgage products provides an interesting example of the different ways that housing finance systems can evolve. Van Order (2000) adopts a contrary view for the US in suggesting that the trend towards unbundling might actually be reversed. Unbundling has created information problems for secondary market institutions. Primary lenders have superior knowledge of the performance of the loans that they sell on to the secondary market. Thus we have classic cases of adverse selection and moral hazard. However, improved access to, and processing of, information to remove this problem reduces the need for specialisation in origination, servicing and investment, thus rebundling might occur. Van Order notes that the extent of any rebundling will depend upon the secondary market charter and regulations.

There are some interesting implications of improved information for the study of household behaviour in the mortgage market, the major focus of this book. Chapter 7 discussed the possibility that mortgage instruments and consumers might be mis-matched ('mis-selling'). At least for some transitional period, such agency problems might be endogenous to the evolution of a complex housing finance system. However, such mismatching is most likely when credit risk is not individually priced. Customised contracts will be optimal. Thus the ultimate degree of heterogeneity in a system of more complete markets would make such mis-matching less likely. The spread of automatic underwriting in the US offers the possibility of individually priced products. Technological advances might then facilitate the efficient repackaging of this heterogeneous debt for investors. So the evolving mortgage market may match borrowers' preferences in different ways, compatible with more complete markets.

Each housing finance system has its own developmental issues. In the UK the debate is in terms of obtaining the benefits of the US model with its prevalence of long-term fixed rate debt, leading to a less volatile housing market. There is an existing basis for securitisation in the UK, which might facilitate the supply and adoption of long-term fixed rate instruments. The adoption of the FRM might also be encouraged by some implicit or explicit FRM subsidy, as in the US. One suggestion has been changes in the funding arrangements of lenders, to achieve a better matching of assets and liabilities. This could be assisted by making fixed rate mortgage-backed bonds of interest to pension funds (Maclennan *et al.* 1998). Discussion in this book has noted reasons why we might observe a variety of mortgage contracts, so that long-term fixed rate debt might not suit all. Defining the issue in terms of encouraging borrowers to adopt a long-term perspective on financial planning might lead to different ideas.

Modifying inflationary and interest rate expectations to reflect a low inflation environment, thus encouraging borrowers to take a long-term view is another possibility. The paradox here is that a flat yield curve, with stable expectations, might render the choice between fixed and variable rate debt irrelevant. Competition between UK lenders that has resulted in a proliferation of often heavily discounted deals may have also encouraged a short-term perspective on the choice of mortgage instrument. The spread of more flexible mortgage repayment vehicles could assist in overcoming capital market imperfections and liquidity constraints that might shift the borrowers' focus to the long term, though for this to work borrowers might need to be protected against possible default. Securitisation and the increased integration of mortgage markets with international capital markets might ultimately dictate the borrowers' menu of mortgage contracts.

Securitisation of mortgage debt will become an increasingly important phenomenon in many housing finance systems. Securitisation requires a number of preconditions to develop into a sustainable market. Legal underpinnings, macroeconomic stability and competitive mortgage markets are all necessary. A standardised mortgage product must be available, so that similar mortgages can be pooled. This ensures that cash flows are more predictable and investment companies can more readily apply due diligence. Origination must be based upon clear and known underwriting standards with the ability to ascertain the credit risk of borrowers. There is the problem here that securitisation can facilitate standardisation of mortgage products, and favourable primary market developments, but that a self-sustaining market requires these features as a precondition. The discussion in Chapter 1 warned against relying upon securitisation as a universal panacea, and transition and developing economies in particular may require the careful nurturing of their primary markets, and a regard to the critical sequencing of development towards more integrated capital markets.

Previous chapters have discussed the emergence of new market segments, in particular sub-prime lending. From the securitisors' point of view the division between sub-prime and prime lending might become less distinct, with an erosion of the segmented basis of mortgage lending to these markets. Improved information and the general evolution of the housing finance system might offer a central place to flexible amortisation, even for borrowers who are a high credit risk. Ultimately, even the distinction between mortgage borrowing and other debt components might become completely irrelevant. There is even an argument for the demise of securitisation, if markets become more complete. Securitisation need not fade away if it continues to afford benefits of increased liquidity or overcomes information problems, and even in a world of individually priced fully flexible mortgage instruments there may be identifiable stable pools of interest and debt repayments for packaging. These ideas are speculative but invite a consideration of trends in mortgage market developments.

There are at least two cautions to any forecast of more complete markets, and the demise of the mortgage product as we know it. The first is that there are enough existing capital market imperfections and information problems to keep interested academics and practitioners busy for some time. This is especially so in evolving housing finance systems. The second is that teleological predictions are fraught with danger, for example consumer behaviour, lenders' preferences and a continuing need to identify collateral might all sustain clearly distinguished mortgage products. An emerging research issue that reflects upon the factors underpinning the existence of different mortgage contracts is the interaction of housing/ mortgage decisions with consumers' portfolio choices, particularly when those portfolios are not fully diversified. This is already evident in the work of Brueckner (1997) and Fratantoni (1997, 1998). These issues will be of interest and of practical importance for some time.

Other issues

That the literature in mortgage market economics is vast and growing is evidenced by the size of the bibliography in this book. It has not been possible to do justice to all dimensions of mortgage market economics. It is hoped that though the literature appears to be rapidly expanding, this book will have provided some understanding and insight into the key areas of analysis, presented the interesting research questions and usefully expounded on the theoretical and methodological developments that facilitate further study and research. However, it has been necessary to sideline some important issues.

The main focus of this book has been the residential mortgage market in advanced housing finance systems. There is much ongoing work on mortgage market development in transitional economies that has not been discussed here. The commercial mortgage market is also important and involves many issues similar to residential mortgage market analysis, in addition to some characteristics and research questions of its own (e.g. Follain & Ondrich, 1997). Multi-family mortgages in the US, where mortgages are raised to purchase additional property to let is an important issue. In the UK the rapid growth of 'buy to let' and corresponding mortgages merits rigorous research, if only because it reflects upon the investment aspects of housing demand and mortgage finance.

It has not been possible to explore or even mention all possible mortgage designs and their specific purposes. For example, an important mortgage instrument in the US is the reverse mortgage that can generate additional income in retirement. In the UK home income plans and equity release schemes are designed to release housing equity to supplement retirement income. These schemes have been criticised for poor performance and have raised issues relating to mis-matching of products to consumers needs ('mis-selling'). Demographic changes, radical changes in pension systems and concerns over household savings behaviour also make this a pressing research issue. The economics of discrimination in mortgage markets is another area that continues to develop. The organising principle of this book was the key areas of household decision making relating to mortgage choices.

Final thoughts

This book began by noting the international importance of the mortgage market, together with the way that household behaviour was becoming an increasingly central concern. The growth of the securitised mortgage market was also seen to have implications for the welfare of households. Mortgage demand and its estimation was presented as a central issue in relation to which other household mortgage choices could be considered. Such choices included the selection of mortgage instrument, the decision on how fast to amortise debt and prepayment and default behaviour.

The mortgage choices of households could be viewed through the lens of affordability, or the abstract notion of a perfectly competitive no arbitrage economy. Each of these perspectives offered insights into the household choices that we have noted. Future mortgage and capital market developments in many countries, and even new techniques and data, may shift the balance between these two views. What is certain is that the mortgage market will continue to be an important focus for academic analysis, and for financial and economic policy in many economies. It has proven to be a market capable of the most dramatic and interesting changes, and one of enduring fascination, if only for the intellectual puzzles and practical challenges that its form, behaviour and development present.

Note

1 The address is reprinted in AREUEA Journal (1990, vol. 18, No. 2, pp. 125–44), now *Real Estate Economics*. The reference for the quotation is Follain (1990, p. 126).

Bibliography

Abrahams, S.W. (1997) The new view of mortgage prepayments: insights from analysis at the loan-by-loan level, *J. Fixed Income* 7 (2): 8–21.

Alexander, W.P., S.D. Grimshaw, G.R. McQueen & S.A. Slade (2002) Some loans are more equal than others: third party originations and defaults in the sub-prime mortgage industry, *Real Estate Economics*, 30 (4): 667–97.

Allen, M.T., R.C. Rutherford & M.K. Wiley (1999) The relationship between mortgage rates and capital-market rates under alternative market conditions, *Journal of Real Estate Finance and Economics* 19(3): 211–21.

Alm, J. & J.R. Follain (1984) Alternative mortgage instruments, the tilt problem, and consumer welfare, *Journal of Financial and Quantitative Analysis* 19: 113–26.

Alm, J. & J.R. Follain (1987) Consumer demand for adjustable rate mortgages, *Housing Finance Review* 6: 11–17.

Alvayay, J.R. & Schwartz, A.L. Jr (1997) Housing and mortgage market policies in Chile, *Journal of Real Estate Literature* 5(1): 47–55.

Ambrose, B.W. & R.J Buttimer Jr (2000) Embedded options in the mortgage contract, *Journal of Real Estate Finance and Economics*, 21(2): 95–112.

Ambrose, B.W., R. Buttimer & T. Thibodeau (2001) A new spin on the jumbo/conforming loan rate differential, *Journal of Real Estate Finance and Economics* 23(3): 309–35.

Ambrose, B.W. & C.A. Capone (1996) Cost–benefit analysis of single family foreclosure alternatives, *Journal of Real Estate Finance and Economics* 13: 105–20.

Ambrose, B.W. & C.A. Capone (2000) The hazard rates of first and second defaults, *Journal of Real Estate Finance and Economics*, 20(3): 275–93.

Ambrose, B.W. & M. LaCour Little (2001) Prepayment risk in adjustable rate mortgages subject to initial year discounts: some new evidence, *Real Estate Economics* 29(2): 305–28.

Ambrose, B.W., A. Pennington-Cross & A.M. Yezer (2002) Credit rationing in the US mortgage market: evidence from variation in FHA market shares, *Journal of Urban Economics* 51: 272–94.

Anderson, R.W. & S. Sundaresan (1996) Design and valuation of debt contracts, *The Review of Financial Studies* 9(1): 37–68.

Archer, W. & D. Ling (1993) Pricing mortgage-backed securities: integrating optimal call and empirical models of prepayment, *Journal of the American Real Estate and Urban Economics Association* 21(4): 373–404.

Archer, W., D. Ling & G. McGill (1996) The effect of income and collateral constraints on residential mortgage terminations, *Regional Science and Urban Economics* 26: 235–61.

Archer, W., D. Ling & G. McGill (1997) Demographic versus option driven mortgage terminations, *Journal of Housing Economics* 4: 1051–337.

Artle, R. & P. Varaya (1978) Life-cycle consumption and home ownership, *Journal of Economic Theory*: 38–58.

Arvan, L. & J.K. Brueckner (1986) Efficient contracts in credit markets subject to interest rate risk: an application of Raviv's insurance model, *American Economic Review* 76: 259–63.

Baesel, J.B. & N. Biger (1980) The allocation of risk: some implications of fixed versus index-linked mortgages, *Journal of Financial and Quantitative Analysis* XV(2): 457–67.

Bennett, P., R. Peach & S. Peristiani (1998) Structural change in the mortgage market and the propensity to refinance, Working Paper, Federal Reserve Bank of New York.

Bennett, P., R. Peach & S. Peristiani (2000) Implied mortgage refinancing thresholds, *Real Estate Economics* 28(3): 405–34.

Bennett P., R. Peach & S. Peristiani (2001) Structural change in the mortgage market and the propensity to refinance, *Journal of Money Credit and Banking* 33(4): 955–75.

Ben-Shahar, D. & D. Feldman (2003) Signalling–screening equilibrium in the mortgage market, *Journal of Real Estate Finance and Economics* 26(2/3): 157–78.

Berger, U.N & G.F. Udell (1992) Some evidence on the empirical significance of credit rationing, *Journal of Political Economy* 100(5): 1047–77.

Bergstrom, R. & P.A. Edin (1992) Time aggregation and the distributional shape of unemployment duration, *Journal of Applied Econometrics* 7: 5–30.

Black, D.G., Garbade, K.D. & Silberg, W.L. (1981) The impact of the GNMA pass through programme on FHA housing costs, *Journal of Finance* XXXVI (2): 457–69.

Boleat, M. (1985) *National Housing Finance Systems: A Comparative Study*, Croon Helm Ltd, London.

Boudoukh, J., M. Richardson, R. Stanton & R.F. Whitelaw (1997) Pricing mortgage-backed securities in a multifactor interest-rate environment: a multifactor density estimation approach, *Review of Financial Studies* 10(2): 405–46.

Bourassa, S.C. (1995) The impacts of borrowing constraints on home-ownership in Australia, *Urban Studies* 32(7): 1163–73.

Brady, P.J, G.B. Canner & D.M. Maki (2000) The effects of recent mortgage refinancing, *Federal Reserve Bulletin* July: 441–50.

Breslaw, J., I. Irvine & A. Rahman (1996) Instrument choice: the demand for mortgages in Canada, *Journal of Urban Economics* 39: 282–302.

Britton, E. & J. Whitley (1997) Comparing the monetary transmission mechanism in France, Germany and the United Kingdom, *Bank of England Quarterly Bulletin* May: 152–63.

Brueckner, J.K. (1984) The flexible mortgage: optimal financing of a consumer durable, *Journal of the American Real Estate and Urban Economics Association* 12:136–52.

Brueckner, J.K. (1986) The pricing of interest rate caps and consumer choice in the market for adjustable-rate mortgages, *Housing Finance Review* 5: 119–36.

Brueckner, J.K. (1992) Borrower mobility, self-selection, and the relative prices of fixed- and adjustable-rate mortgages, *Journal of Financial Intermediation* 2: 401–21.

Brueckner, J.K. (1993) Why do we have ARMs?, *Journal of the American Real Estate and Urban Economics Association* 21: 333–45.

Brueckner, J.K. (1994a) The demand for mortgage debt: some basic results, *Journal of Housing Economics* 3: 251–62.

Brueckner, J.K. (1994b) Borrower mobility, adverse selection and mortgage points, *Journal of Financial Intermediation* 3: 416–41.

Brueckner, J.K. (1994c) Unobservable default propensities, optimal leverage and empirical default models, *Journal of Real Estate Finance and Economics* 9: 217–22.

Brueckner, J.K. (1997) Consumption and investment motives and the portfolio choices of home-owners, *Journal of Real Estate Finance and Economics* 15: 159–80.

Brueckner, J.K. (2000) Mortgage default and asymmetric information, *Journal of Real Estate Finance and Economics* 20(3): 251–74.

Brueckner, J.K. & L. Arvan (1986) Risk sharing in the adjustable-rate loan market: are existing contracts efficient?, *Economics Letters* 22(4): 361–64.

Brueckner, J.K & J.R. Follain (1988) The rise and fall of the ARM: an econometric analysis of mortgage choice, *Review of Economics and Statistics*10: 93–102.

Brueckner, J.K. & J.R. Follain (1989) ARMs and the demand for housing, *Regional Science and Urban Economics* 19: 163–87.

Brueggeman G. & J.D. Fisher (1997) *Real Estate Finance and Investment*, 11th edition, McGraw-Hill/Irwin.

Buckley, R., B. Lipman & T. Persaud (1993) Mortgage design under inflation and real wage uncertainty: the use of a duel index instrument, *World Development* 21(3): 455–64.

Buist, H. & T.T. Yang (2000) Housing finance in a stochastic economy: contract pricing and choice, *Real Estate Economics* 28(1): 117–40.

Burton, M., R. Dorsett & T. Young (2000) An investigation of the increasing prevalence of non-purchase of meat by british households, *Applied Economics* 32(15): 1985–1992.

Burton, M., M. Tomlinson & T. Young (1994) Consumers decisions whether or not to purchase meat: a double hurdle analysis of single adult households, *Journal of Agricultural Economics* 45(2): 202–12.

Calhoun, C.A. & Y. Deng (2002) A dynamic analysis of fixed- and adjustable-rate mortgage terminations, *Journal of Real Estate Finance and Economics* 24(1/2): 9–33.

Campbell, T. & J. Dietrich (1983) The determinants of default on conventional residential mortgages, *Journal of Finance* 38 (5): 1569–81.

Cantor, R. & R. Demsetz (1993) Securitisation, loan sales and the credit slowdown, *Federal Reserve Bank of New York Quarterly Review* Summer: 27–38.

Caplin, A., C. Freeman & J. Tracy (1997a) Collateral damage: how refinancing constraints exacerbate regional recessions, *Journal of Money, Credit and Banking* 29: 496–516.

Caplin, A., C. Freeman, S. Chan & J. Tracy (1997b) *Housing Partnerships: A New Approach to Markets at a Crossroads*, Cambridge, MIT Press.

Capone, C. & D. Cunningham (1992) Estimating the marginal contribution of adjustable-rate mortgage selection to termination probabilities in a nested model, *Journal of Real Estate Finance and Economics* 5: 333–57.

Case, K.E. & R.J. Shiller (1989) The efficiency of the market for single family homes, *American Economic Review* LXXIX: 125–37.

Case, K.E. & R.J. Shiller (1990) Forecasting prices and excess returns in the housing market, *AREUEA Journal* XVIII: 253–73.

Chari, V.V. & R. Jagannathan (1989) Adverse selection in a model of real estate lending, *Journal of Finance* 44: 499–508.

Chatterjee, A., R.O. Edmister & G.B. Hatfield (1998) An empirical investigation of alternative contingent claims models for pricing residential mortgages, *Journal of Real Estate Finance and Economics* 17(2): 139–62.

Chinloy, P. (1995) Privatised default risk and real estate recessions: the UK mortgage market, *Real Estate Economics* 23: 401–20.

Cho, M., I. M. Kim & I. F. Megbolugbe (1995) *Simultaneous estimation of housing demand and mortgage demand: an extended two-stage approach with two sequential choices*, Unpublished Working Paper, Fannie Mae Office of Housing Research.

Clapp, J.M., G.M. Goldberg, J.P. Harding & M. LaCour Little (2001) Movers and shuckers: interdependent prepayment decisions, *Real Estate Economics* 29(3): 411–50.

Coles, A. (2001) *Mortgage Markets: Why US and EU Markets Are So Different*, European Mortgage Federation.

Collin-Dufresne, P. & J.P. Harding (1999) A closed form solution for valuing mortgages, *Journal of Real Estate Finance and Economics* 19(2): 133–46.

Cooper, L. (2002) Mortgage Assets Expand the Market, *Risk Magazine*, November, Risk Waters Group Ltd (http//www.risk.co.uk).

Cotterman, R.F. and J. Pearce (1996) The effects of the Federal National Mortgage Association and the Federal Home Loan Mortgage Corporation on conventional fixed rate mortgage yields, In *Studies on Privatising Fannie Mae and Freddie Mac*: 97–168. Washington, DC: US Department of Housing and Urban Development.

Cox, D.R. (1972) Regression models and life tables (with discussion), *Journal of the Royal Statistical Society* 34: 187–220.

Cox, J.C., J.E. Ingersoll Jnr & C.A. Capone Jnr (1985) A theory of the term structure of interest rates, *Econometrica* 53(2): 385–407.

Cox, D. & T. Jappelli (1993) The effect of borrowing constraints on consumer liabilities, *Journal of Money Credit and Banking* 25: 197–213.

Cragg, J.G. (1971) Some statistical models for limited dependent variables with applications to the demand for durable goods, *Econometrica* 39(5): 829–44.

Cunningham, D.F. & C. Capone (1990) The relative termination experience of adjustable to fixed rate mortgages, *Journal of Finance* 45(5): 1678–703.

Dale-Johnson, D. (1995) Introduction: deregulation and reform of housing finance markets: recent lessons from Western and Central Europe, *Real Estate Economics* 23(4): 395–400.

Deng, Y., J.M. Quigley & R. Van Order (1996) Mortgage default and low down payment loans: the costs of public subsidy, *Regional Science and Urban Economics* 26(2): 263–85.

Deng, Y., J.M. Quigley & R. Van Order (2000) Mortgage terminations, heterogeneity and the exercise of mortgage options, *Econometrica* 68(2): 275–307.

De Sarbo, W.S. & J. Choi (1999) A latent structure double hurdle regression model for exploring heterogeneity in consumer search patterns, *Journal of Econometrics* 89(1–2): 423–55.

Deutsch, E. & H. Tomann (1995) Home ownership finance in Austria and Germany, *Real Estate Economics* 23(4): 441–74.

Devaney, M. (2000) Regulation, moral hazard, and adverse selection in appraisal practice, *The Appraisal Journal*: 180–83.

Devaney, M. & K. Pickerill (1990) The integration of mortgage and capital markets, *Appraisal Journal*: 109–13.

Devereaux, M.P. & G. Lanot (2003) Measuring tax incidence: an application to mortgage provision in the UK, *Journal of Public Economics* (forthcoming).

Dhillon, U.S., J.D. Shilling & C.F. Sirmans (1987) Choosing between fixed and adjustable rate mortgages, *Journal of Money Credit and Banking* 19: 260–67.

Dhillon, U.S., S. Upinder, J.D. Shilling & C.F. Sirmans (1990) The mortgage maturity decision: the choice between 15 year and 30 year FRMs, *Southern Economic Journal* 56: 1103–16.

Diamond, D.B. Jr (1980) Taxes, inflation, speculation and the cost of home ownership, *AREUEA Journal* 8: 281–98.

Diamond, D.B. Jr & M.J. Lea (1992) Housing finance in developed countries: an international comparison of efficiency, *Journal of Housing Research* 3(1): 1–271.

Dicks, M.J. (1989) The housing market, *Bank of England Quarterly Bulletin* February: 66–75.

Dicks, M.J. (1990) A simple model of the housing market, *Bank of England Discussion Paper No. 49*.

Disney, R., A. Henley & D. Jevons (2002) House price shocks, negative equity and household consumption in the UK in the 1990s, Working Paper, University of Wales, Aberystwyth.

Dokko, Y. & R.H. Edelstein (1991) Interest rate risk and optimal design of mortgage instruments, *Journal of Real Estate Finance and Economics* 4(1): 59–68.

Dougherty, A. & R. Van Order (1982) Inflation, housing costs and the consumer price index, *American Economic Review* 72(March): 154–65.

Drake, L. M. & Holmes, M.J. (1997) Adverse selection and the market for building society mortgage finance, *The Manchester School* LXV(1): 58–70.

Duca, J.V. & S.S. Rosenthal (1991) An empirical test of credit rationing in the mortgage market, *Journal of Urban Economics* 29: 218–34.

Duca, J.V. & S.S. Rosenthal (1994) Do mortgage rates vary based on household default characteristics? Evidence on rate sorting and credit rationing, *Journal of Real Estate Finance and Economics* 8: 99–113.

Dunn, K.B. & J.J.McConnell (1981) A comparison of alternative models of pricing GNMA mortgage-backed securities, *Journal of Finance* 36(2): 471–84.

Dunn, K.B. & C.S. Spatt (1985) Prepayment penalties and the due-on-sale clause, *Journal of Finance* 40: 293–308.

Dunn, K.B. & C.S. Spatt (1988) Private information and incentives: implications for mortgage contract terms and pricing, *Journal of Real Estate Finance and Economics* 1: 47–60.

Dunsky, R.M. & J.R. Follain (2000) Tax-induced portfolio reshuffling: the case of mortgage insurance deduction, *Real Estate Economics*, 28(Winter): 549–80.

Earley, F. (2000) Is the UK too different to join the euro?, *European Mortgage Review* September: 1–4.

Ebrill, L. & U.M. Possen (1982) Inflation and the taxation of equity in corporations and owner occupied housing, *Journal of Money Credit and Banking* XIV(1): 33–47.

Efron, B. (1977) The efficiency of Cox's likelihood function for censored data, *Journal of the American Statistical Association* 72: 557–65.

Efron, B. & J. Tibshirani (1993) *An Introduction to the Bootstrap*, Chapman and Hall, New York.

Elmer, P.J. & S.A. Seelig (1999) Insolvency, trigger events and consumer risk posture in the theory of single family mortgage default, *Journal of Housing Research* 10(1): 1–25.

Elton, J.E. & M.J. Gruber (1991) *Modern Portfolio Theory and Investment Analysis*, 4th edition, John Wiley & Sons Inc:, New York, Chichester.

Engelhardt, G.V. (1996) Consumption, down payments, and liquidity constraints, *Journal of Money, Credit and Banking* 28: 255–71.

Engelhardt, G.V. & C.J. Mayer (1996) Intergenerational transfers, borrowing constraints and saving behaviour: evidence from the housing market, *Journal of Urban Economics* 44: 135–57.

Epperson, J., J. Kau, D. Keenen & W. Muller (1985) Pricing default risk in mortgages, *AREUEA Journal* 13 (3): 152–67.

European Mortgage Federation (Hypostat) (1999) *Mortgage and Property Markets in the European Union and Norway*.

Follain, J.R. (1990) Mortgage choice, *AREUEA Journal* 18(2): 125–44.

Follain, J.R. (1991) The federal tax subsidy to housing and the reduced value of the mortgage interest reduction, *National Tax Journal* 44: 147–68.

Follain, J.R. & R.M. Dunsky (1997) The demand for mortgage debt and the income tax, *Journal of Housing Research* 8(2): 155–200.

Follain, J.R. & J. Ondrich (1997) Ruthless prepayment? Evidence from multifamily mortgages, *Journal of Urban Economics* 41: 78–101.

Follain, J.R., L.O. Scott & T.L.T. Yang (1992) Micro foundations of a mortgage prepayment function, *Journal of Real Estate Finance and Economics* 5(2): 197–217.

Forrest, R. & A. Murie (1995) *Housing and Family Wealth*, Routledge, London.

Foster, C. & R. Van Order (1984) An option based model of mortgage default, *Housing Finance Review* 3(4): 351–72.

Foster, C. & R. Van Order (1985) FHA terminations: a prelude to rational mortgage pricing, *Journal of the American Real Estate and Urban Economics Association* 13: 371–91.

Foster, C. & R. Van Order (1990) Estimating prepayments, *Secondary Mortgage Markets*, Winter.

Fratantoni, M.C. (1997) Housing wealth, precautionary saving, and the equity premium, Mimeo, Johns Hopkins University.

Fratantoni, M.C. (1998) Homeownership and investment in risky assets, *Journal of Urban Economics* 44: 27–42.

Fratantoni, M.C. (2001) Homeownership, committed expenditure risk and the stockholding puzzle, *Oxford Economic Papers* 53(2): 241–59.

Friedman, M. (1980) How to save the housing industry, *Newsweek*, 26 May: 80.

Gabriel, S. (1987) Housing and mortgage markets: the post 1982 expansion, *Federal Reserve Bulletin*, December.

Gabriel, S.A. & S.S. Rosenthal (1993) Adjustable-rate mortgages, household mobility and homeownership: a simulation study, *Journal of Real Estate Finance and Economics* 7: 29–41.

Giliberto, S. & T. Thibodeau (1989) Modelling conventional residential refinancings, *Journal of Real Estate Finance and Economics* 2: 285–99.

Gillingham, R. (1983) Measuring the cost of shelter for home-owners: theoretical and empirical considerations, *Review of Economics and Statistics* 65(2): 254–65.

Goebel, P.R. & K.C. Ma (1993) The integration of mortgage markets and capital markets, *Journal of the American Real Estate and Urban Economics Association* 21(4): 511–38.

Goodman, J.L. (1992) Adjustable-rate mortgages and the aggregate demand for mortgage credit, *Journal of Housing Economics* 2(1): 1–16.

Goodman, A.C. & R.W. Wassmer (1992) Optimal mortgage design when transactions costs constrain mobility, *Journal of Housing Economics* 2(1): 17–37.

Green, W.H. (1993) *Econometric Analysis*, 3rd edn, Prentice Hall International, London.

Green, R.K & M. LaCour Little (1999) The truth about ostriches: who never refinances their mortgage and why they don't, *Journal of Housing Economics* 8: 233–48.

Green, R.K. & J.D. Shilling (1997) The impact of initial year discounts on ARM prepayments, *Real Estate Economics* 25(3): 373–86.

Green, J. & J.B. Shoven (1986) The effects of interest rates on mortgage prepayments, *Journal of Money, Credit and Banking* 18(1): 41–50.

Guiso, L. & T. Jappelli (2002) Private transfers, borrowing constraints and the timing of homeownership, *Journal of Money Credit and Banking* 34(2): 315–39.

Guiso, L., T. Jappelli & D. Terlizzese (1996) Income risk, borrowing constraints, and portfolio choice, *American Economic Review* 86(1): 158–72 .

Haddaway, L. (1998) Loan rangers guide, *Money Management* January: 25–34.

Hall, J. & R. Urwin (1989) A disequilibrium model of mortgage lending, *Bank of England Discussion Paper No. 37*.

Haney, R.L. Jr (1988) Sticky mortgage rates: some empirical evidence, *Journal of Real Estate Research* 3(1): 61–73.

Harberger, A.C. (1971) Three basic postulates for applied welfare economics, *Journal of Economic Literature*, September 9(3): 785–97.

Harding, J.P. & C.F. Sirmans (2002) Renegotiation of troubled debt: the choice between discounted payoff and maturity extension, *Real Estate Economics* 30: 475–503.

Harrison, D.M., T.G. Noordewier & A. Yavas (2004) Do riskier borrowers borrow more?, *Real Estate Economics* (forthcoming).

Haurin, D. (1991) Income variability, homeownership and housing demand, *Journal of Housing Economics* 1: 60–74.

Hausmann, J.A. & F.M. Scott Morton (1994) Misclassification of a dependent variable in a discrete response setting, Mimeo, Massachusetts Institute of Technology, Cambridge, MA.

Hayashi, F., T. Ito & J. Slemrod (1988) Housing finance imperfections, taxation, and private saving: a comparative simulation analysis of the United States and Japan, *Journal of the Japanese and International Economies* 2: 215–38.

Hayre, L. & A. Rajan (1995) Anatomy of prepayments: the Salomon Brothers prepayment model, Working Paper, Salomon Brothers, New York, NY.

Heffernan, S.A. (1997) Modeling British interest rate adjustment: an error correction approach, *Economica* 64: 211–31.

Heffernan, S.A. (2002) How do UK financial institutions really price their banking products?, *Journal of Banking and Finance* 26: 1997–2016.

Hendershott, P.H. (1981) Real user costs and the demand for single-family housing, *Brookings Papers on Economic Activity* 2: 401–44.

Hendershott, P.H. & S.U. Hu (1981) Inflation and extraordinary returns of owner occupied housing: some implications for capital allocation and productivity growth, *Journal of Macroeconomics* 3(2): 795–812.

Hendershott, P.H. & S.U. Hu (1983) The allocation of capital between residential and non-residential uses, taxes, inflation and credit market constraints, *Journal of Finance* XXX VIII (3): 795–812.

Hendershott, P.H. & W.C. Lafayette (1997) Debt usage and mortgage choice: the FHA conventional decision, *Journal of Urban Economics* 41: 202–17.

Hendershott, P.H. & Lemmon, R.C. (1975) The financial behavior of households: some empirical estimates, *Journal of Finance* 30: 733–59.

Hendershott, P.H. & J. Shilling (1989) The impact of the agencies on conventional fixed rate mortgage yields, *Journal of Real Estate Finance and Economics* 2 (June): 101–15.

Hendershott, P.H. & R. Van Order (1989) Integration of mortgage and capital markets and the accumulation of residential capital, *Regional Science and Urban Economics* 19: 189–210.

Henderson, V.J. & Y.M. Ioannides (1983) A model of housing tenure choice, *American Economic Review* 73: 98–113.

Hendry, D.F. (1984) Econometric modeling of house prices in the United Kingdom, in Hendry, D.F. & K.F. Wallis, *Econometrics and Quantitative Economics*, Basil Blackwell, Oxford.

Hendry, D.F. & G.J. Anderson (1977) Testing dynamic specification in small simultaneous systems: an application to a model of building society behavior in the United Kingdom, in *Frontiers in Quantitative Economics*, Intriligator, M.D. (ed.), Amsterdam, North Holland.

Herzog, J.P. & J.S. Earley (1970) *Home Mortgage Delinquency and Foreclosure*, New York, National Bureau of Economic Research.

Heuson, A., W. Passmore & R. Sparks (2001) Credit scoring and mortgage securitisation: implications for mortgage rates and credit availability, *Journal of Real Estate Finance and Economics* 23(3): 337–63.

Hicks, P. (2001) *Trends in Mortgages*, Economics, Commerce and Industrial Relations Group, Parliament of Australia, Department of the Parliament Library.

Hillier, B. (1997) *The Economics of Asymmetric Information*, Macmillan Press Ltd, London.

Holdsworth, C. & M.I. Solda (2002) First housing moves in Spain: an analysis of leaving home and first housing acquisition, *European Journal of Population* 18: 1–19.

Holmes, M.J. (1993) The demand for building society mortgage finance in Northern Ireland and Scotland, *Regional Studies* 27(2): 103–8.

Houston, A.L. Jr (1988) A comparison of the reinvestment risk of the price level adjusted mortgage and the standard fixed payment mortgage, *AREUEA Journal* Spring: 34–49.

Huang, D.S. (1969) Effects of different credit policies on housing demand, in I. Friend (editor), *Studies of the Savings and Loan Industry* 3: 1211–39.

Huang, C. & W. Xia (1996) Modeling ARM prepayments, *Journal of Fixed Income*, 5(4): 31–44.

IFC (International Finance Corporation) (2000) Annual Report, *World Bank*.

Institute of Actuaries (I of A) (1999) *Report of the Endowment Mortgage Working Party*, London.

Institute of Actuaries (I of A) (2002) *Report on Prepayment Risk*, London.

Ioannides, Y.M. (1989) Housing, other real estate and wealth portfolios, *Regional Science and Urban Economics* 19: 259–80.

Jackson, J. & D. Kasserman (1980) Default risk on home mortgage loans: a test of competing hypotheses, *Journal of Risk and Insurance* 3: 678–90.

Jaffee, D.M. 1979, Mortgage credit availability and residential construction, *Brookings Papers on Economic Activity* 2: 333–76.

Jaffee, D.M. & B. Renaud (1995) Securitisation in European Mortgage Markets, paper presented to the First International Real Estate Conference, Stockholm, June 28 to July 1. Also published in *Securitization* (Institute of Chartered Financial Analysts of India (forthcoming).

Jaffee, D.M. & B. Renaud (1998) Strategies to develop mortgage markets in transition economies, in Doukas, Murinde and Wihlborg (eds), *Financial Sector Reform and Privatisation in Transition Economies*, North Holland.

Jaffee, D.M. & K.T. Rosen (1978) Estimates of the effectiveness of stabilisation policies for the housing and mortgage markets, *Journal of Finance* 33(3): 933–46.

Jaffee, D.M. & K.T. Rosen (1979) Mortgage credit availability and residential construction, *Brookings Papers Economics Activity* 2: 333–86.

Jaffee, D.M. & T. Russell (1976) Imperfect information, uncertainty, and credit rationing, *Quarterly Journal of Economics*, 90(4): 661–6.

Jenkins, S.P. (1995) Practitioners corner: easy estimation methods for discrete – time duration models, *Oxford Bulletin of Economics and Statistics* 57(1): 129–38.

Jones, L.D. (1993) The demand for home mortgage debt, *Journal of Urban Economics* 33: 10–28.

Jones, L.D. (1994) Home mortgage debt financing of non-housing investments, *Journal of Real Estate Finance and Economics* 9: 91–112.

Jones, L.D. (1995) Net wealth, marginal tax rates, and the demand for home mortgage debt, *Regional Science and Urban Economics* 25: 297–322.

Jones, S.T., N.G. Miller & T.J. Riddiough (1995) Residential mortgage choice: does supply side matter?, *Journal of Housing Economics* 4(1): 71–90.

Jung, A. (1962) Terms on conventional mortgage loans on existing homes, *Journal of Finance* 17: 432–43.

Kalbfleisch. J.D. & R.L. Prentice (1980) *The Statistical Analysis of Failure Time Data*, New York, Wiley and Sons.

Kau, J.B. & D.C. Keenan (1983) Inflation, taxes and housing: a theoretical analysis, *Journal of Public Economics* 21(1): 93–104.

Kau, J.B. & Keenan, D.C. (1995) An overview of the option-theoretic pricing of mortgages, *Journal of Housing Research* 6(2): 217–43.

Kau, J.B., D.C. Keenan, W.J. Muller & J.F. Epperson (1992) A generalized valuation model for fixed rate residential mortgages, *Journal of Money Credit and Banking* 24: 279–99.

Kau, J.B., D.C. Keenan, W.J. Muller III & J.F. Epperson (1993) Option theory and floating rate securities with a comparison of adjustable and fixed rate mortgages, *Journal of Business* 66(4): 595–618.

Kearl, J.R. (1978) Inflation and relative price distortions: the case of housing, *Review of Economics and Statistics* LX(4): 609–14.

Kent, R.J. (1980) Credit rationing and the home mortgage market, *Journal of Money, Credit and Banking* 12(3): 488– 501.

Kent, R.J. (1987) Dynamic credit rationing in the home mortgage market, *AREUEA Journal*, 15(4): 300–20.

Kolari, J.W., D. Fraser, & A. Anari (1998) The effects of securitisation on mortgage market yields: a cointegration analysis, *Real Estate Economics* 26(4): 677–93.

LaCour Little, M. (1999) Another look at the role of borrower characteristics in predicting mortgage prepayments, *Journal of Housing Research* 10(2): 45–60.

LaCour Little, M. (2001) A note on identification of discrimination in mortgage lending, *Real Estate Economics* 29(2): 329–35.

LaCour Little, M. & G.H. Chun (1999) Third party originators and mortgage prepayment risk: an agency problem, *Journal of Real Estate Research* 17(1/2): 55–70.

Lamb, D. (1987) The survey: endowment mortgages, *Money Management* July: 67–85.

Lamb, D. (1989) Special report: the end of endowment mortgages, *Money Management* June: 63–79.

Lambrecht, B., W. Perraudin, & S. Satchell (1997). Time to default in the UK mortgage market, *Economic Modelling* 14: 485–99.

Lamont, O. & J.C. Stein (1999) Leverage and house-price dynamics in U.S. cities, *RAND Journal of Economics* 30: 498–514.

Lea, M.J. (1994) The applicability of secondary mortgage markets to developing countries, *Housing Finance International*, March.

Lea, M.J. (2000) Overview of housing finance systems, *International Housing Finance Sourcebook 2000*, International Union for Housing Finance: 1–13.

Lea, M.J. & S.A. Bernstein (1996) Housing finance in an inflationary economy: the experience of Mexico, *Journal of Housing Economics* 5: 87–104.

Lea, M.J., R. Welter, & A. Dubel (1997) *Study on Mortgage Credit in the European Economic Area*, European Commission, Directorate General XXIV and Empirica.

Lea, M.J. & P.M. Zorn (1986) Adjustable rate mortgages, economic fluctuations, and lender portfolio change, *AREUEA Journal* 14(3): 432–47.

Leece, D. (1995a) Rationing, mortgage demand and the impact of financial deregulation, *Oxford Bulletin of Economics and Statistics* 57(1): 43–67.

Leece, D. (1995b) An econometric analysis of the choice of mortgage design in the United Kingdom, *Applied Economics* 27: 1173–86.

Leece, D. (1997) Mortgage innovation in the 1990s: theoretical and empirical issues, *Journal of Property Finance* 8(3): 226–45.

Leece, D. (2000a) Household choice between fixed and floating rate debt: a binomial probit model with correction for classification error, *Oxford Bulletin of Economics and Statistics* 62(1): 61–82.

Leece, D. (2000b) Choice of mortgage instrument, liquidity constraints and the demand for housing debt in the United Kingdom, *Applied Economics* 32: 1121–32.

Leece, D. (2000c) Inappropriate sales in the financial services industry: the limits of the rational calculus?, *Managerial and Decision Economics* 21: 133–44.

Leece, D. (2001a) Regressive interest rate expectations and mortgage instrument choice in the United Kingdom housing market, *Real Estate Economics* 29(4): 589–614.

Leece, D. (2001b) The impact of mortgage market innovation on housing demand and household gearing in the United Kingdom: a simultaneous equation model, *RICS Cutting Edge Conference*.

Leece, D. (2001c) The expectations in behaviour and the behaviour in expectations: a fresh look at the results of surveys of interest rate expectations, *Paper presented to INQUIRE Annual Seminar, September*.

Lekkas, V., J.M. Quigley & R. Van Order (1993) Loan loss severity and optimal mortgage default, *Journal of the American Real Estate and Urban Economics Association* 21(4): 353–71.

LeRoy, S.F. (1996) Mortgage valuation under optimal prepayment, *Review of Financial Studies* 9: 817–44.

Ling, D.C. & G.A. McGill (1998) Evidence on the demand for mortgage debt by owner-occupiers, *Journal of Urban Economics* 44: 391–414.

Linneman, P. & S. Wachter (1989) The impacts of borrowing constraints on home ownership, *AREUEA* Journal 17(4): 389–402.

Linneman, P., I.F. Megbolugbe, S.M. Wachter & M. Cho (1997) Do borrowing constraints change U.S. homeownership rates?, *Journal of Housing Economics* 6: 318–33.

Maclennan, D. (1990) Paper presented at the first conference of the LBS housing research group, London, September.

Maclennan, D., J. Muellbauer & M. Stephens (1998) Asymmetries in housing and financial market institutions and EMU, *Oxford Review of Economic Policy* 14(3): 54–80.

Mattey, J. & N. Wallace (2001) Housing price cycles and prepayment rates of U.S. mortgage pools, *Journal of Real Estate Finance and Economics* 23 (2): 161–84.

Mayer, C.J. & G.V. Engelhardt (1996) Gifts, down payments, and housing affordability, *Journal of Housing Research* 7(1): 59–77.

Mayer, C.J. & D. Genesove (1997) Equity and time to sale in the real estate market, *American Economic Review* 87: 255–69.

McCall, B.P. (1996) Unemployment insurance rules, joblessness, and part-time work, *Econometrica* 64: 647–82.

McConnell, J.J. & M. Singh (1994) Rational prepayments and the valuation of collateralized mortgage obligations, *The Journal of Finance* 49(3): 891–921.

McCulloch, J.H. (1982) Risk characteristics and underwriting standards for price level adjusted mortgages versus other mortgage instruments, *Housing Finance Review* 5: 65–97.

Mealli, F. & S. Pudney (1996) Occupational pensions and job mobility in Britain: estimation of a random effects competing risks model, *Journal of Applied Econometrics* 11(3): 293–320.

Meen, G.P. (1989) The ending of mortgage rationing and its effects on the housing market, *Urban Studies* 26: 240–52.

Meen, G.P. (1990) The removal of mortgage market constraints and the implications for econometric modelling of U.K. house prices, *Oxford Bulletin of Economics and Statistics* 52(1): 1–20.

Mella-Barral, P. & W. Perraudin (1997) Strategic debt service, *Journal of Finance* 52(2): 531–56.

Meltzer, A.H. (1974) Credit availability and economic decisions: some evidence from the housing and mortgage markets, *Journal of Finance* 29(3): 763–77.

Meyer, B.D. (1987) Semi Parametric Estimation of Duration Models, PhD thesis, MIT.

Miles, D. (1992) Housing and the wider economy in the short and long-run, *National Institute Economic Review* February: 64–77.

Miles, D. (1994) *Housing, Financial Markets and the Wider Economy*, John Wiley & Sons, Chichester.

Milevsky, M.A. (2001) *Mortgage Financing: Floating Your Way to Prosperity*, IFID Centre, Research Report, 01–01, 25 March.

Moriizumi, Y. (2000) Current wealth, housing purchase, and private housing loan demand in Japan, *Journal of Real Estate Finance and Economics* 21(1): 65–86.

Muellbauer, J. & A. Murphy (1997) Booms and busts in the UK housing market, *Economic Journal* 107: 1701–27.

Munchau, W. (1997) Government awaits a swing in public opinion, *Financial Times*, London, 21 November.

Narendranathan, W. & M.B. Stewart (1993) Modelling the probability of leaving unemployment: competing risks models with flexible base line hazards, *Applied Statistics* 42(1): 63–83.

Nellis, J.G. & J.A. Longbottom (1981) An empirical analysis of the determination of house prices in the United Kingdom, *Urban Studies* 18 (February): 9–21.

Nellis, J.G. & R. Thom (1983) The demand for mortgage finance in the United Kingdom, *Applied Economics* 15: 521–29.

Neven, D. & L.H. Roller (1999) An aggregate model of competition in the European banking industry, *International Journal of Industrial Organization* 17: 1059–74 .

Noordewier, T.G., D.M. Harrison & K. Ramagopal (2001) Semivariance of property value estimates as a determinant of default risk, *Real Estate Economics* 29: 127–59.

Nordvik, V. (1995) Prices and price expectations in the market for owner occupied housing, *Housing Studies* 10(3): 365–81.

O'Connell, B. & B. Leung (1996) Mortgage securitisation in Australia: its adoption, driving forces and impediments, *Mimeo*, Syme Department of Accounting, Monash University, Australia.

Office of Fair Trading (OFT) (1995) OFT131–Mortgage Repayment Methods, April, Office of Fair Trading, London.

Office of Housing Research Working Paper, Fannie Mae, Washington, DC, 1996.

O'herlihy, C.J. & J.E. Spencer (1972) Building societies behavior, 1955–1970, *National Institute Economic Review* 61: 40–52.

Ortalo-Magné, F. & S. Rady (1998) Housing fluctuations in a life-cycle economy with credit constraints, Discussion Paper No. 296. *Financial Markets Group*, London School of Economics.

Ortalo-Magné, F. & S. Rady (1999) Boom in and bust out: young households and the housing price cycle, *European Economic Review* 43: 755–66.

Ortalo-Magné, F. & S. Rady (2002) Housing market dynamics: on the contribution of income shocks and credit constraints, Discussion Paper, University of Wisconsin, February.

Ostas, J.R. (1976) Effects of usury ceilings in the mortgage market, *Journal of Finance* 31: 821–34.

Ostas, J.R. & F. Zahn (1975) Interest and non-interest rationing in the mortgage market, *Journal of Monetary Economics* 1(2): 187–89.

Page, A. (1964) The variation of mortgage interest rates, *Journal of Business* 37(3): 280–94.

Pais, A. (2002) Securitisation and rate setting in the UK mortgage market, Mimeo, City University Business School.

Pavlov, A.D. (2001) Competing risks of mortgage termination: who refinances, who moves and who defaults?, *Journal of Real Estate Finance and Economics* 23(2): 185–211.

Pereira, J.A.A., D.P. Newton & D.A. Paxson (2002) UK fixed rate repayment mortgage and mortgage indemnity valuation, *Real Estate Economics* 30(2): 185–211.

Pereira, J.A.A., D.P. Newton & D.A. Paxson (2003) Fixed-rate endowment mortgage and mortgage indemnity valuation, *Journal of Real Estate Finance and Economics* 26(2/3): 197–221.

Peristiani, S., P. Bennett, G. Monsen, R. Peach & J. Raiff (1997) Credit, equity and mortgage refinancings, *FRBNY Economic Policy Review*, July: 83–99.

Perraudin, W.R.M. & B.E. Sorensen (1992) The credit-constrained consumer: an empirical study of demand and supply in the loan market, *Journal of Business and Economic Statistics* 10: 179–92.

Peters, H.F., M.P. Scott & D.J. Askin (1984) Prepayment patterns of conventional mortgages: experience from the Freddie Mac portfolio, *Secondary Mortgage Markets*, February.

Phillips, R.A., E. Rosenblatt & J.H. Vanderhoff (1996) The probability of fixed and adjustable rate mortgage termination, *Journal of Real Estate Finance and Economics* 13(2): 95–104.

Phillips, R.A. and J.H. Vanderhoff (1992) Adjustable rate mortgages and housing demand: the impact of initial rate discounts, *Journal of Real Estate Finance and Economics* 5: 269–79.

Phillips, R.A. & J.H. Vanderhoff (1994) Alternative mortgage instruments, qualification constraints and the demand for housing: an empirical analysis, *Journal of the American Real Estate Association* 22: 453–77.

Plaut, S.E. (1986) Mortgage design in imperfect capital markets, *Journal of Urban Economics* 20: 107–19.

Posey, L.L. & A. Yavas (2001) Adjustable and fixed rate mortgages as a screening mechanism for default risk, *Journal of Urban Economics* 49: 54–79.

Poterba, J.M. (1984) Tax subsidies to owner occupied housing: an asset market approach, *Quarterly Journal of Economics* XCIX: 729–52.

Pryke, M. & C. Whitehead (1991) Mortgage backed securitisation in the UK: a wholesale change in housing finance?, *Land Economy Monograph*, 22, Department of Land Economy, University of Cambridge.

Quercia, R.G. & M.A. Stegman (1992) Residential mortgage default: a review of the literature, *Journal of Housing Research* 3 (2): 341–79.

Quigley, J.M. (1987) Interest rate variations, mortgage prepayments and household mobility, *Review of Economics and Statistics* 119 (4): 636–43.

Quigley, J.M. & R. Van Order (1990) Efficiency in the mortgage market: the borrower's perspective, *AREUEA Journal* 18(3): 237–52.

Quigley, J.M. & R. Van Order (1991) Defaults on mortgage obligations and capital requirements for US savings institutions: a policy perspective, *Journal of Public Economics* 44(3): 353–70.

Quigley, J.M. & R. Van Order (1992) More on the efficiency of the market for single family homes: default, Center for Real Estate and Urban Economics, University of California, Berkeley, Mimeo.

Quigley, J.M. & R. Van Order (1995) Explicit tests of contingent claims models of mortgage default, *Journal of Real Estate Finance and Economics* 11: 99–117.

Ranney, S.I. (1981) The future price of houses, mortgage market conditions, and the returns to homeownership, *American Economic Review* 71(3): 323–30.

Richard, S.F. & R. Roll (1989) Prepayments on fixed rate mortgage-backed securities, *Journal of Portfolio Management*: Spring: 73–82.

Riddiough, T.J. & S.B. Wyatt (1994) Strategic default, workout and commercial mortgage valuation, *Journal of Real Estate Finance and Economics* 9 (1): 5–22.

Riley, J.G. (1987) Credit rationing: a further remark, *American Economic Review* 77(1): 224–7.

Roche, E.P. (1999) Loans around the world, *SMM Online*, April.

Rosen, H.S. (1979) Housing decisions and US income tax: an econometric analysis, *Journal of Public Economics* 11: 1–23.

Rosenthal, L. (1997) Chain formation in the owner occupied housing market, *Economic Journal* 107 (March): 475–88.

Rosenthal, L. (1999) House prices and local taxes in the UK, *Fiscal Studies* 20(1): 61–76.

Ross, S. (1999) *An Introduction to Mathematical Finance*, Cambridge University Press, Cambridge, UK.

Ross, S.L. (2000) Mortgage lending, sample selection and default, *Real Estate Economics* 28(4): 581–622.

Roth, H.L. (1988) Volatile mortgage rates: a new fact of life?, *Economic Review*, Federal Reserve Bank of Kansas City: 1–28.

Rothenberg, J. (1983) Housing investment, housing consumption, and tenure choice, in R.E. Grieson (ed.) *The Urban Economy and Housing*, Lexington Books: 29–55.

Rothschild, M. & J.E. Stiglitz (1976) Equilibrium in competitive insurance markets: an essay in the economics of imperfect information, *Quarterly Journal of Economics* 80: 629–49.

Rudolph, P.M. & J. Griffith (1997) Integration of the mortgage market into the national capital markets: 1963–1993, *Journal of Housing Economics* 6: 164–83.

Sandor, R. & H. Sosin (1975) The determinants of mortgage risk premiums: a case study of the portfolio of a savings and loan association, *The Journal of Business* 48 (1): 27–38.

SA-Aadu, J. (1987) Consumer welfare under the adjustable rate mortgage: some empirical evidence, *AREUEA Journal* 15(3): 132–51.

SA-Aadu, J. (1988) Legal restrictions, credit allocation, and default risk under fixed and adjustable rate mortgages, *Housing Finance Review* 7: 225–47.

SA-Aadu, J. & I.F. Megbolugbe (1995) Heterogeneous borrowers, mortgage selection, and mortgage pricing, *Journal of Housing Research* 6(2): 333–48.

SA-Aadu, J. & J.D. Shilling (1994) Tests of borrowers' perceptions in the adjustable mortgage market: do borrowers view ARM contracts as distinct, *Journal of Urban Economics* 36: 8–22.

SA-Aadu, J. & C.F. Sirmans (1989) The pricing of adjustable rate mortgage contracts, *Journal of Real Estate Finance and Economics* 2: 253–66.

SA-Aadu, J. & C.F. Sirmans (1995) Differentiated contracts, heterogeneous borrowers, and the mortgage choice decision, *Journal of Money Credit and Banking* 27: 498–510.

Sanyal, A. (1994) Ammunition for ARMs: a panel data approach to prepayment modelling, *The Journal of Fixed Income* 4(3): 96–103.

Schoenbeck, M. (1999) ARM borrowers match loans to their uncertainty tolerances, Money Market Trends, SMM Online, Freddie Mac: 26–7.

Schwab, R.M. (1982) Inflation expectations and the demand for housing, *American Economic Review* 72(1): 143–53.

Schwartz, E.S. & W.N. Torous (1989a) Valuing stripped mortgage-backed securities, *Housing Finance Review* 8(4): 241–51.

Schwartz, E.S. & W.N. Torous (1989b) Prepayment and the valuation of mortgage-backed securities, *Journal of Finance* 44(2): 375–92.

Schwartz, E.S. & W.N. Torous (1991) Caps on adjustable rate mortgages: valuation, insurance and hedging, in *Financial Markets and Financial Crises*, editor R.G. Hubbard, Chicago, University of Chicago Press.

Schwartz, E.S. & W.N. Torous (1992) Prepayment, default, and the valuation of mortgage pass through securities, *Journal of Business* 65(2): 221–39.

Schwartz, E.S. & W.N. Torous (1993) Mortgage prepayment and default decisions: a Poisson regression approach, *Journal of the American Real Estate and Urban Economics Association* 21(4): 431–49.

Scott, W.H. Jr, A.L. Houston, Jr & A. Quang Do (1993) Inflation risk, payment tilt and the design of partially indexed affordable mortgages, *Real Estate Economics* 21(1): 1–25.

Shefrin, H.M. & R.H. Thaler (1988) The behavioural life-cycle hypothesis, *Economic Inquiry* 26: 609–43.

Simon, R. (2002) Hybrid mortgages offer the best of two worlds, *Real Estate Journal*, Wall Street Journal Online, 15 January.

Skinner, F. (1999) Mortgage redemption fees: modelling redemption fees and incentives on UK home mortgages and modelling variable and fixed rate lending, Office of Fair Trading, Research Paper 18, November.

Slemrod, J. (1982) Down-payment constraints: tax policy effects in a growing economy with rental and owner occupied housing, *Public Finance Quart* 10:193–217.

Smith, D.J. (1987) The borrower's choice between fixed and adjustable rate loan contracts, *AREUEA Journal* 15(2): 110–16.

Spero, R. (1993) Chip off the old block, *Money Management* February: 20–24.

Sprecher, C.R. & E.S. Willman (1993) ARMs versus FRMs: which is better?, *The Real Estate Finance Journal* 8: 78–83.

Stanton, R. (1992) Rational prepayment and the valuation of mortgage-backed securities, Working Paper, University of California, Berkeley.

Stanton, R. (1995) Rational prepayment and the valuation of mortgage-backed securities, *Review of Financial Studies* 8: 677–708.

Stanton, R. & N. Wallace (1998) Mortgage choice: what's the point?, *Real Estate Economics* 26(2): 173–205.

Stanton, R. & N. Wallace (1999) Anatomy of an ARM: the interest-rate risk of adjustable rate mortgages, *Journal of Real Estate Finance and Economics* 19(1): 49–67.

Statman, M. (1982) Fixed rate or index-linked mortgages from the borrower's point of view: a note, *Journal of Financial and Quantitative Analysis* XVII (September): 451–57.

Stein, J.C. (1995) Prices and trading volume in the housing market: a model with down payment effects, *The Quarterly Journal of Economics* 110: 379–406.

Stephens, M. (2000) Convergence in European mortgage systems before and after EMU, *Journal of Housing and the Built Environment* 15: 29–52.

Stiglitz, J.E. & A. Weiss (1981) Credit rationing in markets with imperfect information, *American Economic Review* 71(3): 393–410.

Summers, L.H. (1981) Inflation, the stock market and owner occupied housing, *American Economic Review, Papers and Proceedings* May: 429–34.

Swan, C. (1973) Comment on the markets for housing and housing services, *Journal of Money Credit and Banking* 5(4): 960–72.

Szerb, L. (1996) The borrower's choice of fixed and adjustable rate mortgages in the presence of nominal and real shocks, *Real Estate Economics* 24(1): 43–54.

Templeton, W.K., R.S. Main & J.B. Orris (1996) A simulation approach to the choice between fixed and adjustable rate mortgages, *Financial Services Review* 5: 101–17.

Thaler, R. & H.M. Shefrin (1981) An economic theory of self-control, *Journal of Political Economy* 89(2): 392–406.

Titman, S. & W.N. Torous (1989) Valuing commercial mortgages: an empirical investigation of the contingent claims approach to pricing risky debt, *The Journal of Finance* 44: 345–73.

Todd, S. (2001) The effects of securitisation on consumer mortgage costs, *Real Estate Economics*: 29(1): 29–54.

Tucker, M. (1991) Comparing present value cost differentials between fixed and adjustable rate loans: a mortgage simulation, *The Financial Review* 26: 447–58.

Upinder, S., J.D. Dhillon, J.D. Shilling & C.F. Sirmans (1987) Choosing between fixed and adjustable rate mortgages, *Journal of Money Credit and Banking* 19(1): 260–7.

Vandell, K.D. (1995) How ruthless is mortgage default? a review and synthesis of the evidence, *Journal of Housing Research* 6: 245–64.

Vandell, K.D. & T. Thibodeau (1985) Estimation of mortgage defaults using disaggregate loan history data, *AREUEA Journal* 13(3): 292–316.

Vanderhoff, J. (1996) Adjustable and fixed rate mortgage terminations, option values and local market conditions: an empirical analysis, *Real Estate Economics* 24(3): 379–406.

Van Order, R. (1990) The hazards of default, *Secondary Mortgage Markets* Fall: 29–31.

Van Order, R. (2000) The U.S. mortgage market: a model of dueling charters, *Journal of Housing Research* 11(2): 233–55.

Von Furstenberg, G. & R.J. Green (1969) Default risk on FHA-insured home mortgages as a function of the term of financing: a quantitative analysis, *Journal of Finance* 24: 459–77.

Von Furstenberg, G. & R.J. Green (1974) Home mortgages delinquency: a cohort analysis, *Journal of Finance* 29: 1545–48.

Wade, P.J. (2002) Canadian mortgage debt grows amid interest queries, Real Estate News and Advice, *Realty Times* (**http://realtytimes.com**).

Wilcox, J. (1985) A model of the building society sector, Bank of England Discussion Paper, No. 23.

Williamson, S. (1986) Costly monitoring, financial intermediation, and equilibrium credit rationing, *Journal of Monetary Economics* 17(1): 159–79.

Williamson, S. (1987) Costly monitoring, loan contracts, and equilibrium credit rationing, *Quarterly Journal of Economics* 102: 135–45.

Yang, T.L. (1992) Self-selection in the fixed rate mortgage market, *AREUEA Journal* 20: 359–91.

Yang, T.L.T. & B.A. Maris (1996) Mortgage prepayment with an uncertain holding period, *Journal of Real Estate Finance and Economics* 12(2): 129–94.

Yezer. A.M.J., R.F. Phillips & R.P. Trost (1994) Bias in estimates of discrimination and default in mortgage lending: the effects of simultaneity and self-selection, *Journal of Real Estate Finance and Economics* 9: 197–215.

Zorn, P.M. (1989) Mobility-tenure decisions and financial credit: do mortgage qualification requirements constrain homeownership, *AREUEA Journal* 17(1): 1–15.

Zorn, P.M. & M.J. Lea (1989) Mortgage borrower repayment behavior: a microeconomic analysis with Canadian adjustable rate mortgage data, *AREUEA Journal* 17(1): 118–36.

Zumpano. L.V., P.M. Rudolph & D.C. Cheng (1986) The demand and supply of mortgage funds and mortgage loan terms, *AREUEA Journal* 14(1): 91–109.

Index